Jewish Life in
21st-Century Turkey

NEW ANTHROPOLOGIES OF EUROPE
Daphne Berdahl, Matti Bunzl, and Michael Herzfeld,
founding editors

INDIANA SERIES IN SEPHARDI AND MIZRAHI STUDIES
Harvey E. Goldberg and Matthias Lehmann, editors

Jewish Life in 21st-Century Turkey

THE OTHER SIDE OF TOLERANCE

Marcy Brink-Danan

Indiana University Press
Bloomington & Indianapolis

This book is a publication of

Indiana University Press
601 North Morton Street
Bloomington, Indiana 47404-3797 USA

iupress.indiana.edu

Telephone orders 800-842-6796
Fax orders 812-855-7931

♾ The paper used in this publication
meets the minimum requirements of
the American National Standard for
Information Sciences—Permanence of
Paper for Printed Library Materials,
ANSI Z39.48-1992.

Manufactured in the United States of
America

Library of Congress Cataloging-in-
Publication Data

Brink-Danan, Marcy.
  Jewish life in twenty-first-century Tur-
key : the other side of tolerance / Marcy
Brink-Danan.
     p. cm. — (New anthropologies of
Europe) (Indiana series in Sephardi and
Mizrahi studies)
  Includes bibliographical references and
index.
  ISBN 978-0-253-35690-1 (cloth : alk.
paper) — ISBN 978-0-253-22350-0 (pbk. :
alk. paper) 1. Jews—Turkey—Istanbul—
History—21st century. 2. Jews—Turkey—
Istanbul—Identity. 3. Istanbul (Turkey)—
Ethnic relations. I. Title.
  DS135.T8B75 2012
  305.892'40561—dc23

                              2011021187

1 2 3 4 5 17 16 15 14 13 12

For Sagi, Ari, Eitan, and Zohar

CONTENTS

CONTENTS

PREFACE

The Ends and Beginnings of 1992

"Jews?" Mete Tapan, Istanbul city planner, had to think for a minute. "One knows they are there but they don't even comprise 1% of the population. No one knows how they vote or what their interests would be. They don't count."

—*Fleminger 2003*

Although there has not been an official census of Jews in Turkey since the 1960s, recent population estimates range from 18,000 to 25,000 (Tuval 2004:xxxiii; Toktaş 2006a:123), making Turkey today home to the highest number of Jews outside Israel in the lands that once comprised the Ottoman Empire. Jews in Turkey constitute a negligible fraction of Turkey's overall population of approximately seventy million people and, as described by the city planner, Turkish Jews don't "count" for much in the polling booth. Nonetheless, over the past few decades Jews in Turkey have taken on an increasingly public role, brokering Turkish diplomatic ties with Israel. As Turkey's model minority, they also have advocated for the republic as it has vied for European Union accession.

During the early years of the Turkish Republic, the process of becoming Turkish and the fear of not being perceived as Turkish enough engendered a profusion of effacing social practices among Jews and other minorities in Istanbul (Bali 2001). Just over half a century later, European Union overtures set the stage for Jews to stand symbolically (and publicly) for the tolerated "Other" in Turkish society. This role was consolidated in 1992 with a Turkish-led international celebration of the five-hundred-year anniversary of Jews finding refuge from the Spanish Inquisition in the lands of the Ottoman Empire. According to the statement of purpose of the Quincentennial Foundation, an organization led by Jewish and Muslim Turkish elites, the commemoration not only celebrates the 500th anniversary of the arrival of the Sephardic [Spanish] Jews on Turkish soil in 1492, but also the remarkable spirit of tolerance and acceptance which has characterized the entire Jewish experience in Turkey. This spirit is not an insulated instance of humanitarianism; throughout its history Turkey has welcomed people of different creeds, cultures and backgrounds. The Jewish community of Turkey is a part of this tradition.[1]

This description, with its claim that Turkey's national spirit is infused with a cosmopolitan regard for others, set the agenda for a public awareness campaign to improve Turkey's international image. If, due to their small numbers and historically low profile, Turkish Jews were previously not considered meaningful players in the Turkish political scene, this campaign, with its museums, academic treatises, and heritage tours, offered them a public platform from which to count as a quintessentially, and quincentennially, tolerated minority. In 1991, Turkey had officially upgraded relations with Israel to the embassy level (Elazar and Weinfeld 2000:367); Quincentennial celebrations, attended by Turkish and Israeli politicians, gathered momentum at the same time that Turkey's relations with Israel were warming. In parallel, the 1990s witnessed an increase in Jewish contributions to Turkish efforts to court Europeans, who made Turkish officials' recognition of their country's own heterogeneous population a central condition for Turkey's acceptance into the European Union.

Partially due to the Foundation's sponsorship and energetic activities, academic publication about Ottoman and Turkish Jewry experienced a florescence around the Quincentennial.[2] Stanford Shaw's *Jews of the Ottoman Empire and the Turkish Republic* is dedicated to "the Muslim and Jewish Turks of the Republic of Turkey, in celebration of five hundred years of brotherhood and friendship 1492–1992" (1991:frontispiece). Shaw ends his book with reference to the Quincentennial Foundation and its activities and officials, as if Turkish Jewry ceased to exist after this date. Shaul Tuval's *ha-Kehilah ha-Yehudit be-Istanbul, 1948–1992* (*The Jewish Community in Istanbul, 1948–1992*) (2004) collects, for the first time, comprehensive demographic and statistical research about modern Turkish Jewry, yet the Quincentennial year likewise ends his story. The cover of his book borrows the Foundation's imagery (a painting of Spanish exiles arriving at the empire) and its motto: "An Example to Humanity."

These chronicles, and many others that appeared contemporane-
ously, were not only timely in terms of the commemoration but also overdue in the intellectual realm; both Jewish and Turkish Studies canons
had largely overlooked the stories of modern Turkish Jews. However, in
these accounts, 1992 appears as the denouement of Turkish Jews' happy
story. In fact, the celebratory events marked, in a dramatic fashion, a
new beginning. Life under Ottoman rule had afforded Jews a degree of
autonomy that was maintained by keeping to themselves and paying
their taxes. Proto-republican political reforms and the new republic's
assimilating policies conditioned Turkish Jews (and other minorities)
to downplay difference in public. If, historically, Turkish Jews kept a low
profile,[3] now they (or, more correctly, their officials and other prominent
figures) have changed tactics. Quincentennial fever engendered a role
reversal in which Jews could be called upon to perform publicly the
very differences (languages, accents, rituals, beliefs, musical traditions,
and so on) they had endeavored to keep private for so long. This book
enters the scene to document, through ethnography and archival analysis, Jewish life in Turkey since 1992. If portrayals of Turkish Jewry end
felicitously at the Quincentennial, this work invites the reader to stick
around after the party, to enjoy the afterglow of merriment but also to
clean up (at least analytically) the mess created during the festivities.

I developed sections of this book as a fellow at the Center for Jewish History (CJH) in New York in 2003–2004. Studying the archives of
the Quincentennial Foundation's American arm, held by the American Sephardi Federation at CJH, allowed me to draw a clear picture of
the chronology and dissemination of the Turkish tolerance trope, with
"trope" here being understood as a style of historical discourse (White
1982). Mallet's work (2008) on the history of official self-representations
among Turkish Jews meticulously details this process and contextualizes
the rise of the tolerance trope against the realpolitik of the late 1980s and
early 1990s, a period that has been noted for improved Israel–Turkish
relations, Turkish overtures to the European Union, and local political
change. As someone with little exposure to the world of public relations
but with a deep interest in how texts travel, I found it striking to see how
press releases about Turkish tolerance generated by the Foundation's
public relations group spread like wildfire across American Jewish and
general news venues in anticipation of the Quincentennial celebrations.

Although some have seen increased anthropological attention to historical tropes as an encroachment on the historian's purview (and sometimes at the expense of more traditional ethnographic fieldwork) (see Tsing 2009:61), a basic understanding of the tolerance trope is central to understanding the way Jews understand their past and present as Ottoman subjects and Turkish citizens. At the same time, working on this project strengthened my convictions about the importance of putting media and archival evidence into dialogue with ethnographic observations of peoples' lived experience. The book grew out of notes and recordings collected during ethnographic field research conducted over the course of a year (2002–2003) and during shorter visits in 2007 and 2009. During my fieldwork in Istanbul I attended community functions, theatrical productions, wedding ceremonies, religious rituals, committee meetings, retreats, gatherings of a Jewish study group, and press nights at the Jewish paper. In the early months of fieldwork, I passed through metal detectors and double doors at kosher restaurants, Jewish schools, and synagogues with my passport in hand as identification. Later in my fieldwork process, I came to know the security guards as friends (or, more importantly, they came to know me); instead of exchanging identifying documents, we swapped kisses on two cheeks as I passed more easily through the guarded passages that limn Istanbul's streets and Jewish spaces.

Throughout my research in Istanbul and in the years that have followed, I have tried to square the mellifluous representations generated by the Quincentennial Foundation, and by community officials more generally, with a more cautious dictum Turkish Jews shared with me on numerous occasions: "Our life here is very secure. The Jews are happy. But, just in case, don't mention the fact that you are Jewish to anyone outside of the community." If on one hand the success of the Quincentennial campaign proved the successful integration of Jews into Turkish society, on the other hand this success relied on their celebration of a public face of difference in spite of an everyday performance of Turkishness. What to make of this tension between public and hidden transcripts (Scott 1990)?

In making sense of Turkish Jews' cosmopolitanism and their tolerance for tension, I have relied heavily on linguistic anthropological methods of conversation and discourse analysis and on an overarching semiotic analytical framework. Semiotics, a theory of meaning that focuses on the way signs are created (and debated), has lent me analytical tools through which to decode ironic enactments of Turkish Jewish identity and erasures of difference that stand in dramatic contrast with the community's own public pronouncements. I find this model useful for understanding how to make sense of changing meanings in which cosmopolitanism is historically and contextually anchored but also regularly unmoored and set upon new waters of interpretation.

Ethnography, with its attention to lived experience, allows us to observe the tensions inherent in the ways people with cosmopolitan ways of being actually make sense of these options. As some have argued, "cosmopolitanism is not just—or perhaps not at all—an idea. Cosmopolitanism is infinite ways of being" (Pollock et al. 2002:12). While in theory it may appear that we all have infinite ways of being, what appears to be chaos is governed by a sophisticated—and sometimes contradictory—set of constitutional, political, juridical, and discursive rules that order our lives. In addition to providing the first English-language ethnography about contemporary Turkish Jewry, this book has an underlying goal of understanding how Jews in Turkey make sense of present and past understandings of tolerance, citizenship, and belonging, transforming multiple possibilities into a lived cosmopolitanism.[4]

ACKNOWLEDGMENTS

The following fellowships and institutions generously supported research for this book: Fulbright-Hays, National Foundation for Jewish Culture, Maurice Amado Foundation for Sephardic Studies, Eastern Consortium of Persian and Turkish, Mellon Foundation, Institute of Turkish Studies, Barnard College Alumnae Fellowship, and Brown and Stanford Universities. A fellowship at the Center for Jewish History allowed me regular access to the archives of the American Sephardi Federation (ASF), which holds an invaluable collection of documents relating to the American Branch of the Quincentennial Foundation; special thanks is due to Randall Belinfante, ASF librarian/archivist. A Cahnman Publication Subvention Grant of the Association of Jewish Studies supported the completion of this book.

At Indiana University Press, Janet Rabinowitch and Rebecca Tolen helped bring this book to publication, with editorial assistance from Brian Herrmann and Maureen Epp. Matti Bunzl and Michael Herzfeld, editors for the New Anthropologies of Europe Series, as well as Matthias Lehmann and Harvey Goldberg, editors for the Series in Sephardi and Mizrahi Studies helped locate this book in its appropriate milieus. Harvey Goldberg and Esra Özyürek offered useful feedback on an earlier version of this manuscript, for which I am most grateful.

My training in anthropology began at Barnard College (Columbia University) and at Ben-Gurion University, where I learned the trade from outstanding mentors such as Marco Jacquemet, Paula Rubel, Abraham Rosman, Morton Klass, Lesley Sharp, Elaine Combs-Schilling, Fran

Markowitz, and Aref Abu-Rabia. I would never have ended up in an anthropology class were it not for my theater professor, Mark Sussman—himself a student of Barbara Kirshenblatt-Gimblett—who recognized that my interest in performance lay in its deeply social aspects. A special debt is owed to the faculty members with whom I worked most closely at Stanford University: Carol Delaney, Aron Rodrigue, Miyako Inoue, and Penelope Eckert. My education at Stanford was also enriched by the teaching of Paulla Ebron, Ian Hodder, Sylvia Yanagisako, Renato Rosaldo, Hayden White, and Ann Stoler, and by friendship with students in my cohort.

Colleagues at Brown University, especially those who have participated in the Judaic Studies faculty seminar and in our informal anthropology writers' group, have helped me refine many of the ideas in this book. Because I am a faculty member in two departments (Judaic Studies and Anthropology), acknowledging the individuals with whom I work daily would be very long indeed, but I hope you know that talking and thinking with you has made my job more enjoyable. At Brown, I also enjoyed the camaraderie and intellectual stimulation of fellows at the Cogut Center for the Humanities. Writing dates with Ruti Ben-Artzi, Paja Faudree, Jessaca Leinaweaver, and Pauline Jones Luong made the scribbling process a bit less lonely.

My work has thus far enjoyed a multi-disciplinary audience of peers in various forums, including the annual meetings of the American Anthropological Association, the American Ethnological Society, the Israeli Anthropological Association, the Middle East Studies Association, the Association for Jewish Studies, and the World Union of Jewish Studies. Unique opportunities for dialogue also came in the form of invitations to present talks at the Sorbonne (Paris), King's College (London), the University of Michigan (Ann Arbor), and the University of California (Los Angeles), as well as at the Frankel Institute for Advanced Jewish Studies Early Career Workshop and the Modern Jewish Studies group at the Association for Jewish Studies meetings. I especially thank Julia Cohen for her extended notes on the historical questions raised in an earlier version of my introductory chapter, circulated at the Modern Jewish Studies Workshop in 2009.

It has been a special pleasure to have an ongoing dialogue with ethnographers of Jewish life in the form of the Council for the Anthropology of Jews and Judaism, a group of the American Anthropological Association, which I have co-chaired with Matti Bunzl since 2007. Although the list of participants over the years is too long to list here, it is this group's unique tenacity and dedication to the study of contemporary Jewish life that buoys many of my intellectual pursuits.

Mersi to friends made during my fieldwork research, including, in no particular order, Izzet, Lusi, Reni, Beki, Emil, Rahel, Murat, Luiza, Shila, Sinto, Lina, Shayna, Ilene, and so many others. Our ongoing relationships, whether online or face to face, are a constant reminder of why I love anthropological fieldwork. Thanks to Baruh Pinto, for sharing with me his companionship, coffee, and intellectual pursuits.

As so many researchers in Istanbul know, Rıfat Bali, an independent scholar, is a constant source of moral and practical support for scholarship on minorities in Turkey. Over our decade of acquaintance, Rıfat's productivity has been an inspiration; in the time it has taken me to complete this one book, he has penned so many of his own works, reaching a wide audience by writing in Turkish, English, and French.

I owe my father, Stuart Brink, thanks for teaching me the value of cultural comparison and a love of language. My mother, Joyce Brink, always thought I'd be a great artist and has nonetheless supported a different kind of career path. Sara Reinstein read a penultimate version of this manuscript with a poet's eye. Thanks also to Rebecca Brink for her reading of this work when it was in a much earlier stage. To Gertrude, Larry, Susan, Sarah, Kenneth, and Michael Brink, Arnold and Dorothy Goldstein: I hope I have made you proud.

My husband, Sagi Brink-Danan, always wanted me to write "I couldn't have done it without you" in my first book. Regarding my family, "There is little doubt that without them I could have written more and, who knows, maybe even have gotten smarter" (Scott 1990:xviii). Knowing this, I am still glad that I have Sagi and our children, Ari, Eitan, and Zohar, to anchor my academic occupations (and preoccupations) in the everyday life of a partner and mother, reminding me that I work to live, rather than the inverse.

Parts of this text have been published in earlier versions as journal articles and are reproduced here with kind permission from *American Anthropologist*, the *Political and Legal Anthropology Review* (PoLAR) and the *Anthropological Quarterly*. Some images and ideas presented here also appear, albeit in different form, in the following edited collections: *Orienting Istanbul: Cultural Capital of Europe?* (Deniz Göktürk, Levent Soysal, and İpek Türeli, eds.; 2010) and *Itinéraires sépharades: Complexité et diversité des identités* (Esther Benbassa, ed.; 2010).

Jewish Life in
21st-Century Turkey

Introduction

This is a book about the tensions inherent in Turkish Jewish life at the turn of the twenty-first century. These tensions arise from a number of contradictions: Jews in Turkey publicly celebrate a long history of co-existence and tolerance in the region, yet live with ongoing security concerns bred by anti-Semitism and periodic attacks against members of the community and their institutions. Since the creation of the Turkish Republic nearly a century ago in 1923, Jews have enjoyed full citizenship in Turkey with all its rights and responsibilities, yet their patriotism and indigenousness are regularly questioned by Muslim Turks. Jews are privy to what I call "cosmopolitan knowledge" about different symbolic and cultural systems (Brink-Danan 2011). They have learned about difference by comparing their lives to the ways Jews outside of Turkey live and to the ways Jews have lived in the past, yet they perform and disavow this difference at different times and on different stages. In Turkey today, cosmopolitanism is both celebrated and reviled, and Jews regularly find themselves performing a patriotic role as citizens while also embodying cosmopolitan difference in order to represent themselves as the good minority. It is this final dynamic that commands the lion's share of this study: How do Jews in Turkey manage the tensions between their cosmopolitanism and patriotism, between their difference as Jews and their sameness as Turkish citizens? What kind of cultural habits does this tension breed?

An example of the tension between difference and sameness can be found in the way many Jewish families in Istanbul today follow the biblical command to mark their doorposts with a *mezuzah,* a small ritual object that contains a text from Deuteronomy emphasizing the unity of God, embedded in an injunction to outwardly signify this belief:

> Hear, O Israel,[1] the Lord is our God, the Lord is One. Blessed is His name, whose glorious kingdom is forever and ever. Love the Lord your God with all your heart, and all your soul, and all your might. These words that I command you shall be upon your heart. Repeat them to your children, and talk about them when you sit in your home, and when you walk in the street; when you lie down, and when you rise up. Hold fast to them as a sign upon your hand, and let them be as reminders before your eyes. Write them on the doorposts of your home and at your gates.

Several years ago I attended an educational session preparing Jewish couples in Istanbul for marriage. These sessions, created to counter assimilation and a perceived decrease in knowledge about Jewish ritual practice, are mandatory for all couples marrying through the Turkish Rabbinate. At the meeting, each couple received a *mezuzah* complete with a parchment upon which this injunction was handwritten. In describing the gifts that the couples would take home, the session organizer focused on the central significance of the *mezuzah* by emphasizing its monetary and symbolic value. The hand-inscribed parchments, without which the *mezuzah* is not considered kosher (fit for use), are expensive and not produced in Turkey.

The rabbi leading the session described the *mezuzah*'s symbolic role as protector of the Jewish home:

> Many of you have fancy electronic security systems in your apartment. Here is a low-tech security system made specifically for the Jewish home. It is a security system for a Jewish future and for a Jewish life. Every time you move to a new house, your children will watch you put the *mezuzah* up on the doorpost and learn of the importance you place on Jewish values and customs.[2]

A murmur then echoed throughout the auditorium. The audience became increasingly noisy until one woman raised her hand to ask the rabbi, "Are we supposed to put the *mezuzah* on the inside or outside of our homes? In my parents' house it is on the inside. I've heard that the outside is the proper place." Although Orthodox interpretations of Jewish law dictate that the *mezuzah* be visible to passers-by on the street,

FIGURE 1

Pamphlet describing how to affix a *mezuzah*.
Collection of the author.

many Turkish Jews refuse to outwardly signify their Judaism. By affixing the *mezuzah* behind the door, that is, by marking the *inside* of the doorframe, Turkish Jews fulfill the commandment without displaying difference in public. At the woman's question, the rabbi paused and then attempted to reassure her, saying that "the proper place is on the outside. Don't be afraid to attach it outside your home. If you are really afraid that people will know that Jews live inside, that is, if it is a security concern, you can put it on the inside." Then, with a shrug and a smile, the rabbi smoothed out the tension in the room by adding, "I'm not a policeman. Personally, I won't say anything." The crowd responded with laughter but continued to mumble quietly for a few minutes, processing the irony of a *mezuzah* as at once a symbolic security system and a potential trigger for anti-Semitic threats and even violence. There have been recent efforts on the part of certain members of the community to encourage "proper" placement of the *mezuzah,* including the circulation in 2002 of a Turkish- language pamphlet on the "Mitzvah of Hanging the *Mezuzah*." Nonetheless, Turkish rabbis maintain an ambiguous attitude toward this practice.

How much difference is tolerable in the public sphere? The tension engendered by the discussion of local intentions and cosmopolitan knowledge around the "correct" placement of the *mezuzah* speaks to a broader concern about the limits of visibility that Turkish Jews find acceptable. In the Turkish context (Çaha 2005) and elsewhere in Europe, this question burns with ever-increasing intensity as politicians and pundits alike debate tolerance, multiculturalism, and the public nomination of religious difference. There seems to be no end to the curiosity, concern, and controversy about the politics and meanings of headscarves on women, for example, and other religious markings in Europe's public sphere (Asad et al. 2009; Bowen 2007; Mahmood 2005; Scott 2007).

Turkish reckonings with cosmopolitanism have certainly gained attention in recent years, with the term itself increasingly appearing in travel brochures touting Istanbul in particular as a "meeting of civilizations" and celebrating its "religious mosaic" (Bali 2010). In August 2002, the Turkish Parliament passed legislation allowing Kurdish-language broadcasting and instruction. The passing of this legislation created openings and possibilities in the Turkish public sphere for the recognition of the region's historical polyglot multiplicity. Although many regard this change as lip service to European Union demands (Spolsky 2004), such policy shifts seemed to signal a new era in which Turkey would celebrate multiculturalism through an acknowledgement of its citizens' cosmopolitan tongues. However, since then linguistic controversies, such as those that ensued following the performance of Kurdish songs in 2002 by popular musician Sezen Aksu in a concert entitled "The Turkish Mosaic," or the use of Kurdish in parliament by representative Ahmet Türk in 2009, suggest the real tensions between juridical and popular notions of cosmopolitan rights. The assassination in 2007 of Hrant Dink, a Turkish Armenian journalist and human rights advocate, by a teenage nationalist, provoked contradictory responses, such as a memorial rally of over fifty thousand Turks under the banner "We are all Armenians" on one hand, and a photo, leaked to the media, of Turkish police proudly posing with Dink's murderer under a waving Turkish flag on the other. These examples and others suggest that cosmopolitanism is simultaneously thriving and under attack in Turkey. How might we understand the role that Turkish Jews, their officials, and their institutions play in the ongoing debate about cosmopolitanism, difference, and tolerance that today is the focus of so much public debate in Turkey, the European Union, and elsewhere (Blommaert and Verschueren 1998)?

"Welcome to the new Europe, where Jews are no longer persecuted but revered as cosmopolitan ancestors" (Boyer 2005:523). Jews increasingly occupy a special role in European claims to cosmopolitanism, especially as a foil against which to compare tolerance for other kinds of differentiated citizens (Peck 2006:154–174). Are Jews in Istanbul revered as ancestral remnants of a lost cosmopolitanism? As capital of the Ottoman Empire, Constantinople was home to large populations of Armenians, Greeks, and Jews and notable for its religious and linguistic diversity; as such, Ottoman cosmopolitanism was defined by a co-existence of religious difference. The creation of the nation-state in 1923 and the relocation of the government capital to Ankara shifted the demographic and symbolic composition of the city (Çınar 2005) and left behind what has been called a "depopulated cosmopolis" (Komins 2002). Nonetheless, the megalopolis remains home to an incredible variety of political, religious, and class affiliations. One recent aspect of Istanbul's public life includes a rapidly growing nostalgia for a lost cosmopolitanism (Neyzi 2002; Mills 2007, 2010; Özyürek 2006, 2007; Potuoğlu-Cook 2006; Bali 2010; Türeli 2010), or what is often called the Ottoman "mosaic." Recently, it has been argued that the "mosaic" model might be better replaced by the metaphor of *ebru*—Turkish paper marbling—in which identity is seen as porous and mixed (painterly) rather than hard-edged (like tiles) (see Durak 2007). Festivals, exhibitions, and concerts celebrating religious difference, tolerance, and multiculturalism increasingly punctuate Istanbul's landscape (Yardımcı 2007). For example, on a recent stroll down Istiklal Caddesi (Independence Avenue), a popular shopping thoroughfare on Istanbul's European side, I noticed a shirt displayed in the window of a small clothing store. By replacing letters in the city's name with a Christian crucifix, a Jewish star, and an Islamic crescent, this cultural artifact captures a moment in which the symbols of cosmopolitanism (that is, religious difference) are increasingly fashionable in formerly Ottoman cities (Mills 2010:9; see also Silverstein and Makdisi 2006).

If "demonstrations of knowledge about Others are expressed as confirmations of Constantinopolitan cosmopolitanism" (Örs 2006:90), it would follow that this form of cultural capital would be regularly de-

FIGURE 2
Shirt for sale in shop window, Istanbul.
Marcy Brink-Danan, 2007.

ployed in public. Given their public face as Turkey's ideal cosmopolitans, one might expect Turkey's Jews to be colorful peacocks, parading their multicultural feathers down Istiklal Caddesi toward an area formerly known as Pera (now Galata), where Jewish, Greek, and Armenian shops and cafés once lined the streets. However, outside of media reports, official celebrations of difference, and their political corollaries, Turkish Jews make great efforts to erase material evidence of Jewish linguistic, ritual, and physical differences that might suggest cosmopolitanism. The

Jews of Istanbul exhibit flexibility in switching between a number of different linguistic and social codes. These codes shift valence depending on interlocutor and context, politics, and perception. Despite the idyllic official discourse of Turkish tolerance, Istanbul's Jews today gather in homes, schools, and synagogues unmarked as Jewish spaces (see Neyzi 2002:142). Visitors to Jewish sites in Istanbul march through metal detectors while armed guards check passports and identity cards; security cameras record the scenes, perched like watchful birds above the barbed wire and cement barricades that secure Istanbul's Jewish institutions. I became convinced that this tension was indicative of a kind of knowledge about different ways of being in the world, but that this tension would also challenge some of my assumptions about cosmopolitanism itself.

Tolerance and Citizenship: Jews as Turks or Foreigners?

How do people come to be seen as "different," in direct contradiction to their apparent legal or political equality as citizens of a given state? In spite of the sometimes-celebratory public mood of difference recognition, it often seems that members of the majority culture or society lack knowledge about the concrete conditions, tensions, and experiences of the lives of actual cosmopolitans (Brink-Danan 2010). In everyday interactions, I regularly observed a contest of claims worked out between Muslim Turks (even those recently arrived in Istanbul) and Turkish Jews (with centuries-long genealogical ties to the city) in which the former imagined the latter to be transient non-Turks and as such, implicitly non-local.

In 2007, I noticed a poster hanging in the Jewish Museum of Turkey; commissioned by the Istanbul Metropolitan Municipality, the Istanbul Tourism Atelier, and Istanbul 2010: European Capital of Culture Agency, the slogan "mono love, multi culture" was emblazoned above the word "Istanbul," with the city's historic names testifying to its mythical cosmopolitanism. If locality is to be understood through an anthropological examination of cosmopolitanism, the term "local" demands unpacking (see Geertz 1973). One may question the literal use of "local," given that all people are "locatable": "Since anthropologists now gener-

mono LOVE multi CULTURE

Licus / Ligos / Lykos / Lygos / Bizantium / Buzantion / Buzantiya / Vizention
Bizantion / Antonia / Augusta / Antonina / Antoneinia / Neas Romes
Roma Bizanti / Roma Constantinum / Roma Orientum / Nea Rome
Constantinopolis / Taht-ı Rum / Tekfurye / Konstantiniyye
Beldetü'l- Tayyibe / Darü'l Hilafe / Darü'l İslam / Der-Aliyye / Çar'gorot
Konstantine Grad / Miklagard / Vezendovar / Yağfurye / Yankoviçe
Escomboli / Estambul / Estefanye / İslambol / İstimpoli / Sitanbul

İSTANBUL

FIGURE 3
Poster for Istanbul 2010: European Capital of Culture,
displayed at the Quincentennial Foundation Museum
of Turkish Jews (Jewish Museum of Turkey).
Marcy Brink-Danan, 2007.

ally claim that their distinctiveness rests on a method (fieldwork) rather
than an object (non-European cultures), this sense recommends itself to
them: fieldwork defines privileged access to the local" (Asad 1993:8). But
who defines locality in Turkey? In Turkey, use of the term *yerli* functions
as a semantic claim to indigenousness:

> (Anatolian villagers) consider themselves *yerli* (native), in contrast to *göç-*
> *men* (immigrants). *Yerli* is an interesting word, composed of *yer* (earth,
> ground, place) and the suffix -li (lı, lu, lü), which means "belonging to" or
> "relating to" and in this context is an identity marker . . . *Yerli* thus means
> those who come from that particular piece of earth. (Delaney 1991:204;
> see also Mills 2010:1)

What (and who) defines the way Jews relate to a particular land,
that cosmopolis that has been called Byzantium, Constantinople, and

Istanbul, among other names? Jewish life in Asia Minor dates to the fourth century BCE, and today's Jewish community comprises multiple origins due to the palimpsest of Jewish migrations to the region over time. The dominance of Sephardi cultural and linguistic identification has a number of causes, including the mass migration of immigrants from the Iberian peninsula to the Ottoman Empire in 1492, which overwhelmed extant Jewish populations. Sephardic Jews sought—and found—refuge in the Ottoman Empire during the fifteenth century when Sultan Beyazit II "welcomed" Jewish exiles from the Iberian Peninsula, gladly populating his territory with skilled and grateful subjects and purportedly critiquing the intelligence of Christian monarchs who would expel such useful human capital as the Jews (Benbassa and Rodrigue 2000:7). Even before the expulsion of Jews from the Iberian Peninsula, Rabbi Yitzhak Sarfati, himself a German refugee living in Ottoman lands, had issued a call to Jews throughout Europe to "leave the torments they were experiencing in Christendom and to seek safety and security in Turkey" (Lewis 1984:135–136). Although Beyazit's declaration has been widely assumed to be apocryphal (Mallet 2008:89) and the rabbi may have been coerced by the Sultan to write the letter (Inalcık 2002:5), these origin myths of Turkish tolerance form the basic pillars of Ottoman Jewish historiography and are still widely recounted today. The idea that Jews were in the Ottoman Empire and Turkey "by choice" rather than "by conquest" (Cohen 2008:103–104) was consolidated around the four-hundred-year anniversary of Jewish migration to the Ottoman Empire and contributed to the conflation of multiple Jewish cultures under the heading of Sephardi identity; this conflation was repeated in the five-hundred-year celebrations as well.

Given this history, the vast majority of Jews in Istanbul today identify as "Sephardic," that is, they say they trace their ancestry from Spain. Spanish-sounding surnames, such as Amado, Niego, and Ventura are common among today's Turkish Jewish families. Indeed, many elderly Turkish Jews still speak Judeo-Spanish (also known as Musevici, Espanyolca, Ladino, Judezmo, Spanyolit),[3] a "fusion language" whose phonology, grammar, and lexicon are primarily Spanish, but which incorporates elements of Hebrew, French, Arabic, Aramaic, Italian, Turkish, and Greek (Harris 1982, 1994). As noted by Stein (2006:499), "as late as the Second World War, 85 percent of Turkish Jewry ... identified Ladino as their native language."

Scholars of Turkey and the Ottoman Empire increasingly problematize the question of tolerance and difference (Barkey 2008; Baer et al. 2009), arguing that we should not assume that tolerance or difference meant the same thing under various regimes, in distinct locales, or over time. The need to understand the shifting meaning of these terms is not just an academic preoccupation but a necessary corrective to the tendency of politicians and journalists to assume that tolerance and difference are themselves timeless and universal ideals. Under Ottoman rule, Jews and Christians occupied a clearly differentiated—but protected—social position with collective rights and responsibilities under the Islamic "pact of toleration" accorded them due to their status as "People of the Book." This law was unevenly implemented over the centuries of Ottoman rule but it uniformly recognized Jews as different, not equal: "Nothing in the political system of the Ottoman Empire called for different groups to merge into one. The difference was a given and accepted as such" (Rodrigue and Reynolds 1995). As a reader of Ottoman Jewish history and an observer of the lives of Jews in the Turkish Republic, I was confronted with the question of how tolerance of difference has been enacted, interpreted, and taken up in recent Turkish discussions; the question became one of the puzzles that this book attempts to solve.

Furthermore, should Turkish Jews today be subject (or privy) to tolerance because of their difference or in spite of it? The very question of "tolerance" of "difference" takes on a meaning in the context of empire (and under different conditions of empire), such as that of the Ottomans, that is quite distinct from its meaning in a nation-state. As Marc Baer has shown with the case of the Dönme, followers of seventeenth-century messianic leader Shabbatai Tzevi (an Ottoman convert from Judaism to Islam), the rise of powerful national ideologies undercut tolerance of cosmopolitanism and difference (2010). After four centuries in which an Islamic code for minorities recognized Ottoman Jews as a corporate identity, in 1923 Jewish community officials exchanged differentiated special status for universal citizenship in the nascent Republic of Turkey, effacing communal autonomy for the promise of emancipation. Adopting the French political model of *la-*

icité, the founders of the Republic of Turkey imagined a public sphere dramatically emptied of religious symbolism. While a muted version of Sunni Muslim identification was nonetheless incorporated into the vision of a secular Turkish Republic, the languages, practices, and beliefs of Turkey's religious and ethnic minorities took on a marked and taboo character.

Despite the loyalist attitude of many Jews, including committed advocates of Turkism such as Galante, Tekinalp (né Kohen) and others, the early years of the Republic of Turkey saw an increase in decidedly intolerant anti-minority xenophobia, in which minority languages were banned and devastating riots occurred (especially outside of Istanbul). Further, the *Varlık Vergisi,* an excessive tax instituted during World War II, pilfered small Jewish (and other minority) businesses to the point of bankruptcy (Benbassa and Rodrigue 2000:184) and is cited as a major impetus for Jewish emigration from Istanbul (Bali 2005; Mills 2010:189). *Varlık Vergisi* is commonly translated as "Capital Tax" or "Wealth Tax;" we might, however, consider an alternate translation of *varlık* as "presence," which focuses attention on the devaluation—both financial and political—of minority presence during this time. Keyder described this period (1910 to the 1950s) as one in which non-Muslims were "eliminated and driven away . . . their property, as well as the positions they vacated, became part of the dowry of the new state that could be distributed to the rest of the population" (1997:40).

Despite these hardships, some non-Muslims, albeit a tiny fraction at less than 1 percent of the population today, remained in Turkey. According to statistics, it is assumed that there are currently sixty to sixty-five thousand Armenians, twenty to twenty-five thousand Jews, and three thousand Greeks remaining in Turkey (Karimova and Deverell 2001). Moreover, their traces of difference were overwhelmingly erased from the national narrative when the Republic of Turkey redefined the status of its minorities as full citizens. After centuries during which Jews and Christians in the Ottoman Empire enjoyed protected status, the Jewish community exchanged inequality for universal citizenship under the new republic.

The Jewish community in Istanbul today is not segregated legally or politically from general Turkish society or its institutions. However, as many historians have noted, this juridical position of equality was (and continues to be) imperfectly matched by widespread discrimination, social rejection, and suspicion of "foreigners."

As Jews in Istanbul reckon with difference in the present political milieu, they remain aware of a backdrop of historically contingent cosmopolitanisms built with a logic distinct from that of the present regime. On one hand, present-day discussions of "tolerance" for Jews in Turkey are necessarily influenced by the deep history of (shifting) Ottoman usages of the term; on the other, not only has the term "tolerance," as a "word in motion" (Gluck and Tsing 2009), taken on new meanings in global usage (Blommaert and Verschueren 1998), the terms of citizenship and therefore of toleration have also been dramatically altered.

Turkey, the Middle East, Europe, and the Jews

News commentaries, political debates, and academic conferences function as arbiters in debates about Turkey's place in the world. In some contexts, Turkey (and research about it) is squarely located in the Middle East. In others, it is vigorously defended as European. Since its inception, the Turkish Republic has been imagined through its Western orientation and therefore as deviant with regards to "real" Middle Eastern countries.

At the same time, Turkey's ongoing (and contested) negotiations for inclusion within the European Union elucidate the unstable processes inherent in the creation and refiguring of world areas and their boundaries (see Appadurai 1996; Abu-Lughod 1989; Gupta and Ferguson 1997; and Herzfeld 1997). Lingering doubts about whether Turkey should be accepted into the European Union necessarily inform Jewish life in Turkey and, as such, this ethnography. Turkey has long been imagined as the seam between East and West, and its marginal status has long been theorized (Todorova 1997). But can Istanbul's continental straddle offer a model for cosmopolitanism beyond the clichéd bridge between East and West, between Europe's margins and centers? Anthropologist Zeynep Gürsel's brilliant ethnographic film, *Coffee Futures* (2009), uses the popular ritual of reading coffee fortunes as an opportunity to talk with Turks about their predictions for relations between Turkey and the European Union. As the skeptical fortune-tellers and political leaders featured in the film insist, there is no way to know when and if Turkey will join the European Union (see also Mandel 2008:11–13). I likewise make no predictions about Turkey's acceptance or rejection from the European Union, although like so many, I am wary of the terms of the process itself. However, this book adds a critical element beyond the project of prognostication: a mapping of how discursive categories such as Turkish, foreign, Jewish and European come to exist, change, and exert power in society. I detail the spaces of contestation for Turkish Jews in an ambiguously defined region, highlighting the rhetorical and symbolic claims through which their urban cosmopolitan identity is formed (see also Örs 2006). These negotiations open up a discussion about the relationship between geographic and cultural locations, a topic that recurs throughout this book. How does a study of Turkish Jews call these boundaries further into question? What cultural assumptions must we rely upon if we take Turkish Jews as our research subjects? Where (in the world) do we locate such subjects?

Locating Jews in geographic space is never a simple task, especially when that location is so widely contested as Turkey is today (Navaro-Yashin 2002). If only a century ago there were nearly a million Jews living in the Islamic world outside of Iran, now the Turkish Jewish community is one the largest of the few remaining in what is regularly seen as a "Muslim milieu." Given that there are so few examples of continuing Jewish communal life in the Islamic world, one would think that the story of Turkish Jewry would be sought after and demanded by scholars and laypeople alike. However, both Turkey and Turkish Jewry have tended to fall through the cracks as not-quite-Middle Eastern and not-quite-European.

Framing modern Turkish Jewry through an area studies approach as "Middle Easterners" or "Europeans" has other serious flaws, given the mass out-migration of one-third of Turkey's Jewish community after the establishment of the State of Israel as well as patterns of exodus in times of economic crisis, anti-minority activities, or political turmoil (Tuval 2004:59–63; Mallet 2008:537–538). Jews from Turkey living in Israel, for example, generally call themselves "Sephardic" (Spanish) and are uncomfortable with the designation "Mizrahi" (oriental or Middle Eastern) (Goldberg and Bram 2007:232). Locating cosmopolitans is not as simple as choosing one geographical or cultural assignment over another. Chapter 2 introduces the reader to Baruh, a Jew with whom I conducted research in Istanbul between 1999 and 2002. Soon after I left Istanbul, Baruh moved to Jerusalem to live near his only daughter and her family. I later visited Baruh in Israel, only to find that he had packed his Turkish life into a shipping container in order to recreate, in a new, slightly smaller space, his apartment in Istanbul. The home smelled the same, although everything was slightly brighter in the sunnier spot, a two-hour flight from where I had seen it last. Baruh speaks to his Israeli-born granddaughters in English, his daughter in French, and the greengrocer in Hebrew. Is he still a Turkish Jew? Turkish Jews have an ambiguous relationship with Israel as an imagined homeland where they do not actually live (see Levy 1997; Levy and Weingrod 2005). Complicating this relationship are the lukewarm, and often contested, relations the Turkish government maintains with Israel, as well as a widespread Turkish antipathy to Zionism.

Although many people with whom I worked in Istanbul have since moved away from Istanbul, this book outlines movement not only in physical space but also through symbolic terrains. How do we define Jewish locality and culture areas? How do narratives of language, literacy, and religion and diaspora play a role in these definitions?[4] The sorting through of meaning and classification of "us" and "them" is an ongoing cultural process of organizing information; defining what is classifiably local and what is absolutely foreign draws my analysis toward the negotiation of cosmopolitan identities and their related semiotic strategies, described in this book through the Turkish Jewish case.

Fieldwork in Istanbul

Istanbul, divided by the Sea of Marmara into European and Asian banks, has Jewish neighborhoods on both sides. The Jewish population has been classified by geographical origin prior to arrival in the Ottoman Empire, with groups having come from Byzantium, Italy, Eastern Europe, Portugal and Spain. However, over 90 percent of the present community claims descent from the Iberian Peninsula, with ancestors arriving in the Ottoman Empire at the time of the Spanish Expulsion. The shift in population centers of the Jewish communities in the Turkish Republic shows a sharp decline in the communities outside Istanbul and reflects their increased urbanization: over 90 percent of Turkish Jews live in urban centers—mostly in Istanbul—with an estimated 1,500 in Izmir and small communities in Ankara, Bursa, Adana, and Antakya (Tuval 2004:1; Weiss 1975:169).

Jews regularly enact their cosmopolitanism not where they eat, sleep, or work, but rather in a handful of buildings and streets in what was once Pera, but today is called Galata, Beyoğlu, or Karaköy. The neighborhood itself was home to the offices of the Istanbul 2010: European Capital of Culture Agency, the planning center for activities held in honor of Istanbul's designation for 2010, which through its multiple projects imagined the urban landscape as transformed into a stage for Turkey's European-ness (Brink-Danan 2010). During my ethnographic fieldwork conducted between 2001 and 2003, I often came to this area to visit the Jewish Museum, for a meeting at the Offices of the Chief Rabbinate, or to attend a function at Neve Shalom synagogue. Pera—a nineteenth-century nexus for Muslims, foreigners, and non-Muslim Ottoman subjects—served as a test case for European-style modernization: banks, widened streets, and other architectural innovations marked the area as progressive (Karmi 1996; Bartu 1999). Early twentieth-century Jewish elites tied their fate to this neighborhood's Westernizing elite as a claim and path to modernization (Kastoryano 1992:258). Evidence of this era survives in the architectural formation called the Kamondo Steps,[5] named for its sponsor, Abraham Kamondo, a Jewish Ottoman banker whose alliances with major European Jewish figures, such as the Rothschilds and Baron de Hirsch, opened a path to the West for Ottoman Jewry. Seni has noted the Kamondos' impact on the

> urban fabric of Istanbul . . . where the family business began. Their influence derived principally, although not solely, from a real-estate empire centered mainly in Galata, the European section of the city. The family also played an important role in transforming the city in other ways, for example, in the development of a system of transportation. (1994:664)

Made famous by French photographer Cartier-Bresson, the Kamondo Steps signal a "Europeanist" moment in a changing architectural and human landscape of Ottoman minorities, but the tale of Istanbul's Jews does not end there. The pirouetting curves of the stairs link Constantinople to Istanbul, recalling how Turkish Jews have continually remained connected to the rest of what many now simply call "Europe."

Highlights of this long relationship include the presence of Romaniote Jews in the Byzantine Empire; the already-mentioned influx of Jews to the Ottoman Empire after their expulsion from the Iberian Peninsula and the maintenance of Judeo-Spanish as this community's lingua franca until the mid-twentieth century; the introduction of French as an elite Jewish language with the arrival of the Alliance Israélite Universelle (AIU) schools in Constantinople and throughout the Ottoman Empire (a process precipitated by Kamondo and his sympathizers). With genealogical roots in Spain and a legacy of French education, Turkish Jews reveal European influences in their linguistic practices, travel itineraries, and musical styles (Dorn 1991). The Turkish Jewish case thus illuminates debates about geographic and cultural boundary-drawing in interesting ways: Turkish Jews now largely live in Istanbul, have a history of embracing things they consider "Western," and maintain a commitment to Turkish secularism (seen as a European project by its supporters and detractors alike; see Houston 2001).

Given its history, it is not surprising that Galata today is the staging ground for performances of Europeanness upon which Istanbul's Jews—and other Turks—act out their role as cosmopolitans. However, I would argue that this role is not shaped by nostalgia. Rather, Jews (or their officials) are motivated by the very practical goal of using Istanbul's landscape as a site through which to argue for Turkey's—and their own—deep ties to Europe. One indication of this is visible in the recent marking of the Kamondo Steps with a plaque acknowledging their creator, and in the Kamondo Mausoleum Rehabilitation Project, supported by the Istanbul 2010 European Capital of Culture Agency (Gültekin 2009:38).

As tourists learn, to see the sites of Galata (the Kamondo Stairs, the Jewish Museum, the Neve Shalom synagogue) is to take a nostalgic tour of Turkish Jewish history. However, if one wants to visit Jews living in Turkey today, then Galata is the wrong destination. The majority of Jews now live in neighborhoods such as Şişli, Nişantaşı, Gayrettepe, Göztepe, or Etiler (Tuval 2004: 85–87). These demographic shifts map the changing socio-economic status of Istanbul's Jews and reflect larger social changes that have altered the overall pattern of residence in the city (Varol 1989; Kastoryano 1992). Twenty-first-century Istanbul lacks a Jewish center; Jews in Istanbul do not live in a neighborhood enclave with the synagogue at its hub and all community activities revolving around it. One could, for example, visit a Jewish home in the working-class neighborhood of Şişli, where a family of four lives in a dark railroad apartment, fries cheaply bought fish in a kitchen the size of a closet and rides public transportation to a menial labor job at a large clothing factory. Meanwhile, the owner of that factory, also a Turkish Jew, resides in an opulent *site* (a condominium-like gated community) an hour's drive out of Istanbul near Tarabya Bay and is served sushi and other delicacies by live-in maids and cooks. While the working-class Jew struggles to get scholarships for her daughter's school fees, the wealthy one guarantees his children's academic success with English tutors, exam preparation, and full-time chauffeurs who shuttle them between the most exclusive private schools and clubs.

The challenge of deciding where to live while conducting research revealed a basic demographic reality of the Jewish community in Istanbul: there were areas of higher and lower Jewish residency but no dominant rule about one place where Jews congregate. Therefore, I ended up living in Beşiktaş, a central area within walking distance of two different synagogues, one in the textile district and the other a waterfront synagogue next to a kosher restaurant. I could travel easily from Beşiktaş by bus and ferry to other centrifugal areas of Jewish life. Following Jews as they moved around Istanbul's landscape, I might find myself window shopping at an elite mall or at a supermarket where I could buy soy sauce, tofu, and shitake mushrooms among giant glossy images of Atatürk in a tuxedo, or I might go with Jewish friends to a bohemian café owned by the friend of a left-wing sociology student. I might travel to a wholesale novelties district, where Jewish customers greet the owners of the business with the Arabic *asalaam aleikum* (peace be upon you) of the pious Muslim merchants working beside them.

Although there remain few areas where Jews are likely to live in dominant groups, inversely, some neighborhoods are defined by populations with which Jews rarely cohabit: ultra- nationalist areas, religious Muslim neighborhoods, squatter towns, and so forth. Now lined with music shops and artists' studios, areas of Istanbul once inhabited by Jews and other minorities, such as Galata and Kuzguncuk (see Houston 2001:17–34; Mills 2006, 2010), became hip and quaint when emptied of them. At the same time, claims to property in former Jewish neighborhoods have become politically sensitive in light of the needs of new residents who now call these seemingly abandoned places home. For example, the Jewish community owns a plot of land that they wish to develop for a community center, but the area has been built up with *gecekondu* (squatter settlements) by migrants from outside Istanbul (see White 2002), and Jewish officials don't want to enter the political fray that would ensue if ownership of this land was contested.

Given Turkish Jews' dispersal throughout the socio-economic and geographic map of the city, how does one locate the community? Indeed, is it fair to call Jews in Istanbul a "community?" In contrast to Tuval's study (2004) of the Jewish community in Istanbul between 1948 and 1992, which featured demographic and political analyses largely based on his work with documents and interviews with community elites (as would befit his status as a retired Israeli public servant and former consul to Istanbul), my ethnography aims to tell the story of a broader spectrum of Turkish Jewry, their concerns and contemporary issues. As I will recount in further detail elsewhere in this book, the social and political positions of Jews within the community—and within Turkish society more broadly—impact their stakes in performing knowledge of difference. However, despite variations in local Jewish life, I comfortably refer to Jews in Turkey as a "community" (in Turkish, *cemaat*), given the centralized authority of the chief rabbi, the claims to a general unity of geographic origin (Iberian), and centripetal residence patterns (the vast majority of Turkish Jews live in Istanbul).[6] Unlike Jewish communities in a number of global locales, in which a multiplicity of options for social and religious organization exist, the Turkish Jewish community is centralized, comprehensive, and, for those who critique its leadership, censuring. For those who trespass beyond the boundaries of acceptable community limits, no alternate branches, sects, or leaders exist outside the rabbinate's auspices. For example, a couple who wants to be married in a Jewish ceremony must register with the rabbinate.

While there are no alternatives to nominal orthodoxy in today's Turkish Jewish scene, I observed a diverse range of practices and philosophies in the Turkish Jewish community. Some Jews kept kosher and attended synagogue every week, whereas others only attended synagogue services for the last five minutes of Yom Kippur, the day of atonement considered by many Jews to be the holiest day of the year. Of the forty synagogues in Istanbul, about twenty have active members, staff, and rabbinic leadership. While a small group of Jewish students (fewer than one thousand) attend Jewish schools, the majority study at state and private schools and attend Turkish universities. Turkish and English are the primary languages of instruction at the Jewish schools, with basic Hebrew also being taught a few hours a week. For Jewish boys, basic tutoring in Hebrew takes place in sessions with the local rabbis in preparation for their Bar-Mitzvah, the coming-of-age ritual for boys. Although constituting a small fraction of the Turkish population, the Jewish community of Istanbul today has a strong infrastructure, maintaining a handful of kosher restaurants and butchers, its own school, hospital, museum, and press.

Sephardic Jews have been described as both traditional and open to modernization (Stillman 1995; Lehmann 2005). Because of their different historical trajectories, Sephardic and Ashkenazi Jews reacted to political and cultural emancipation with quite distinct social reforms (see Stillman 1995). The ultra-Orthodox practices of Eastern European Jews arose in response to reformist Jewish movements as a way to maintain authority and to protect themselves from assimilation. However, in Sephardic communities throughout North Africa and the Middle East, no alternative reformist movements were created. Although Sephardic Jews took up assimilationist opportunities, the cultural expectations of the lands where they lived allowed (if not required) Jews to continue to maintain certain boundaries, which kept them from the general population. For example, the emancipatory practices in the Ottoman Empire that allowed Jews to learn French as pupils of the Alliance schools did not make them more like their neighbors but less so. Sephardic Jewish communities did not see a rise in ultra-Orthodox practice until Jews from the Balkans, North Africa, and the Middle East began arriving in Israel, where the missionary zeal of Chabad (and other Ashkenazi sects) succeeded in convincing them to become stricter in their adherence to and interpretation of Jewish law (Stillman 1995). I observed a similar trend among a handful of followers of a Chabad rabbi who has lived in Istanbul for a decade now.[7]

Before I began fieldwork I was warned, "If you want to learn about Jewish life in Istanbul, don't look in the synagogue." In sharp contrast to a 2006 study by the Turkish Economic and Social Studies Foundation, in which nearly 60 percent of Turks described themselves as "very religious" or "extremely religious," most Jews I met in Istanbul saw themselves as devoutly secular: social connections, community folk dancing, or playing basketball was more central to their Jewish identity than attending synagogue or keeping Jewish dietary laws (*kashrut*). Community centers draw Jewish youth together for a range of cultural, educational, and social activities, including folk dancing, sports, theater, and holiday celebrations. A *yetişkin gençler* (young adult) group created in the first few years of the twenty-first century lacked affiliation with any particular synagogue or Jewish social club. Its aim was to bring "marriageable" Jews together from different parts of Istanbul for social events with the aim of promoting endogamous (intra-Jewish) unions. This group maintains an online discussion group and throws parties in different venues in Istanbul.

Many Jews leave Istanbul during the summer for their residences on a collection of nine islands (Princes' Islands), all accessible from Istanbul by boat within an hour. Due to the high concentration of religious minority residents, the islands have been called an "open air ethnographic museum of pluralism and multiculturalism" (Schild 1998, 2004).[8] This perception of the islands' "foreignness" is echoed in the title of a film about Burgaz Ada (one island in this archipelago) called *Nearby Yet Far Away—The Isle of Burgaz* (Hazar 2004). Another island, Büyük Ada, provides a car-free and breezy retreat from Istanbul's congested and hot summer months. The island has two active synagogues, kosher restaurants, and large pool clubs whose membership is comprised almost entirely of Jews. On warm Friday nights during the summer, after families have gone to synagogue or eaten a meal with family, friends and relatives crowd the teahouses and streets surrounding the clock tower in the central square near the ferry dock. The island is a unique example of Jewish public space, and although young people have begun spending less time there, it remains a popular symbol of Jewishness and religious difference in Turkey. A man who has a summer home on the island regularly brings his business partner, a Muslim. The friend always makes the same joke about how foreign the place seems, saying, "Thanks for bringing me to the island. I got to visit another country without renewing my passport!"

A frequent example of Turkish Jewish "mixed" language refers to the arrival of Jews at Büyük Ada by ferry: "El vapur esta yanaşeyando a la skala de Büyük Ada" ("The ferry is approaching the Büyük Ada dock." The syntax of the sentence is recognizably Judeo-Spanish while the nouns and verb root for "approaching" are borrowed from Turkish). While lounging around a pool at a largely Jewish club on Büyük Ada, a Turkish friend who heard about my project exclaimed, "We [the Jews] have no culture here. Come back in five years; there'll be no Jews left in Turkey."

Demographic trends indicate that the Turkish Jewish community is similar to many other Diasporic Jewish communities (outside of Israel) in exhibiting a decline in numbers over time (Schmelz et al. 1983), attributable to a number of factors: migration, low birthrate, an aging population, and out-marriages resulting in non-Jewish identification of offspring. The intercensal change in Jewish population between 1945 and 1955 was 40 percent, largely due to mass emigration to Israel (see Weiker 1988). Between 1923 (the foundation of the Turkish Republic) and 1965, the number of Jews in Istanbul alone dropped from 47,000 to 30,831. Between 1945 and 1965, the percentage of Jews who called Judeo-Spanish their mother tongue decreased from around 62,000 (81 percent of the community) to 12,772 (33 percent) (Weiss 1975:168). Turkish Jews regularly complained to me about the high rates of assimilation, intermarriage (long frowned on in Turkish Jewish society, which historically prioritized endogamous marriage) and a low birthrate (Toktaş 2006a:129–130). One sixty-year-old Turkish Jew described the problem thus: "If every year or so we have one *brit milah* [Hebrew; ritual infant male circumcision], that is, one boy is born every few years, who will he marry when he grows up?" This man's children have since moved to Israel. One married an Israeli; the other is still searching for a Jewish mate.

Despite these seemingly bleak demographics and negative prognostications, this ethnography is neither nostalgic nor romantic; it does not engage with salvage anthropology in pursuit of saving the heritage of Turkey's dying community (cf. Salzmann and Gürsan-Salzmann 2010). If there was one trend I observed among Turkish Jews, it was that their history taught them to be ready for change. Political philosopher Seyla Benhabib, a Sephardic Jew from Turkey whose work on cosmopolitanism enjoys wide circulation, gave this response to an interview question about how her family history caused her to view the world: "It makes me aware of the fragility of good political institutions. I never take them for granted ... It makes me very attentive to what I would like to call practices of good governance and state-building, and makes me realize how fragile and unpredictable the course of history is" (2003).

Turkish Jews share a history of expulsion and migration across borders both political and cultural; this is evident in the legacy of community-wide multilingualism. Rodrigue writes that "The polyglot orientation of the Jews has survived to this day, in spite of the process of Turkicization begun seriously under the republic" (1990:172). During fieldwork I found myself using many languages with Jews in Istanbul. Sephardic multilingualism demanded that I speak French and/or Judeo-Spanish with grandparents, Turkish with middle-aged members of the family, and English with young students eager to practice.[9] Sometimes I was mistaken for an Israeli and greeted in Hebrew, a language learned by many Turkish Jews during their massive out-migration to Israel during the 1950s (only to find that a longing for Istanbul or a better job prospect drew them back to Turkey). Years of education in multiple languages and the constant negotiation between religious laws and secular citizenship have created a true semiotic awareness among Turkish Jews.

In this light, I recall the assertion that "The distinction between geography and anthropology largely rests on a distinction between the 'outer knowledge' given by observation of 'man's' place in nature (geography) and the 'inner knowledge' of subjectivities (anthropology)" (Harvey 2000:534). This book draws on research conducted in multiple sites (albeit largely within Istanbul); however, a larger goal of the project aims to map the travel not only of people but also of ideas, of "knowledge schemas" adapted from other historical times (as such, vertically multi-sited) as well as from other places (horizontally multi-sited). The Jews in this multitudinous city have amassed an encyclopedic knowledge of culturally significant (and at times, oppositional) references that allow them to negotiate social and political change. Simply put, today's Turkish Jews are deeply cosmopolitan because of their collective and enduring knowledge of difference, their recognition of optional social codes for belief and behavior, and perhaps most centrally, because of their awareness of the importance of context and performance in the enactment of these codes.

Cosmopolitanism as Knowledge:
A Reevaluation of the Term

What kind of cosmopolitanism do Turkish Jews exhibit? A spatial definition of the cosmopolitan is one who "moves across global space"; a
social definition sees this character as never belonging to a single community; a political cosmopolitanism imagines humans as citizens of the
world; a structural understanding of cosmopolitanism views the phenomenon as an elitist position from which to look down on locals; a
moralizing cosmopolitanism demands that one "show solidarity with
strangers"; and finally, an essentialist definition of cosmopolitanism sees
each human as transcending social systems and classifications (Rapport
and Stade 2007:232–233). While this list might seem exhaustive, none
of these definitions accounts for the central quality of cosmopolitanism I observed in Istanbul: reflective knowledge of how to interpret and
manage difference.

In popular European theorizations of the cosmopolitan and the local during the early 1990s, cosmopolitans are described as "seek[ing]
out contrast rather than cultural uniformity and cultivat[ing] skills in
navigating foreign cultural terrains" (Hannerz in Rapport and Stade
2007:227). This way of imagining the cosmopolitan derives from a view
that in order to become cosmopolitan one has to actively pursue difference. But what if the person and his or her community have already
been marked as "different?" Some of the most negative uses of the term
"cosmopolitan" have been applied to Jews. Of the use of the term as an
epithet, Beck writes, "The Nazis said 'Jew' and meant 'cosmopolitan'; the
Stalinists said 'cosmopolitan' and meant 'Jew'" (2006:3; see also Richardson 2008:17). This sense of the term carries negative implications
in the minds of those who claim that Jews are never loyal patriots (see
Beck 2002). Does one need to choose to be cosmopolitan? There seems
nothing inherently ethical in recognizing difference once the element
of choice is taken away (Benhabib 2006:20). For millennia Jews (Boyarin
and Boyarin 1993; Habib 2004; Haskell 1994; Shokeid 1988; Levy 1997,
1999; Levy and Weingrod 2005) and other Diasporics (Clifford 1994)
have been confronted with contrasting symbolic systems whether or
not they chose them or sought them out. Thousands of years in and
of Diaspora might well breed cosmopolitan skills in "navigating for-

eign cultural terrains" right at "home" (Hannerz in Rapport and Stade 2007:227).

What does the experience of Jews in Istanbul illuminate about cosmopolitanism that studies of Jamaicans (Wardle 2000), Sindhis (Falzon 2004), and Turks in Germany (Mandel 2008) have not? The Turkish Jewish case minimally challenges two tenets of cosmopolitanism as (1) an individualistic pursuit, and (2) a choice, and therefore an ethical orientation. The Turkish Jewish case provides an important corrective to the tendency to see cosmopolitanism exclusively through the lens of Kantian universalism. One productive reason for calling Turkish Jews "cosmopolitan" is that their collective experience challenges the way in which theorists of cosmopolitanism regularly assume an individual subject in search of universal ethics. An excessive focus on the individual as the object of cosmopolitan imaginings may derive from the fact that so much work on cosmopolitanism traces its definition along pre-drawn contours outlined by Kantian philosophy. This kind of Kant-infused anthropology of cosmopolitanism, in Rapport's words, "aspires to a global moral environment where more and more might know their lives as their own achievement—continually preferred, and possibly exchanged—not an ascription" (Rapport and Stade 2007:226). This seems a particularly Christian, or Pauline, understanding of how we (or more correctly, how Christians) come to be who we (they) are in the world. But why must we cling to an exclusively Kantian definition of the cosmopolitan as a "transcendent individual" (Rapport 1997)? To borrow from an earlier disciplinary debate, when we anthropologists speak about "culture" today, do we remain married to nineteenth-century definitions of culture that anchor our disciplinary history, or do we acknowledge the changes in meaning this term has undergone (Kuper 1999)? Like the term "culture," the very definition of what is "cosmopolitan" has inevitably changed over time, and we benefit from considering its historical (or theological) roots as useful but not all-encompassing (Habermas 1997:126). Would it not be more intellectually fruitful to adjust the theoretical imaginary to the evidence that challenges and confronts our comfortable models?

By imagining cosmopolitans as transcendent individuals, we negate the genealogical ties that govern so much of Jewish community life, both in Turkey and in Diaspora more generally. This model also ignores the fact that for so many Jews their identity is understood (by themselves and others) to be the inverse of what Rapport and others imagine as cosmopolitan: ascribed rather than achieved. As Appadurai noted over a decade ago, global identity, whether cosmopolitan or not, doesn't necessarily develop out of free will and the ever-expanding choice of individuals (1996). Rather, global identities display a remarkable degree of essentialism and collectivist imaginings. This is especially true in Turkey, where conversions to Judaism are not authorized by the local rabbinate. Turkish Jews often invoke the terms *mozotros* (Judeo-Spanish for "we" or "ours") or *bizimkiler* (Turkish for "ours") to describe members of the Jewish community as an ascribed group that has functioned for millennia to inspire and inform Jews' cosmopolitanism. If cosmopolitanism isn't something you choose, as the Jewish case seems to imply, the argument that it is a moral or ethical orientation (Appiah 2006) is called into question.

My ethnographic observations of Turkish Jews in Istanbul reveal that cosmopolitan ways of being frequently conflict and contradict each other and are therefore censored. I began to think about this worldview as one type of lived cosmopolitanism: an awareness of multiple audiences, some of whom might be antipathetic ones. Applied more broadly, this scenario complicates the notion that cosmopolitanism requires a public nomination of difference (Calhoun 2002); it may well be that lived cosmopolitanism is observable only by accounting for knowledge of what should be kept private. The privatization of cosmopolitanism has been tied to the emergence of the nation-state out of multi-ethnic or multi-religious empires. Being a Turkish cosmopolitan means not only knowing about different ways of being, but knowing in which *contexts* one should perform difference. This leads to "disemia," or "the expressive play of opposition that subsists in all the varied codes through which collective self-display and self-recognition can be balanced against each other" (Herzfeld 1987:114). In addition to describing the awareness of competing symbolic systems that has been characterized as "double consciousness" (Du Bois 2008),[10] what I call "cosmopolitan knowledge" is a third (and critical) consciousness—or intersubjectivity—that acts as an interpretive superstructure around social rules about when to perform or disavow one's cosmopolitan identity.[11]

An overarching goal of this book will be to illuminate, through ethnographic example, how individuals and groups negotiate change and multiplicity in their world through cosmopolitan knowledge. Central to this concept is the idea, derived from the century-old semiotic theory that still invigorates anthropological studies, that signs are made up not just of symbols and the things they stand for (the dyad of signifier–signified, proposed by de Saussure [1986]). Rather, signs come to have meaning in the world because of a third element, that is, the sense made of the relationship between signifier and signified, that we habitually assign to them. As an early and seminal figure in the study of semiotics, Peirce (1931) focused not just on what things seem to stand for but on the process behind meaning-making itself: how signs come to be interpreted as they are, how they were interpreted in the past, and how they might come to be interpreted in the future. His tripartate model included the representamen (the sign's form), the interpretant (the sense made of the sign), and the object (to which the sign refers).

Cosmopolitan knowledge is therefore not only an awareness of otherness but also an interpretive stance that recognizes and re-inscribes difference by performing or erasing it. We might consider this a "triple consciousness," the superstructure of awareness from whence cosmopolitans make sense of the possibilities and limits that doubleness inheres. Without a fundamental examination of this third kind of consciousness—that is, the sense made of doubleness, and the interpretation, production, and performance of knowledge of difference—a reckoning of lived cosmopolitanism is incomplete. I thus consider the issue of reflective knowledge not as one of the missing pieces that would allow us to define cosmopolitanism, but rather, as a prerequisite for understanding the phenomenon altogether.

Chapter Overview

In the chapters that follow, I explore how knowledge about difference shapes the lives of Jews in Istanbul. Each chapter takes up an aspect of cosmopolitanism to show not only how an ethnography of this community benefits from this theoretical frame but also how the community's practices illuminate something about cosmopolitanism. Rethinking cosmopolitanism along the lines of knowledge of difference and the tensions this engenders suggests a shift at the level of theorizing the phenomenon. It also, however, suggests a shift in method. Studying cosmopolitanism as knowledge performed and erased from public requires attention to the theatricality of micro-discourses, family narratives, and casual conversations as well as to the rhetorical style of public pronouncements.

The book opens with a discussion of the mythologization of Ottoman tolerance and the impact of this rhetoric on today's Turkish Jewish community. Despite assertions that Turks have "amnesia" regarding pre-republican history, there is a rapidly growing interest in recovering the Ottoman past (Özyürek 2007). Among Turkish Jews, for example, it is possible to trace the emergence of a nostalgia that imagines minority citizenship in the Turkish Republic as a legacy of Ottoman forms of religious tolerance. Since its establishment, the Turkish Republic has implemented a shifting range of official policies with regard to its minority populations. These policies redefine basic ideas about Turkish citizenship and have implications for the way in which Turkish Jews envision their difference. As Jews in Istanbul consider the role of religious difference in the present political milieu, they remain aware of a backdrop of historically contingent terms for tolerance built according to logic different from that of the present regime. Through analysis of the Quincentennial Foundation's public relation campaign, chapter 1 systematically examines the creation of a popular rendering of Turkey as a land of "tolerance and love" that draws on Ottoman terms of citizenship and belonging. By beginning the book with a description of this popular discourse and its dissemination, I also point to where the discourse exists in tension with Turkish Jews' lived experience. This focus reveals the sometimes awkward relationship between discourse analysis and ethnography, and also frames the rest of the book with a question: How does public discourse, the patterned and crafted statements that display regularity and consensus (Foucault 1972:38), intersect with the smaller, more intimate conversations, silences, and secrets that are the sites of everyday contestations about the ways things are, were, and should be?

Jews in Turkey are quite used to people assuming they are strangers as soon as they introduce themselves. Chapter 2 shows how Turkish Jewish names signify difference in the present and explores how those differences accrue mythical meaning over time. I discuss the processes through which seemingly local, native, or indigenous people—in this case, Turkish Jews—are reclassified as foreigners. I also explore naming as a process through which the subjects of reclassification themselves understand present-day ontologies—ideas about what things exist or can be said to exist, and how such things should be grouped according to similarities and differences—as historically informed and context dependent. By studying moments of categorical reassignment, I detail the processes that drive the classification of names as indices of belonging or exclusion. Anthropologists increasingly study military, juridical, and economic ontologies that reorder, relocate, and restrict human (and non-human) groups. I illuminate a quiet but powerful space, that of naming, through which classifications are made and undone. Here I shift the definition of cosmopolitanism away from its current obsessions with global movement of money and bodies. I focus instead on cosmopolitanism as a meta-pragmatic awareness of difference, as manifested specifically in naming practices among Turkish Jews.

Reading cosmopolitan difference with Jews in mind allows comparative endeavors that at times represent Jews as having attained, through assimilation, a certain acceptance in the broader Diasporic settings in which they live. For example, in addressing the notion that Muslims are Europe's "new Jews," it has been argued that "Islamophobia . . . is a genuine political issue, part of a wide-open debate on the future of the Muslim presence in Europe. Anti-Semitism, by contrast, is not. This is not to downplay the dangers of the new anti-Semitism but to recognize that it operates on a completely different level" (Bunzl 2005:506). How might we understand the level on which anti-Semitism in Turkey currently operates? By examining the pragmatics of cosmopolitanism, one quickly discovers its limits. If the tolerance trope is increasingly familiar to observers of Turkish Jewish life, so too is the community's impenetrability to visitors and other non-intimates. When confronted with the tension between the pervasive tolerance trope and constant attention to "security," Turkish Jews claim that security measures began as a response to the 1986 attack in which twenty-one people were massacred by Palestinian sympathizers at Istanbul's largest synagogue, ironically named Neve Shalom (Hebrew; Oasis of Peace). Since then, episodes of periodic violence (especially attacks on synagogues in 1992—the Quincentennial anniversary—and 2003) and ongoing threats have challenged the right of Jews to feel safe in the space that they, in their own rhetoric, have called home for over five hundred years.

If Jews feel at home in Turkey, why do they place so much emphasis on security? What does security since Neve Shalom tell us about perpetual peace and cosmopolitan ideals? The publishing house, schools, and synagogues are unmarked as Jewish spaces; visitors must present identification and pass a security check to enter. Moreover, the Jewish community manifests a distinction between private Judaism and public Turkism in a number of ways, ranging from the wearing of Judaica (such as necklaces with Hebrew or Stars of David) underneath their garments to the placement of *mezuzot* on the inside of the threshold of their homes. Chapter 3 portrays the dangers involved in claiming a cosmopolitan identity and the political situations in which this claim might be censored. These dangers are both physical (such as attacks on persons and institutions) and social-symbolic (such as political exclusion, social ostracism, and discrimination). Here I focus on the historical demands toward assimilation (Turkicization), the relationship of Turkish Jews to Israel, and anti-Semitism in Turkey. In this light, I investigate the conditions in which Jews in Istanbul consider themselves reluctant cosmopolitans and the relationship between tolerance and security. I focus on the role of practices that allow the Turkish Jewish community to maintain its "appearance of disappearance," including community border maintenance, social alignment, and differentiation in architecture, language, clothing, and naming practices.

The year 2002 was a historic one for the Jewish community of Turkey. For the first time in nearly half a century, a new chief rabbi was to be installed. Further, this was the first time the rabbi would be chosen through a community-wide democratic election rather than by a small committee of elites (Brink-Danan 2009). The term for chief rabbi in Turkey, *hahambaşı*, is a combination of the Turkish *baş*, "head," and the Hebrew *haham*, "scholar." The composite title announces the figure of chief rabbi in Turkey as responsible both to a small community of co-religionists (*dindaşlar*) and to a republican government and its officials. The changing role of the chief rabbi reflects shifting local, national, and global ideas about how Turkish Jews are supposed to relate to the broader society, and the democratic election of 2002 was no different. Chapter 4 focuses on the 2002 election and inauguration of Turkey's chief rabbi, emphasizing how it was a dense site for the enactment of a "politics of presence" (Phillips 1994) in which democracy is seen not only as a practice through which to debate ideas but a discursive move to represent collective difference in the public sphere. As such, observing the performative nature of minority politics illuminates how these alternative discursive spheres relate to the broader contexts in which they occur.

In chapter 5 I bring together concerns about cosmopolitan ideologies and their performative enactment in social and ritual spaces. Through descriptions of various meetings, including musical performances, parent-teacher association meetings, and a pre-marriage information session, I show how these ritualized spaces offer the community a variety of stages upon which to perform cosmopolitan knowledge. This chapter is organized to give the reader a taste of the range of performative spaces in which Turkish Jews find themselves.

Between the relentless retelling of Turkish tolerance of Jewish difference in official community representations and the repetition of episodes in which I was warned about the enduring risks inherent in public Jewishness, I had a sinking feeling that I would be left without a story; unless, perhaps, the production of cosmopolitan knowledge, its kaleidoscopic playfulness and pride, fear, and silences was a tale worth telling. I interpret Jews' reluctance about displaying difference as an invitation to reconsider cosmopolitanism and its changing value in Turkey (see also Mills 2008:385). Considering the poetics of silence and irony, the book's penultimate chapter examines how an imaginative use of language allows Turkish Jews to maintain a register of intimacy even when they are speaking the same language as non-Jewish Turks. This chapter further explores the ethics of reporting about a community that would rather represent itself, showing how I, as an ethnographer, wrestle with their code of secrecy.

This book offers a window into the lives of a population that observers of the contemporary Turkish scene have overwhelmingly overlooked. In the ethnography that follows, I balance description of the diversity of life in Istanbul with that of social structures and experiences that Turkish Jews share. I do not define cosmopolitans as free-floating agents of individualism, but as participants in a broad social structure through which difference is marked, defended, and reproduced concomitantly with cosmopolitan knowledge. After documenting, through ethnography, the lives of Turkish Jewish cosmopolitans, the book discusses the broader implications of this study for our understanding of Turkish Jewish life since 1992 and for our ideas about difference in the public sphere.

Turkey has garnered special attention as a test case for the public/ private divide around which the new force of political Islam has increasingly mobilized since the 1990s (White 2002), challenging the secular nature of public life and driving secular idols (for example, the Turkish Republic's founder, Atatürk) from the public sphere into the home (Özyürek 2004; Navaro-Yashin 2002). This has engendered an exciting new critical literature about Turkish nationalism and the Turkish state, but one that largely takes up these questions from the perspective of the majority and its central institutions (Özyürek 2007). This book contributes to this literature by looking at Turkish nationalism and the Turkish state from the perspective of a quantitatively small but symbolically important group, showing how republican ideology has been embraced and rejected by different groups in the country.

This book chronicles the everyday cultural negotiations of a twenty-first-century Jewish community whose story has been largely ignored by scholars in both modern Jewish and Turkish studies. In describing an understudied Jewish community, I aim to fill the lacunae in knowledge about contemporary Jewish life in Turkey, with its deep history of cosmopolitanism and unique ways of dealing with difference. By offering a picture of the Turkish Jewish community's present concerns, I detail cosmopolitanism's tensions as they play out along several axes. These axes of tension include those obtained between political discourses of tolerance and everyday experiences of intolerance, between Jews as foreign and indigenous Turks, between Turkish Jews' sense of security and fear, between private and public performances of self, and between the anthropologist's representations and those generated by her subjects.

An analysis of the particular tensions observable in the Turkish Jewish case brings into view broader theoretical assertions about cosmopolitanism itself. This ethnography, therefore, aims at a double purpose of description and theoretical intervention, a duality whose tensions I have attempted to overcome by offering a historical and ethnographic context for readers outside of Turkish and Jewish studies as well as signposting, in lay terms, the conversations in which I participate as an anthropologist. As I will argue throughout this work, cosmopolitanism relies on knowledge about different ways of being and, perhaps more importantly, understanding in which contexts one should (and should not) perform difference. By studying Jews in Istanbul, I show how without a fundamental examination of the production and interpretation of knowledge of difference, a reckoning of lived cosmopolitanism—tensions and all—is incomplete. I thus consider the issue of tension not as a symptom of cosmopolitanism's failure but rather, as an essential site for understanding the phenomenon altogether.

ONE

Tolerance, Difference, and Citizenship

As Turkey continues its half-century march toward joining the European Union, its Jews have been singled out as living proof of Turkey's fulfillment of the Union's "recognition of diversity" criterion. Public efforts toward "recognition of diversity," however imperfectly matched with celebrations of national and pan-European identity, have become a pillar of European self-definition (Soysal, Bertilotti, and Mannitz 2005:27). Jews, particularly, occupy a central role in European claims to cosmopolitanism, especially as a foil against cries of intolerance made by other differentiated citizens and their champions (Peck 2006:154–174). Playing their part in international arenas, Jews regularly proclaim Turkey's eternal hospitality and tolerance for difference to a global audience as counterpoint to European politicians' regular criticisms of Turkey's treatment of Armenians, Kurds, and Islamists.[1] This shift on the part of Turkish Jews—from a quiet, assimilating posture to a more public performance of difference—marks a change in the way they represent themselves and is but one reflection of the myriad ways in which Turkey's European Union overtures, its rapprochement with Israel and the United States, and other global political shifts have set the stage for Jews to stand symbolically for the tolerated Other. Istanbul, home to the vast majority—over 90 percent (Tuval 2004:xxxiii)—of Turkey's Jews, is the obvious theater for the Jewish community to perform this role.

As stages for cosmopolitanism, urban centers capitalize on the symbolic power of the city to trump the nation-state context, especially in the public imagination (Örs 2006:81). Istanbul's re-signification echoes trends across Europe's urban landscapes, in places such as Berlin (Peck 2006), Krakow (Kugelmass and Orla-Bukowska 1998), and Vienna (Bunzl 2003), where Jewish museums, musical performances, and memorials are key sites through which cities enact their tolerance of diversity. Gruber notes,

> More than half a century after the Holocaust, an apparent longing for lost Jews—or for what Jews are seen to represent—is also evident. In a trend that developed with powerful momentum in the 1980s and accrued particular force after the fall of communism in 1989–90, Europeans . . . have stretched open their arms to embrace a Jewish component back into the social, political, historical, and cultural mainstream. (2002:4)

To be a European city, it seems, is to "have" Jews. Those who are aware of the history of Jews in the Ottoman Empire and in Turkey are generally able to repeat a story of Ottoman welcome and Turkish tolerance. Although there is long-standing debate about the relative tolerance of Christian and Islamic regimes, many assume that the Turkish tolerance discourse is natural, given the striking contrast between the relatively peaceful experience of Jews in the empire (and under Islam more broadly) and the sometimes blood-stained history of Jews in Eastern Europe (see Cohen 1994; Bat Ye'or 1985). Ottoman and Turkish Jews never lived in ghettos and were never persecuted in a wholesale manner. Ottoman political structure had a place for them as a tolerated minority; further, Jews became full citizens with the shift to a secular republic.

But how did Jews come to engender the role of the *good* minority in today's discussions about Turkish qualifications (or lack thereof) for candidacy in the European Union? The process of becoming a good minority reflects a dedicated campaign of self-representation among Turkish Jews that has been sustained over decades (if not centuries, if we consider Jews' desire to be "good Ottomans"; see Cohen 2008). One group that has taken responsibility for building representations of Turkish Jews as a good minority has been the Quincentennial Foundation (QF), an organization formed in the 1980s to commemorate the five-hundred-year anniversary of the expulsion of Jews from Spain in 1492 (see also Baer 2000; Mallet 2008).

Historians invoke the term "a usable past" (Roskies 1999) to describe how individuals, communities, and nations seek to interpret the

past in light of current concerns and future desires. The QF has publicly resurrected the memory of the Spanish expulsion and the legacy
of Jewish life in the Ottoman Empire. As I noted in the preface, through
conducting research in the archives of the American Branch of the QF,
held at the Sephardi Federation in New York, I was privileged to learn
how a group of Turkish Jews and Muslims has interpreted the story
of Turkish Jewry and disseminated it to an audience largely ignorant
of this history.

In this vein, this chapter describes the ongoing invocation of Ottoman tolerance among Turkish Jews in Istanbul today observable across
the sites of the QF's activity, including in academia, heritage tourism
and, most enduringly, in the creation and maintenance of a Jewish museum in Istanbul. By engaging with the tolerance discourse, my purpose
is neither to congratulate nor to demonize Turkey, nor is it to offer a
comparison of regimes that have been "good" or "bad" for the Jews. I do
not see the mythologization of the Ottoman past or of Turkish tolerance
as a question of false or true representation; instead, I see it as a strategy
for the management of diversity (Barkey 2008:27), illuminating the way
Turkish Jews' self-representations are shot through with tensions that
invite ethnographic observation and analysis.

The Quincentennial Foundation:
The Official Story of Turkish Jewry

Over a decade of fieldwork engagement with Turkish Jews, I observed
that members of this community were acutely aware of their history,
repeating the number "five hundred" like a mantra intoning the years
that have passed since their expulsion from Spain. The expulsion is commonly invoked in discussions of Sephardic culture and in performance.
For example, a half-dozen music groups sing in Judeo-Spanish at concerts around the city and for community affairs. These performances
inevitably mention the five-hundred-year inhabitation of Jews in the Ottoman Empire and the Republic of Turkey; such references are often pro
forma, as even mentioning the number "five hundred" around community members is destined to draw a certain amount of weary eye-rolling.

Nineteen ninety-two was not the first time Turkish Jews undertook
celebrations with a patriotic public face and struggled with the tensions

this process created. Between the nineteenth and twentieth centuries, historiography of the Ottoman Jews was largely hagiographic, applauding the tolerance and the beneficence of the Ottoman sultans. One reason offered for this consistency in representation is that historians of the Ottoman Empire once largely relied on a small sample of the same sources, namely the chronicles of Elijah Capsali and Joseph Sambari (Mallet 2008:62). Celebrations of the four hundredth year of Ottoman Jewish life choreographed performances of loyalty, as Jews aimed to represent themselves as model Ottoman patriots, at home in the empire and abroad: "Ottoman Jews found that the centenary offered them a means through which they could endeavor to reinforce their relationship to their state, and to fashion themselves new as Ottomans" (Cohen 2008:95). Claiming a direct link to the centennial celebrations of the past, a journalist for Şalom, the Turkish Jewish newspaper, announced in 1982 that an event should be scheduled for the five hundredth anniversary, modeled on what had been done in 1892 (Mallet 2008:457).

Nineteen ninety-two was marked around the globe by commemorations (and critiques) of Columbus's journeys. For Turkish Jewry, this year was a time for them to reassert, as Abraham Galante (a Turkish Jewish patriot and intellectual) had in the 1930s, that "Turks and Jews are as indivisible as fingernails and fingers" (Mallet 2008:7). The QF's claim that Turkey's national spirit is infused with a cosmopolitan regard for the Other set the agenda for a public awareness campaign to improve Turkey's international image. This campaign was built around a notion of Jewish gratitude for Ottoman and Turkish hospitality and dovetailed with warming relations with both Israel and the United States (and the "West" more generally). The QF began its activities by hiring a public relations firm, the GCI Group, to help them network with international academic institutions,[2] Jewish organizational leaders and fundraisers,[3] and tourism offices and museums.[4]

Early correspondence (1989–1991) between the QF and American Jewish organizations, educators, and reporters reveals a general lack of knowledge about Ottoman and Turkish Jewish history. Discussing the history of Ottoman Jewry, specifically focusing on the 1492 expulsion and subsequent welcoming of the Jews to Turkey, the chair of an American Jewish organization wrote, "The reality is that we are fundamentally inadequately uninformed about this historic event of modern-day relevance."[5] This audience, the uninitiated, is the QF's prime target, as a board member wrote:

> The problem is what is presented to the world, to those who think Turkey is what one has for Thanksgiving, is the picture of a town with crooked streets and crumbling buildings, colorful vegetable markets and horse carts . . . but where is modern Turkey with its apartments and wide boulevards, daring bridges and snarled traffic, high-rises and hotels and the newly verdant parks along the golden horn and booming industry alongside the quaint little fabric shops? It is difficult to make a synthesis of both . . . yet that is what our people want to project.[6]

The QF's successes, recorded in ten bimonthly status reports created by their public relations group,[7] include the projection of their message through a lecture series on the five-hundredth-anniversary story, distribution of QF educational curricula, sponsored participation in academic conferences, and publication of thousands of articles. Museums were courted to sponsor in-house exhibitions, socialites convinced to host a gala event at the Plaza Hotel in New York City, and Jewish organizations encouraged to send their constituents on Jewish-themed tours of Turkey. These contacts, initiated by the public relations group and the QF's board members, establish the QF's desire to promote a narrative of Turkish–Jewish co-existence in academia, tourism, and museum exhibitions.[8] Each of these interrelated public relations projects speaks to the goal of creating a representation of Turkey and the Ottoman Empire as a place where minorities (specifically Jews) were tolerated.

Academia: Teaching Tolerance

A primary school curriculum, created in conjunction with the QF for Jewish day schools in the United States,

> takes the student step by step through the Sephardic story, beginning with the background information on Jewish life in Spain up to 1492, followed by the early years in the Ottoman Empire. It then proceeds through carefully planned units which focus on economic, political, religious life and all other dimensions of the Jewish experience in the Ottoman Empire and Modern Turkey.[9]

These efforts offered an important corrective to the Ashkenazi (Eastern European)-centric curricula of most Jewish American institutions.

Academic proliferation of the QF's official story in America, which cost around $25,000 for curriculum development, extended beyond the scope of primary school education; the QF's officers organized academic conferences, book publications, and university lectures around the themes of Turkish Jewish tolerance. In a request to a leading Sephardic studies scholar at Yeshiva University in New York to join the executive board, the QF director wrote: "We know that the story the QF wishes to tell is one close to your heart."[10] What followed was a deal with Yeshiva University which pledged that "All lectures in the Sephardic Studies Department in 1991–1992 will be on some aspect of Turkish Jewry."

An academic advisor to the Foundation suggested that a "scholarly work be done on Jews in Turkey—a book about the story we're celebrating—which the foundation would support."[11] Correspondence between the QF and the Memorial Foundation for Jewish Culture illustrates how the latter was persuaded to allocate monies toward a "grant to a scholar doing research/book on the 500th anniversary story." Slowly, yet with the authority of academic scholarship, the anniversary story accrued legitimacy as articles, papers, classes, and books began to focus on the tolerance of the Turks (both Ottomans and republicans) toward the Jews throughout history. At least eight academic publications dealing with Turkish Jewish or Sephardic topics benefited from the QF's financial support (Mallet 2008:473). As mentioned earlier, most publications about Turkish Jewry were concentrated around the Quincentennial years (1991–1993), and accounts published in those years regularly cite the activities of the QF as the culmination of Turkish Jewish experience. While on one hand, this emphasis on Sephardic Jewry was long overdue (see Gerber 1995), the content of many of these publications relies on a heavy-handed rendering of Ottoman tolerance (see, for commentary, Benbassa and Rodrigue 2000:194). The QF-sponsored conference proceedings, collected in a book entitled *Studies on Turkish-Jewish History: Political and Social Relations, Literature, and Linguistics: The Quincentennial Papers* (Altabé, Atay, and Katz 1996) opens with a letter from then-President George Bush congratulating Turkey for its historical example of tolerance and ends with paeans, in the form of poetry, to the Ottoman Empire and the Republic of Turkey. One such example, which appears in *The Quincentennial Papers* in English, Ladino, and Turkish, reads as follows:

Homage to Our Turkish Brethren

Oh, most noble Turk! Compassionate savior of the Sephardim.
Our friendship dates back to when you dwelled in Nishanpur
Beside the remnants of the ancient tribes of Naphtali and Zebulin,
As is told by the Medieval Jewish traveler, Benjamin.

Osman brought you to Anatolia and Mehmet to Istanbul.
Your valiant men instilled terror in Christendom.
Blind to their own savagery, they called you cruel,
Ignoring the justice with which you ruled.

Not so, we Sephardim. We remember what Beyazıt decreed,
His protection to our forefathers from Aragon and Castile,
Echoing Mehmet's words upon conquering the Byzantine.

"The God of the heavens has delivered unto me many lands,
and given me the mission to protect the descendants of Abraham
to give them sustenance and to provide for them a vast refuge . . .
Therefore, come to Istanbul, if you are so inclined,
to live in the shade of the fig tree and the vine."

Such were the words that came from the Fatih's lips,
Words that welcomed the exiled Jews.
When other ports banned their pestilent ships,
When the frontiers of other nations closed,
You opened your doors, you gave us a home.

Grandees of Spain, the flower of our ancient race
Now victim of envy, fanaticism, and hate,
Humbled and hungry, persecuted and debased,
The Sultan was wise enough to appreciate.

Our forefathers brought many skills to the East,
But most important of all was the will to work,
The desire to prosper and live in peace.
We were allowed to do so, thanks to the Turk.

The benevolence granted by your forefathers did not end in 1492,
For five hundred years we have lived side by side, Turk and Jew;
We have shared your destiny, we have eaten your food;
Our Spanish is enriched by your words, our music by your tunes.

And so on this five hundredth anniversary of 1492,
We wish to express to you our gratitude.
The One God, whom we both revere, brought us together.
May the harmony we have known last forever.[12]

Having carefully studied the academic accounts produced out of this campaign prior to my fieldwork in Turkey, I came to Istanbul with an idyllic picture of cosmopolitanism and tolerance that stood, many times, in contrast to the omnipresent security concerns I encountered among present-day Istanbul Jews, who were consistently wracked with doubt about their own differences and displays thereof. Only in retrospect did I realize that the driving icon of tolerance that shaped the narrative of many of these histories precluded other (possibly dissenting) academic engagements. The lack of engagement with more troublesome (i.e., intolerant) episodes in Ottoman and Turkish history, questions of second-class citizenship, and changing relations among the Jews of Turkey, as well as with other minority histories in the region, left me fundamentally unprepared for what I would encounter in Istanbul.

Tourism: Traveling Tolerance

In order to promote general and Jewish tourism to Turkey, the QF contacted Jewish professional organizations to ask what needed to be done to achieve this goal. A director of the United Jewish Appeal responded by explaining,

> We do not travel to Turkey much on pre-missions . . . this is partly due to the lack of promotional material and information about Turkey, its Jewish community, history, etc. I believe it would be in the interest of both your organization as well as the government tourist operation to consider producing material that reflects what we know to be the enormous appeal that Turkey represents where Jewish history and interest are concerned.[13]

He reiterated the importance of a "story," emphasizing that it needn't be an "elaborate public relations campaign, but merely some handy and attractive brochures relating to Jewish travel to Turkey and travel to Turkey in general."[14] Despite protests to the contrary, a major public relations campaign was indeed mounted. Not only did QF materials promote a given interpretation of Turkish history with special attention to its Jewish inhabitants, the means through which the message was conveyed were attractive and far-reaching.

In the heritage-tourism arena, the QF emphasized the value of telling the co-existence story's unique aspects, stressing Turkey's democratic political structure (in contrast to other Muslim-majority states) and its history of cosmopolitanism and hospitality. This theme was picked up by travel writer Tom Brosnahan, whose Jewish Heritage Sites of Turkey was published by the QF in 1992 (Mallet 2008:474) and is reproduced online at his website.[15] In a similar vein, in 1992 the Turkish Ministry of Tourism published a twenty-six-page brochure with the title "Turkey: The Land of Tolerance and Love" that was distributed in hotels and on airlines (Mallet 2008:474).

During the campaign to promote tourism, the QF came up against anti-Turkish press regarding the Armenian and Kurdish populations in Turkey. In response, a member of the QF penned a note to the group's public relations committee detailing what he considered a novel idea involving the Turkish government's donation of Turkish vessels (such as ships and airlines) to an upcoming heritage tour. He bemoaned the bad publicity in the United States and Europe,

> engendered, in part, by highly vocal indigenous minority groups that have been able to gain the attention of the media. These groups have focused attention upon civil conflicts that they have characterized as atrocities. They have painted Turkey as a barbaric, backward inhumane society that abuses the helpless. Under these circumstances, we should not let pass an opportunity to achieve a well-deserved public relations coup by having the Turkish government replicate an historic act of kindness towards perhaps the most oppressed minority the world has ever known.[16]

He continued by contrasting the negative reports with the idyllic history of the Ottoman's tolerant welcome of the Jews of Spain and suggested that sending modern-day transport to "rescue" Jewish heritage tourists from Spain in 1992 could be a tourism and media coup:

> The Quincentennial Celebration in 1992 would give a message heard in all parts of the world by declaring that it would again send ships to receive Jews from Spain—Jews who traveled to that land in sorrowful remembrance of the evil that was perpetrated upon them by the combination of the Spanish Monarchy and Church 500 years ago.

Although this dramatic vision of tourism theater was not realized, the QF nonetheless shaped their official tours around the "tolerance" narrative, inviting Jewish leaders and journalists to participate on sponsored tours, complete with QF-trained guides to act as interpretive guides for all groups. In addition to tours for individuals and synagogue groups, there were tours specifically designed for journalists (sponsored in conjunction with the Turkish national carrier, Turkish Airlines). The QF created an expanded itinerary, including destinations such as Çanakkale, Bursa, Izmir, and Sardis, explaining, "This expanded itinerary is particularly important if we are to generate excellent travel stories."[17]

The reporters were selected based on their affiliations with well-respected media with large circulation. According to GCI's reports, the firm

> invited primarily Jewish media for the first journalist trip because in our professional judgment, it is easier to gain immediate and positive results with the media which have an immediate interest in the story . . . In addition, we feel it essential that the Jewish media in the U.S. have an excellent understanding of the story and are our allies up to and including 1992.

These group vacations, which the QF called "spokesperson tours," were described as presenting the program's message directly to "special interest groups" and to "journalists and key individuals . . . invited to Turkey to witness the facts for themselves" (Güleryüz 1992:27). As a form of public memory, heritage tours are vulnerable to both "shared and contested aspects of memory at the same time" (Özyürek 2006:9). The tension between the QF's constant public pronouncements of how comfortable Jews are in Turkey and the realities of their reluctant cosmopolitanism gave pause to many a visitor. A participant in a QF heritage tour described the Turkish welcome as "not all it's cracked up to be" when compelled by locals to hide his Jewish identity:

> On a bus ride to our hotel, we were told that "Public displays of Jewish nationalism are not encouraged." This same scene would repeat itself, but in a different manner. It's easy to co-exist peacefully when you're invisible! . . . It is my custom to always wear a kipa. As we left the synagogue, the sexton (shamash) chased after me and asked me kindly to remove my kipa while in the streets. An odd request in a peaceful country![18]

Museums: Exhibiting Tolerance

If academic treatises and tourism clustered around the 1992 celebrations, the QF also undertook projects that were intended to endure as a "legacy for the 500th anniversary and beyond" (Güleryüz 1992:26–27), namely, the renovation of the Ahrida synagogue (dating from the fifteenth century) and the preservation of a green space with a monument by Yavuz Gorey, a Turkish sculptor who studied with a German artist who had taken refuge in Turkey following the Nazi rise to power (Reisman 2006:96). The most central and lasting effect of the QF, however, was the institution of a Jewish museum in Istanbul.

The museum, officially named the Quincentennial Foundation Museum of Turkish Jews but often referred to simply as "The Jewish Museum of Turkey," was created by the QF in the defunct Zulfaris synagogue and is quietly nestled at the terminus of a dead end street in Karaköy, Istanbul. In 2003 I observed a group of young Turkish Jewish adults during an organized tour of the museum. The museum's director explained to the tour group that the history of the expulsion and the arrival on Ottoman soil was likely "familiar" and that these sections were intended to "educate the general public." The museum's curator then introduced the goals of the museum to an audience he perceived as already familiar with the exhibition's historical narratives; he explained he was compelled to create the museum after the 1986 synagogue bombing, when the general population in Turkey (as well as the international press) recorded its shock at the revelation, through a newsworthy event, that Jews *still lived* in Istanbul. The museum's director also explained that while the museum serves the local Jewish population, it is really intended to "present the face of Judaism to the outside," as a platform for Jews to have a political presence through which they advocate, in no uncertain terms, for Turkey to be seen as civilized, tolerant, and modern.

Since the 1990s, Turkish intellectuals, Islamists, and others have been debating multiculturalism against the backdrop of years of one-party and military rhetoric that long emphasized the unity of Turkish identity. The desire to represent multiculturalism has resulted in the staging of major exhibitions dedicated to Turkish history, focusing specifically on the early republican period and showcasing the everyday lives of Jews, Greeks, Armenians, Kurds, and Alevis to "make statement(s) about the multicultural nature of the Turkish Republic and the intimate connections of such diverse citizens to each other, as if they formed one family" (Özyürek 2006:70).

If the museum falls into line with other recent Turkish representations of history in local exhibitions, it departs from the general theme and museum narratives of Jewish museums elsewhere in the world. In conversation with the director of Istanbul's Jewish Museum, I was proudly told that all other Jewish museums "have a sad tone . . . but here we have a positive story. The museum promotes Turkey as a place which is *not* anti-Jewish and *not* anti-minority."[19] Of course, this museum is not the first to take up the organizing frame of tolerance. But analysis of the Museum of Tolerance (MOT) in Los Angeles reveals that in many cases, tolerance talk demands what historian Salo Baron (1928) famously called a "lachrymose" conception of Jewish history as "bad to the Jews." In the logic of the MOT and others, this lachrymose history demands that we learn from Jewish experience to be tolerant of those subjects who occupy similarly abject positions (Brown 2006). The Jewish Museum of Turkey expresses a radically different sentiment about Jewish history, a markedly anti-lachrymose interpretation of the Ottoman Empire's and Republic of Turkey's exemplary tolerance for their Jewish subjects, as reflected in the QF's assertion that "Jewish history is full of sad events which are marked by commemorations and memorial services. But now there was a major event to celebrate" (Güleryüz 1992:25). What is striking here is how the term "tolerance," whether used in a lachrymose histori-cal sense (such as that employed by the Museum of Tolerance) or to laud Turkish and Ottoman acceptance (as at the Jewish Museum of Turkey), has the same effect of ossifying a public discourse about the need for a cosmopolitan toleration of the eternal Other. What representative strat-egies does the museum in Istanbul use to exhibit tolerance of the Other?

The main exhibition, which includes Jewish ritual objects (such as a prayer shawl and a candelabra) with a crescent and star (a typical Islamic motif), organizes its themes around the recursive narration of Turkish–Jewish co-existence across social domains: journalism, art, medicine, and even diplomatic service. Exhibition panels contextualize objects within the tolerance trope, as in the following description:

> Jews have been able to live in peace under the religious freedom provided by both the Ottoman Empire and the Turkish Republic. They have been influenced by the prevailing traditions of the society of which they were an incumbent part and they have absorbed aspects of their cultural con-text. This is evidenced in the adoption of Ottoman and Turkish motifs in the design of Jewish artifacts and even in the creation of the liturgical objects. (Kamhi and Ojalvo 1997:10)

FIGURE 4
Gallery at the Jewish Museum of Turkey.
Marcy Brink-Danan, 2007.

"Tolerance terms" recur throughout the panels and saturate sentences, as in the following note from the curator in the catalog: "Yesterday symbolizes a history of *co-existence in peace and harmony that has served as an 'example to humanity'"* (Kamhi and Ojalvo 1997:ix; emphasis added).

The Jewish Museum alternates the word "tolerance" with a vast (although sometimes tenuously related) vocabulary; the terms "Turkish–Jewish friendship," "peace," "religious freedom," "harmony," "co-existence," "mutual respect," "humanitarianism," "civilization," and "equality" permeate its panel texts, catalogs, and related literature. Perhaps more importantly, the images selected and their placement in the building tell a recursive tale of Turkish–Jewish symbiosis. The selection of objects in the main hall displays *only* syncretism (with an emphasis on Jewish borrowing from the Turkish majority frame). The absence of actual Jewish difference or otherness, among other themes, calls attention to the interest of the community elites in representing how much in common they have with fellow Muslim Turks rather than displaying their distinct variety of religious and cultural life.

If the Quincentennial Foundation displayed the tolerance discourse through recursive selection and organization of artifacts around its chosen theme, another technique used for creating a convincing discourse was "erasure of the improper element" (Gal and Irvine 1995), which in this case was episodes in which the Turkish government or its citizens behaved in a way that might be interpreted as intolerant. A volunteer who worked on the project described the censorial strategy with some distaste. Recruited to work on the museum because of her long-standing involvement with the community, she was sent by museum officials to a course on archival museum techniques. She complained about the project, saying:

> I enjoyed the museum course, but the methods I learned there clashed with the community—at least with those people who were organizing the museum for the five-hundred-year celebration. The course taught us about representation and telling stories through exhibition building. I started to clash with the committee when I brought up historical negatives such as the Struma affair, Thrace, or even the *Varlık Vergisi* [Capital Tax].[20] My father's printing company collapsed because of that tax; he couldn't make ends meet for the family on top of paying the government off. Why did he have to pay the government? For being Jewish! The exhibition wasn't following the norms of a professional historical exhibition. When I discussed this with a historian working on the project, he promised me that later, after the big celebration, we would make a proper archive, a professional archive. But I doubted that this promise would be fulfilled; I disassociated myself from the process.[21]

The volunteer's expectations for a "proper" exhibition differed from what she observed to be the process at hand in creating a Jewish museum in Istanbul; she was angered that the tolerance imperative demanded an erasure of "the improper element." Instead of focusing on the devastating consequences of the Capital Tax or other negative episodes in Turkish Jewish history, the museum foregrounds, for example, the humanitarianism of Turkey during World War II. Museum exhibits feature former Consul Ülkümen's receipt of the honor of "Righteous Gentile" at Israel's Holocaust Museum (Yad Vashem) for protecting Jews in Rhodes from deportation by the Nazis, and display photos of German Jewish academics who came to Turkish universities during the same era. Nowhere are the few recent violent attacks against the community discussed or displayed. Anti-Semitism is never mentioned, despite its pervasive grip on Turkish media makers and consumers (see Bali 2001; Schleifer 2004).

Curators reveal how this tolerant milieu encouraged them to Turkify (in Turkish, *Türkleşmek*) by embracing the Turkish language, nation, and its symbols, that is, to become less different. At the same time, in order to claim that Turkey is a tolerant place, Jews have to remain eternally different, that is, be a subject that continues to demand tolerance. In building the exhibition at the Jewish Museum of Turkey, curators ran into a catch-22: erase difference or praise toleration? One way they overcame this tension was by positing difference as something Jews embodied in the *past* (see Fabian and Bunzl 2002).

> Descending the historical staircase, we reach the ground floor arranged as the ethnographic section with reconstructed scenes of birth and circumcision, the trousseau and a wedding ... decorated *ketubboth* (marriage contracts) anda chronological display (1860–1960) of fascinating photos of brides and grooms carry visitors through a kind of "time tunnel." (Kamhi and Ojalvo 1997:47)

At the bottom of the "historical staircase" at the Jewish Museum, visitors enter a basement gallery containing life-size ethnographic dioramas of a wedding, circumcision, and birth, and encounter some free-standing artifacts such as a wooden ritual circumcision chair and synagogue lamps. In addition to the faceless models that remain frozen in posed scenes from a different time in Turkish Jewish history, the remaining space in the basement ethnographic exhibition is covered with black-and-white and sepia wedding photos of Jewish couples taken over a century, ending in 1960. The collection of colorless photos seems to fall in step with a broader trend of using photography to evoke nostalgia for Istanbul's colorful past. As has been suggested about the wide popularity of Turkish photographer Ara Güler's black-and-white photos of Istanbul, which have been featured in recent museum exhibitions, urban installations, photographic books, and essays (see Pamuk 2005), "this mode of seeing perhaps registers metaphorically the city's loss of (cultural) colour" (Türeli 2010:303).

FIGURE 5
Wedding photographs on display at the
Jewish Museum of Turkey, ethnographic section.
Marcy Brink-Danan, 2007.

Turkish Jews who attend the museum enjoy the ethnographic section (especially the wedding photos) and a wall of sepia-toned photos
located upstairs in what was the "women's balcony" when the building
was a synagogue. Indeed, there are few color photos in the museum;
the largest collection are those showing the activities of the Quincentennial Foundation during the celebration of the five-hundred-year
anniversary.

The ethnographic section also contains a small collection of wedding contracts, explaining that the intricately illuminated texts are a
thing of the past and that "nowadays they are plain printed documents."
Each of the themes exhibited in the ethnographic section displays difference as something not only old, but more importantly, as inherently
private. This contrasts with the emphasis on the main floor on the interaction between Jews and Muslims in the public domain, where Jews
appear as subjects of the majority rule and as contributors to Turkish
culture and society in general.

On the museum's Turkish-language website,[22] the curator introduces the collection with an invitation to the Turkish public to take
responsibility for the museum's success: "Türkiyemizin bu ilk ve tek
'Türk Musevileri Müzesi' ni biz kurduk . . . ancak yaşatacak olan sizler-
siniz" (The first and only Jewish museum of "our" Turkey was founded
by us . . . However, it is you who will make it live). Interestingly, this
motto paraphrases a quote attributed to Atatürk: "Cumhuriyeti biz
kurduk, sizler yaşatacaksınız" (We founded the republic, you will keep
it alive). As a way of empowering citizens to take ownership for the
goings-on of the republic (see Paley 2001:19), the statement attributed
to Atatürk still appears in public spaces, as I observed written upon a
banner strung over Beşiktaş Square during the 2002 general election
season.

The curator's note on the museum website encourages Turkish Jews
to make the museum "their own" by searching their closets, cabinets,
and drawers for old objects, letters, and photographs that will augment
the museum's collection. The inheritance they might have left their children could be put to better use as an "example to humanity," which reflects the motto and goal of the Quincentennial Foundation. That goal,
of showing Turkey as an example of humanitarian tolerance toward its

FIGURE 6
"Cumhuriyeti biz kurduk, sizler yaşatacaksınız"
(We founded the republic, you will keep it alive).
Marcy Brink-Danan 2002.

minorities (namely, the Jews), underlines the notion that "exhibitions are fundamentally theatrical, for they are how museums perform the knowledge they create" (Kirshenblatt-Gimblett 1998:3). Nonetheless, it is obvious from the museum's layout (and from interviews with its founders) that its exhibitions were never really intended for locals. Who, then, is this museum's imagined audience?

As I noted after a few visits, the museum mainly hosts Muslim schoolchildren, foreign tourists, and dignitaries. Given the Turkish Jewish community's commitment to broadcasting the tolerance trope to non-Jews as well as to a foreign and influential audience, the stated goals of making a museum of and for the community is often overlooked. The museum's director explained that while the museum indeed serves the local Jewish population, such as visitors from Jewish social clubs and Istanbul's one Jewish school, the museum is really intended to "present the face of Judaism to the outside."

In conversation with me, some Turkish Jews criticized the museum as being stagnant (the exhibits are not updated) and for omitting issues that have been at the forefront of the minds of Turkish Jews for decades: dwindling demographics, assimilation, rising Turkish anti-Semitism, terrorism, geography, Diaspora communities, and Israel. One interlocutor, an editor at the Turkish Jewish press, complained that the omission of important—albeit negative—events made her uneasy, saying, "Why not mention the Neve Shalom attacks, even if to highlight the support of the government after the damage was done?"

However, during an interview, a local Turkish Jewish historian reminded me that the Quincentennial Foundation's goal is not historical accuracy, but a kind of public relations "theater" (see Hill 2000). As documented in the archives of the American Branch of the QF, during the half-decade of its public relations campaign, tolerance was mapped onto every Turkish cultural field (economy, music and arts, medicine, literature, education, and so on), across wide-ranging regime changes, and read into the Turkish "national character." The tolerance narrative became a counterpoint to the brutality of historical Spanish persecutors (especially relevant around the 1992 expulsion commemorations) and to Western stereotypes of Turks as "uncivilized barbarians." This frame of the tolerant Muslim versus the intolerant European echoed rhetoric employed a century prior, in which Jewish subjects argued in their newspapers that the Ottoman Empire "preceded all the so-called civilized nations in its tolerance of religious difference" (Cohen 2008:99).[23] In a speech given during the inauguration of the chief rabbi in 2002, the community president invited attendees to visit the museum, declaiming:

> As we all know, our ancestors who ran from the brutalities of Inquisition in Spain in 1492 found refuge on these lands. They found a home, a homeland where they could live in peace for centuries. A museum in celebration of our 500th year was opened in Karaköy last year and I strongly advise those of you who have not yet been to pay a visit.
>
> What you will see there are glorious pages of our shared history of 500 years. You will see the kind of civilization our ancestors founded on these

lands living in justice and kindness as free people. You will witness a
notion much needed in the world especially after September 11th: The
notion of how people of different cultures and civilizations can co-exist.

... Our community has contributed generously to various stages of European Union accession processes ... The common wish of people living
in this country is to reach the level of modern civilization as glorious
Atatürk himself signaled. I believe that cooperative efforts spent in Turkey's name toward the attainment of equal member status in the European Union will be rewarded ... We, the Turkish Jews, will continue to
work towards this goal.[24]

Foreign museum guests respond to the tolerance trope much in
the way that the museum's curators intended. They engage in its "civilizational discourse" (Brown 2006), equating tolerance of Ottoman and
Turkish Jews with modernity and civilization. Museum visitors have
remarked, "It is amazing to see how tolerant the Turks are; America can
learn something from them"; and, "I was surprised to learn how tolerant
the Turks were even in medieval times; even in Europe the Jews were
treated much worse." As a public relations campaign, the museum projects a civilized society that American and European guests identify as
similar to their own, as reflected in comments in the visitor guestbook.
Examples included a U.S. ambassador to Turkey, who in 2001 wrote,
"The United States and the American people are proud and honored to
stand with Turkey in fostering peace and tolerance among all ... peoples." A British ambassador expressed similar sentiments, noting that
the museum is "a symbol of the significance of religious tolerance for
us all" (Kamhi and Ojalvo 1997:47). Much as Vienna's Jewish Museum
displays Jews as ideal European citizens to the exclusion of new Others (Muslims and/or Africans) (Bunzl 2003), the civilizational message
of the Jewish Museum in Istanbul highlights Turkish Jews' Europeanness and thus prescribes them an ongoing and central role in Turkish
affairs.

The Quincentennial Foundation, in addition to creating a museum
at home, also sponsored traveling exhibitions to bring the tolerance discourse to an international audience. In a press release for the opening
of an exhibition about Turkish Jewry at the Magnes Museum in Berkeley, California, a community historian from Istanbul highlighted his
desire for friendship as a serious goal for the QF:

> This exhibition will not only celebrate and publicize the rich cultural heritage of Turkish Jewry but also the spirit of tolerance which allowed Sephardic culture to flourish in Turkey. As it travels through the United States, it is our fervent hope that the exhibition also will serve to promote Turkish–American friendship and goodwill.[25]

The director of the Magnes Museum at the time[26] responded in kind: "The Magnes is proud to be a participant in this historic observance which celebrates the harmonious relationship between Jews and Turks, and the unique and colorful blend of culture created over five centuries. It is our hope that this exhibit will strengthen our knowledge and relationship with Turkey and its Jewish communities which are so little known in this country." The target audience for the QF story eagerly picked up on its pro-Turkish narrative, embracing the well-packaged account created by the public relations firm handling QF activities in the United States.

In a letter to the chair of the QF, Ambassador Akşin, Permanent Representative of Turkey to the United Nations, imagined tolerance in its liberal incarnation, based on mutual respect and recognition:

> Peace depends on the existence of a tradition of tolerance such as the one that allowed the persecuted Jews to find a safe haven in Turkey five centuries ago.[27] Both Turkey and the Turkish Jews have much to celebrate on this auspicious occasion. The cultural diversity that the Jews brought to Turkey and the contributions of gifted Jewish artists and scholars have done much to enrich Turkey's cultural life. In return, the peace and security offered by the Empire allowed the Turkish Jews to flourish and to prosper.[28]

Like the ambassador, many have viewed the Ottoman arrangement as a proto-multiculturalist formation, extolling the autonomy allowed to non-Muslim communities as a legacy for modern times. The foreword to "A History of the Turkish Jews," a pamphlet created by the QF based on a lecture, argues that Ottoman "humanitarianism" is "consistent with the beneficence and goodwill traditionally displayed by the Turkish government and people toward those of different creeds, cultures and backgrounds. Indeed, Turkey could serve as a model to be emulated by any nation which finds refugees from any of the four corners of the world standing at its doors" (Güleryüz 1992:5–6). This passage brings us to the question of whether, given the changing conditions for citizenship following the fall of the empire and the rise of the republic, we can imagine tolerance as a constant variable. If the Ottoman forms of tolerance were built around the notion that non-Muslim subjects of the empire were inherently unequal (in other words, in need of tolerance by the Muslim rulers), who are the "Turkish government and people" in this conception? The assumption must be that the Turkish government and people are Muslims who tolerate non-Muslims, but this runs counter to the principles that led to the creation of a secular republic under which equal citizenship was extended to all Turks. A basic review of the history of the relationship between Muslims and non-Muslims in the empire, however, reveals that the question of an Ottoman legacy of tolerance being carried over to the republic is problematic.

No one conceptualization of the *dhimmi* (those subject to the pact of toleration; in Turkish, *zimmi*) was applicable throughout the history of the Ottoman Empire (see Barkey 2008). During its early, expansionist years the significant societal cleavage distinguished between the *askeri* (warrior class) and the *reaya* (literally "flock," but here "subjects"). Ottoman policies of recruiting *dhimmi* into the warrior class, including the practices of forced conversion, seemed to have little basis in *shari'a*, if not blatantly contradicting its protection of *dhimmi*. Kunt argues that Islamic law was secondary to imperial concerns during the early Ottoman period. However, during the Islamization of the sixteenth to seventeenth centuries, the line between Muslim and *dhimmi* became more pronounced. This shift included an increasingly strict policy of the military class (*askeri*) being held by Muslims. This trend continued, and "by the 1800s, ambitious non-Muslims were already seeking distinction in society as leaders of national movements" (Kunt 1982:65).

In observing the transition from empire to secular nation-state, many have noted that the old models were not completely erased by the new; indeed, many features of the religious discourses of the Ottoman period were translated to the nation-state (see Braude and Lewis 1982; and Kastoryano 1992). Ottoman *zimmi* became minorities, and the retention of difference, an Ottoman hangover if you will, can be seen in the continued categories of religion and language on Turkish censuses (until 1960) (Elazar et al. 1984) and the marking of religious affiliation on personal identity cards. While the categories of religious and linguistic difference have not disappeared, they have shifted from a collective claim to an individual, that is, confessional, claim.

However, most important here is the basic understanding that these communities were never seen as equal, as they are framed in the current multiculturalist discourse of tolerance, but fundamentally different. The power differential flowed in one direction: assumptions of Islamic superiority dictated that deference of the *dhimmis* be made explicit in their different clothing, architecture, and inability to testify as witnesses in an Islamic court. One historian of Ottoman Jewry explicates this critical qualification of "tolerance" in opposition to the liberal model:

> One can reinterpret the mosaic notion more dynamically, not stressing "minority/majority" or "ruler/ruled," but instead emphasizing the recognition of "difference" and, in fact, the near lack of any political will to transform the "difference" into "sameness." This is not the same as pluralism. The "difference" each group was ascribed, or ascribed to itself in its self-representation, was not articulated on the basis of rights . . . That particular arrangement, therefore, renders invalid all our terms for debate about minority/majority, which are all extraordinarily Europe-centered— and in many cases post-Enlightenment-Europe—centered. (Rodrigue and Reynolds 1995)

Walzer's *On Toleration* (1997) defines various permutations of tolerance through their structural properties (such as multinational empire, international society, consociations, nation-states, and immigrant societies) rather than on the quality or quantity of love with which the term "tolerance" was infused. In the following section, I show that the QF employed the terms "love" and "friendship" as qualifiers for tolerance, enriching it with positive resonance rather than one of neutrality or forbearance. Simultaneously, the insistence on friendly discourse about Turkey demanded the excision of historical events that stood outside the tolerance narrative.

Tolerance and Citizenship

Modern Turkish citizenship was conditional upon the effacement of particularistic difference on the part of minorities, in a loyal demonstration of Turkish nationalism. Atatürk's address to the Jews of Turkey in 1923 stated no less:

There are some of our faithful people whose destiny has been united
with that of the Turks ruling them, in particular the Jews, who because
their loyalty to this nation and this motherland has been confirmed, have
passed their lives in comfort and prosperity until now, and will continue
to live hereafter in comfort and happiness. (in Shaw 1991)

The public voice of the Jewish community overwhelmingly promotes the tolerance trope. In private, an elderly Turkish Jewish friend
(who lived under the empire and experienced the transition to republicanism) explained: "You have to please everyone: the government, the
rabbis, the community members. The community still operates as if we
were tolerated subjects in the Ottoman Empire, not as if we were equal
citizens. They aren't brave, like the Armenians." Unlike other groups
who have openly challenged Kemalist nationalism, such as Islamists,
Armenians, and Kurds, the Jews have supported a classically republican
Turkish national identity, advocating internationally for Turkey. Striking examples of Turkish Jews' deployment of their particular history
to counter claims of Armenian genocide can be seen from at least the
early 1980s, when a delegation of Turkish Jews nearly thwarted an Israeli
conference on genocide in which the Armenian case was included on
the program (Charny 1984). As recently as 2007, prominent Turkish Jews
challenged the decision of the Anti-Defamation League, an American
organization with the mission of fighting anti-Semitism and bigotry,
which supported a United States congressional resolution (House Resolution 106) calling the tragedies visited upon Armenians "genocide"
(Kamhi 2007).[29] In both cases, opponents to the Armenian case argued
that Jewish support for claims of Turkish genocide would put both the
Turkish Jewish community and the diplomatic relationships between
Turkey, Israel, and the United States at risk. The Jews, in the role of the
"good minority," serve as a powerful foil to the Armenian genocide discourse (Mallet 2008:415–429) in particular, enabling Turkey to display a
history of cosmopolitanism and refute the bad press it so often garners
over the genocide question but also with regard to Kurdish and Islamist
critiques.[30]

Reflecting on an earlier model of liberal tolerance, Walzer considers
French Jewish emancipation through the words of the French Legisla-
tive Assembly's debate on the matter: "One must refuse everything to
the Jews as a nation and give everything to the Jews as individuals"

(1997:39). He adds Sartre's caveat, written in 1944, which claimed that emancipation "annihilates . . . [the] Jew . . . leave[s] nothing in him but the abstract subject of the rights of man and the rights of the citizen." Individuals could in this sense be naturalized and assimilated; Frenchness was in this sense an expansive identity. But France as a republican nation-state could not tolerate "a nation within a nation." The Republic of Turkey, which borrowed many French emancipationist principles (see also Lewis 1953), likewise rejected the value of (and considered a threat) those who would claim a hyphenated national identity. In light of Walzer's remarks, it is possible to interpret the QF's praise for the Ottoman Empire's recognition of collectivist difference as a quiet critique of the monolith of nationalist culture that forces Judaism to be publicly "invisible"; recognized as a private individual identity rather than a collective one (see Eisen 2000).[31] In many ways, community officials (both religious and lay leaders such as those involved with the QF) desperately fear the individualized version of liberal tolerance promised by the founders of modern Turkey. By praising an Ottoman version of tolerance (rather than critiquing the present one), the QF discursively unites the Ottoman Empire's Islam-infused policies with those of the secular Turkish Republic.

My research reveals that in their zeal to tell a *good* story through educational materials, the museum, and tourism, the organizers and participants in the Quincentennial celebrations—perhaps inadvertently—conflated the terms of tolerance particular to the Ottoman and Turkish political entities toward their Jewish subjects and citizens. Some of the communications about the Quincentennial interpreted "tolerance" as a liberal version of individual rights, others lauded the autocratic, collectivist recognition of religious difference as "tolerant," while still others imagined "tolerance" as a code word for cosmopolitanism, democracy, and/or modernity (see Özyürek 2006). Very few of these interpretations acknowledged the power differential in tolerating versus being tolerated (whether in the Islamic system of Muslim/non-Muslim or in the demographically oriented nation-state model of majority and minority). These definitions, when applied universally to the Ottoman Empire and the Republic of Turkey, ignored the real organizational differences between the two political systems and overlooked the internal historical changes *within* each system.

If the organizers and participants of the 1992 celebrations came to the project with the intention of promoting a history of Turkish tolerance, what, then, are the effects of the tolerance discourse on the lives of Turkish Jews themselves? On one hand, the establishment of a museum and the production of other lasting monuments to this history have given the Turkish Jewish community a permanent place on the cultural map of Istanbul. On the other, the overwhelming success of this discourse leaves Jewish community officials with little room to criticize Turkish policies or leaders. Some Turkish Jews see criticism as overdue, especially after the nightmarish attacks on synagogues in 2003 and the ongoing plague of anti-Semitic rhetoric that pervades the Turkish media. This was expressed in a scathing opinion piece published in a leftist Turkish newspaper (*Radikal*) immediately after the 2003 attacks, in which local historian Rıfat Bali critiqued what he saw as the ongoing *dhimmitude* (see Bat Ye'or 2002)—cowardice, vulnerability and a position of inferiority toward Islam—of Turkish Jewry. Playing on the usual sense of the tolerance trope, he argued that Turks should cease to tolerate anti-Semitism:

> Turkish Jews are not *dhimmis* who are in need of protection and tolerance from the Muslim majority. They are citizens of the Turkish Republic. The only expectation is the end of traditionalized tolerance of anti-Semitism. It is high time to say "enough." Unfortunately, only today do we realize that it is actually too late to say that now. (Bali 2003)

How does one square the tolerance trope with the real fears and security measures of contemporary Turkish Jewish life? Security at Turkish Jewish institutions has never been tighter, including at the museum itself. I posit that the tolerance trope of this museum, the most permanent artifact of the QF's work, is more prescriptive than descriptive. As a form of public memory, the tolerance trope is one way that "different groups and individuals in society promote their own versions of memory in order to serve their interests in the present" (Özyürek 2007:9). Turkish Jewish officials would like to see Turkey become a more tolerant place, one in which the small Jewish community need not have metal detectors or security guards at their synagogues or fear for the safety of children at Istanbul's only Jewish elementary school. A leader in the Jewish community has stated that "quiet diplomacy, not contestation, has worked to their advantage compared to the treatment of other minorities. In this way, they have secured permission to construct new synagogues and enhance existing structures, as well as other benefits" (in Adler 2005:132).

In this case, nostalgia for an imagined Ottoman tolerance casts not a backward glance but instead a wishful eye toward the future and a secure legacy for Turkish Jewry. This new politics of friendship between Turkish Jewish elites and their government allows Turkish Jews a more public role than they have previously enjoyed (or even desired). At the same time, public performances of tolerance (and the imagined audiences to which they are played) consolidate the possible "ways of being" for Turkish Jews into a unified, repeatable tale, one that exhibits doubt about otherness at the same time it celebrates tolerance for difference.

The Quincentennial activities need not actually be "representative of the cultural orientations and political aspirations" of the minority individuals who perform them; rather, they are a way of "articulating utopias" (Soysal 2001:22) that speak to the larger society in which they hope to participate, despite their marginality. For example, the Beyoğlu Jewish Rabbinate Foundation recently conducted a survey of Turkish opinions about minorities, using funds from the European Commission. Despite the fact that the survey results indicated 42 percent of Turks "do not want to have Jewish neighbors" (with an increase to 61 percent among those who identify themselves as Muslims) (2009)—or perhaps because of it—evidence of Jews praising Turkish tolerance underscores the (perhaps utopian) aspirations of this tiny community to count for something and to stand "for Europe."

Counting beyond Their Numbers

Jews in Istanbul used the Quincentennial commemorations to participate in the broader political arena to which they have limited access due to their small numbers and disempowered status as a Turkish minority. As a founder of the QF once expressed, "What Turkish Jews lack in numbers they make up in enthusiasm and commitment."

The changing "politics of friendship" (Derrida 1997) between Jews and Turks reveal a new trend that parallels those at play elsewhere in Europe. Partridge has aptly named this process "exclusionary incorporation," by which "previously abject beings become subjects, but in a way that preserves and even depends on their position as outsiders" (2008:668). How do Turkey's religious minorities, those persons whose beliefs, rituals, and languages constitute the difference celebrated, relate to their own exclusionary incorporation? Are they critics or pawns? If historically, the modus operandi of Turkish Jews was to keep a low profile (see Bali 2007), now Jews (or more correctly, their officials) have changed tactics. In an interview with the museum director in 2007, I was told, "The Jews here have been very careful about showing their culture in public. We want to show ourselves in public, not be hidden anymore. We like sharing our culture, but this is a big shift for all minorities [in Turkey]."[32] Perhaps the only way for Jews to perform publicly in Turkey today is as embodied symbols of toleration and difference in seemingly de-politicized venues (such as the museum, public concerts, and visual art exhibitions). The new movement is to use these "cultural" venues as stages from which to advocate publicly for Turkey in an abstract, nostalgic, and uncritical way. However, by choosing the tolerance trope over all others, Turkish Jewish elites engage in a process of de-politicization; tolerance becomes a moral goal, not a political agenda. The tolerance discourse, therefore, hides its goals under a moral or cultural banner, disavowing its political aims (Brown 2006:178; see also Benhabib 1996).

Through image and text, the Jewish Museum in Istanbul performs the politics of Turkish–Jewish friendship. The main exhibition recursively narrates Turkish tolerance: by prominently featuring the Ottoman welcome of expelled Sephardic Jews in 1492, by displaying or highlighting a Jewish ritual object crowned with the crescent and star of the Turkish flag, museum curators act out a story of state tolerance on a local stage. However, the museum's spatial organization reveals a hierarchy of ideas about Jewishness in Istanbul. If the main hall emphasizes the Turkishness of the Jews, the basement ethnographic section focuses on Jewish traditions not shared with the Muslim majority, albeit as cultural "remnants" of difference in the past.

In the service of positive representation, the QF has transformed "tolerance" into an icon that it claims characterizes the total Jewish experience in the Ottoman Empire and Turkey but which necessarily erases—or underplays—other, more negative aspects of that experience. The iconicization of tolerance relies on its ability to serve as an open signifier, absorbing the changing status of the Jews under Ottoman rule and as citizens of the Republic of Turkey. At the same time, such an open range of interpretation muddies the positive and negative valences of tolerance itself. When the terms "tolerance" and "friendship" can be used in so many variations, one becomes increasingly aware that they lack a particularly useful meaning for anthropological analysis. What this case does offer is an excellent study for students of semiotics and ideology, who credit political symbols (in this case tolerance) with the ability to absorb a range of (at times, contradictory) meanings.

What could be wrong with tolerance? Aren't all forms of tolerance better than its alternatives: persecution, expulsion, and annihilation?[33] While the positive aspects of even the most minimal tolerance in any of its organizational forms seem praiseworthy, praise is not the only response one might have to the phenomenon. Rather, by questioning the valences and uses of the term, we can investigate the political and personal dreams and disappointments of Jews in Istanbul.

For example, by engaging with the tolerance trope's "civilizational message" (see Brown 2006), Turkey's Jews perform their Europeanness and ascribe to themselves an ongoing and central role in Turkish affairs, offering the republic "a people to be tolerated" at a time when toleration is on the minds of so many (especially lawmakers in Europe). Rather than demanding the rights that Jews might legally claim as full citizens of the Republic of Turkey, their officials' tolerance discourse asks for favors more reminiscent of Ottoman conditions for citizenship. As such, the past becomes imminently usable, recalling Boym's clever phrase "the future of nostalgia" (2001).

New political and historical settings demand new concepts of citizenship. Nostalgia for an Ottoman concept of citizenship grafted onto the present-day situation of Jews in Turkey expresses the desire for a utopian future without doing the work of figuring out how to make that *politically* possible in today's terms. Mythologizing tolerance without room for critique erases a history of changing power dynamics as well as future opportunities for such. If the tolerance trope rose to prominence at a historically propitious time (both in terms of Turkey's warming international relations and the five-hundred-year anniversary), the 1980s and '90s also included violence and anti-Jewish rhetoric: Islamist parties' ascendancy accompanied by anti-Jewish themes, synagogue bombings, and assassinations of or threats against prominent Turkish Jews (Mallet 2008:449–456). This chapter has highlighted the tension between a hagiographic discourse and the way Jews actually perceived their lives in Turkey at the time this very discourse of tolerance and love was on the rise. Imagining a past without ethnic tensions, without inequalities, and without change does little to make tolerance and friendship real in our world, especially when tolerance blows up, literally, in one's face, as it did when bombs exploded at Turkish synagogues in 2003.

However, it does not take explosives to convey to people on a daily basis who belongs and who does not. In everyday negotiations, Jews are reminded that despite their long history in Istanbul and the once-cosmopolitan ethnic and religious makeup of the city, they are regularly considered foreigners.

TWO

Cosmopolitan Signs: Names as Foreign and Local

Barely a generation ago, there were approximately one million Jews living in the Islamic countries from Morocco to Afghanistan. Some of these Jewish communities had their roots in antiquity, going back before the great Muslim conquests of the seventh century of the Common Era—before most of what today are called Arab countries had any Arabs, *before Turkey had any Turks*.

—*Stillman 1995:59; emphasis added*

How do people become aware that they are strangers in their own lands? Someone must make them so. Sometimes they are forcibly removed. Sometimes they are just reclassified.

—*Tsing 1993:154*

In Istanbul, one quickly observes a wide variety of political, religious, and class affiliations: "The Istanbul cityscape is like a raised Braille script that the traveler can read as a code for the different forces and interests, and the negotiations among them, that characterize the city" (White 2002:4). A space in which social distinctions are commonly encoded and decoded are those interactions—in the bank, in the classroom, at the market—in which people make introductions. Introductions are particularly salient because of the seemingly banal but politically fraught ontological process of marking a name as "Turkish" or "foreign." As other Jews in what are now Muslim-majority lands experience, Jews in their everyday interactions with Muslim Turks are regularly assumed to be foreigners who are either recently arrived or on their way to somewhere else.[1] Despite over half a millennium of living in the region, full Turkish citizenship, and fluency in Turkish, Turkish Jews are regularly reclassified as *yabancı* (Turkish; stranger or foreigner) in everyday interactions with Muslim Turks. If Jews lived in the region now called Turkey "before there were Turks," why are they today considered foreign?

These everyday moments of reclassification offer a productive starting point for examination of how someone knows he or she is a stranger (Secor 2004). Following Georg Simmel's understanding of the role of "strangers" as cultural brokers (1950), sociological literature has focused on how this category of person exhibits a heightened awareness of the arbitrariness of cultural classifications. Through what linguistic and social practices is one made a stranger in the first place? Using the ethnographic example of Turkish Jewry, a focus on names may help parse the process through which populations find themselves reclassified and the sense made of these ontological shifts. Tsing's phrase "just reclassified" (1993) invites an elaboration of how classification works and the social consequences of being grouped with others.

Jews in Turkey are aware of the ways in which they are, in some ways, different from Ottoman and Turkish Jews of earlier generations; they are also aware that they are, in some ways, different from Muslim (and Christian) Turks as well as from Jews in other locales. The cosmopolitan calculus of these differences makes them who they are, but it is an equation that is not fixed and that constantly needs to be recalculated. Over a decade of fieldwork, I have noted that Turkish Jews consider naming a central site through which they negotiate their status as a religious minority. Jews recounted to me the enduring way in which their Jewish names index foreignness in Turkey. Their strategies of double naming (maintaining both a Jewish and a Turkish name), as well as other conscious choices about the retention or rejection of names marked as Jewish, reveal the way names signify modernization, cultural survival, and assimilation. Perhaps more intriguing, however, is the recurrence of names as sites of rich historical memory, that is, the way Turkish Jewish names act as objects through which Turkish Jews unravel the tangled nets of time.

In the symbolic realm of naming, Turks of various religious and political persuasions—Jews included—define "Turkishness" through a

set of unmarked, canonical names achieved through a century of disavowing non-Muslim claims of membership in the Turkish nation. For
example, in 2002 Lusi, a Turkish Jewish student, and I decided to rent
an apartment together in Istanbul. Lusi is a Turkish citizen, speaks and
dresses like the Istanbul urbanite that she is, and is only distinguish-
able from Muslim Turks because her first and last names are regularly
considered "non-Turkish." On meeting her, real estate brokers would
invariably ask, "Nerelisiniz?" (Where are you from?) The situation once
bordered on the farcical when, despite Lusi's insistence on her Turkishness, neither the agent nor his secretary could spell her name while
completing the rental paperwork. Lusi (who uses both the French spelling—Lucie—and the legal, phonetic Turkish one—Lusi) patiently pronounced each letter separately, using the mnemonic spelling technique
of Turkish schoolchildren in which letters are made clear by reference
to Turkish cities: "L" as in Lüleburgaz; "U" as in Urfa; "S" as in Samsun;
and "I" as in Istanbul.

   When I introduced Lusi to Volkan, a waiter at a café I frequented in
Istanbul, he joked with her, "Is that your real name? You can't be Turkish!" During another visit to the café, Volkan asked me if I had figured
out what was "going on" with my roommate. He urged me to spy on her,
saying, "One day, when she isn't looking, take her identity card and see
what it says. I'll bet 'Lusi' isn't her real name. You can't even spell that
name in Turkish!"

   Another example of naming as a site for identity work surfaced during an interview conducted in 2003, in which a Turkish Jewish woman in
her fifties recounted her son's ordeal of living in Turkey with a "foreign"
name:

> Last year my son won an academic award. The university dean congratu-
> lated him on speaking "such excellent Turkish—for a foreigner!" . . . He
> is interested in politics and studied political science in one of the best
> universities in Turkey. Nonetheless, he can't be a politician in Turkey
> with our [Jewish] family name. He feels very frustrated by this as he has
> no interest in living abroad. (Brink-Danan 2009:8)

This woman explained that her son was "completely Turkish" and
that he was offended when she suggested that he consider leaving Turkey
for some place where his name might not hinder his political aspirations.
Sometimes being classified as a foreigner seems a minor inconvenience,

without heavy material consequences; however, in other cases, being marked as foreign, both in the present and the past, engenders more serious results, including economic and political exclusions.[2] The act of marking someone as "foreign" thus opens up questions about the social and material consequences of naming as "a vocabulary of inclusion and exclusion" (Herzfeld 1982:299). But how does this vocabulary acquire power to include or exclude?

Muslim Turks who classify Jewish Turks as "foreigners" through naming dialogues seem to forget past contexts and are likely unaware of the repetition of similar speech events over their lifetime and beyond. But what of the memory of prior contexts held by those being named?

If contested claims between my friend Lusi and Muslim Turks led to awkward moments, fear, or dismay, it is likely because Lusi—and other Jews—regularly interprets these moments by building on a chain of meaning that accrues over time, drawing precisely on those very historical contexts that many Muslim Turks deny in the present. But in the minds of those—in this case, Jews—being classified "out" of the collective, episodes like those between Lusi and real estate brokers or café waiters are not isolated from reclassifying performances in prior contexts. My Jewish interlocutors regularly set individual naming events, even seemingly innocuous ones, into historical relief against a backdrop of socializing discourses that teach Jews to fear being reclassified as foreigners.

Turkish Jewish Names: A History of Shifting Signifiers

In her work on everyday Turkish state-making practices, anthropologist (and Turkish Jew) Yael Navaro-Yashin recounts how she is regularly compelled, like Lusi and so many of my friends, to lecture Turks about the history of non-Muslim minorities in the region:

> As a person of "minority" status in Turkey, I was not perceived as a proper native by many of my own informants, whether Islamist or secularist. In encounters in my own city Istanbul, the first thing that incited curiosity on an everyday basis was my name. (2002:14)

If, when beginning fieldwork in 2002, I found the regularity with which Lusi was considered "foreign" surprising, I soon learned that naming was a critical place for Turkish Jewish identity work, offering a personal and social site for negotiations of belonging and ostracism in the Turkish national project. When I discussed the issue of names with Lusi, she suggested that I interview her grandmother, Naile, who often recalled a dramatic (and traumatic) story about her own mother and a time when having the "wrong" name caused serious problems.

Born in the Ottoman Empire, Naile's mother had been an outstanding student at the French-language schools of the Alliance Israélite Universelle, the Jewish school system that dominated the educational landscape of North African, Middle Eastern, and Balkan Jewish communities from the late nineteenth century until the mid-twentieth century (Rodrigue 1990). At age eighteen, Naile's mother went to Paris to study for a teaching position. Traveling by train during World War I, she reached the French border and encountered guards demanding identification. When signing her name, she had written "Grasya," the Judeo-Spanish name listed on her official identification. On another form of identification, she had written "Juli," the name by which she was known at school. The inconsistency of her signatures raised suspicion. In what Naile imagined to be "another inquisition," the guards questioned Grasya–Juli, who tried to explain that she had two names because she and her community were in the process of "Westernizing." Her protests proved unconvincing: the guards stripped her and hosed her down with icy water so she wouldn't be able to complete her mission to deliver the government secrets they assumed were written in invisible ink on her skin.

After returning to Constantinople to work as a French teacher, Juli (or was she Grasya?) married and bore a child. When choosing her baby's name, she rejected a long-standing Sephardic Jewish kinship-naming pattern of calling a female child after one's father's mother. The couple thus gave their Jewish child neither a Judeo-Spanish nor a French name but chose the most "Turkish" name they could find, that of Ottoman Sultan Abdülhamid II's daughter: "Call her 'Naile,'" they said, "and our child will not suffer."[3]

The symbolic and physical violence of Grasya–Juli's naming story has secured its place in Lusi's family lore, not only serving as a site of historical memory but also pointing to the myth value of Turkish Jewish names that act as critical objects through which Turkish Jews understand difference as it has been enmeshed in nets of time and cultural change. At the beginning of the twenty-first century, when Lusi's name is reclassified outside the Turkish collective through a "where are you from originally" conversation (Beck 2006:165), she recalls her great-grandmother's stories of name-based exclusions in her attempt to make sense of the present social situation. Despite their initial marking of her as a *yabancı*, landlords did not deny Lusi an apartment. Unlike the case of parents in Turkey who gave their children Kurdish names coming under the scrutiny of legal proceedings (Aslan 2009), no overt penalty was enacted on Lusi, despite being considered a stranger, in the interactions I observed. Nonetheless, even when no harm seems implied in being marked as foreign, Lusi's memories of the "Naile story" lead her to wonder what border guards lie in wait for her—what social and material penalties might accompany this ontological assignment.

Name talk such as Naile's story allows Jews in Turkey to recall different conditions for citizenship in changing political and social landscapes, invoking historical contexts in which names signal belonging or ostracism. If "the data of social life plucked from their isolable moments invariably point to lived moments that lie beyond them" (Agha 2005a:1), one way to understand what linguistic data point to is to analyze speech acts that explicitly interpret the way meaning shifts across contexts (Bauman 2005:146).

Jews' names in Istanbul, even the most seemingly "Turkish" ones such as "Naile," signify this community's somewhat baroque history of survival across changing languages, borders, and political regimes. If Turkish Jews now take it for granted that having a name (or using one on official documents) that "sounds Turkish" is desirable, Jewish names in eighteenth- and nineteenth-century Istanbul reflected a conservative cultural practice of retaining "traditional" personal names. These included, for men, biblical Hebrew names or a suffix including God's name. For women, nonreligious names in Judeo-Spanish, Hebrew, Greek, or Turkish—especially ones that described them as "life-giving," "worthy," or "queens"—were popular (Bornstein-Makovetsky 1997:16–17). However, the Europeanization of the Ottoman Empire that began in the late nineteenth century (Benbassa and Rodrigue 2000; Stein 2003) shifted Jewish naming patterns away from what were then considered traditional Jewish names, such as Grasya, and toward an adoption of more modern French or Western European–sounding names, such as Juli (Bornstein-Makovetsky 1997:21).

The positive social value attributed to a "pure" Turkish name reflects the effects of the transition from the polyethnic Ottoman Empire to Turkish republicanism, during which names garnered a new symbolic weight of association. Since its establishment in 1923, the Turkish Republic has implemented multiple policies toward the nationalization of minorities (Baer 2007; Bozdoğan and Kasaba 1997). These policies focus on the definition of "Turkish citizenship" and have implications for the way in which Turkish Jews generally envision their difference as belonging outside of the public sphere. As part of Mustafa Kemal Atatürk's nationalist Westernizing campaign, in addition to the well-known Romanization of the Turkish language and the exchange of the fez for the fedora (Lewis 2001), Turks were compelled by law in 1934 to adopt a family name (Bali 1999; Lewis 2001; see also Scott et al. 2002).

Although as recognized minorities, Jews, Armenians, and Greeks were exempt from this policy (Türköz 2007:901), they responded in a variety of ways ranging from cultural resistance to enthusiastic assimilation. An official statement issued in 1925 by the Turkish Jewish community renounced special privileges in lieu of citizenship in a secular Turkish Republic but here too, families and individuals reacted differently to these changes. The Official Turkish Jewish Community Renunciation of Special Privileges Provided by the Treaty of Lausanne, Article 42, 15 September 1925 (in Shaw 1991) was not without provisions, especially for dealing with questions of marriage and divorce. Whether this renunciation reflected a true desire to assimilate to Turkish policies is unknown; historical research suggests that the Jews had no option but to issue a nationalist pronouncement (Benbassa and Rodrigue 2000:102).

Some Turkish Jews retained their historical names drawn from Hebrew (e.g., Levi), Roman (e.g., Bonofiel), Judeo-Spanish (e.g., Aseo), Greek (e.g., Politi), or Turkish (e.g., Alev). Others complied by retaining part of their historical name and adding a "Turkifying" suffix or prefix to the original name (e.g., -öz; büyük-). Some Turkified their name by translating it into Modern Turkish. Yet others transliterated their name following the rules of Turkish phonetic transcription (e.g., Kohen).

Finally, many replaced their old name with a seemingly unrelated Turkish name. According to a Turkish folklorist, "The change in per-

FIGURE 7
Sign on a bookstore in Istanbul.
Marcy Brink-Danan, 2007.

sonal names in Turkey was probably the most successful component of the complex process of modernization introduced by bureaucrat intellectuals" (Başgöz 1999:214). Nonetheless, the creation of the Turkish Republic was not the first time that local Jews were subjects of reclassifying regimes. As Meltem Türköz (2007) describes, Turkish Jews have memories of a deeper history of regime change and co-occurring symbolic shifts, as in the case of a Turkish Jewish man whose relationship to his name shifted over time. The interviewee, Sami Altındağ, described how his father received a Turkified surname from Atatürk that caused the elder much pride. In his forties, Sami rejected the name as a falsehood, claiming, "I am not Altındağ" (Türköz 2007:902–903). His feelings changed after learning about earlier name changes from an elderly family member; in his estimation, his family had changed names at least twenty times over two millennia. Sami finally had to abandon any notion of retrieving an "authentic" name, explaining, "So I concluded that

Altındağ is as valid a surname as those other surnames [we have carried]" (Türköz 2007:903).

The process of Turkification was marked by an intense bout of creativity around the issue of choosing, retaining, and defending one's new or old name, as depicted in a recent novel by Turkish Jewish author Moris Farhi. In Farhi's novel, a nationalist teacher named Metin interrogates a Jewish student named Moris Alev about the latter's "foreign" moniker:

> "What's your name?" he shouted. Alev told him. Metin snarled, "Moris? Moris? What sort of name is that? All Turkish names have a meaning ... My name, Metin, means 'stalwart.' What does Moris mean?" Well, as you know, Moris comes from the French Maurice, and is an affectation among educated Jews for Moses. So we thought Alev was cooked.
>
> Not in the least. He thought for a few minutes, then spoke slowly as if Metin was a dimwit. "The surname is Moriz, sir. Written with a 'z.' Not Moris with an 's.' It was misspelled by the registrar of births, sir. As you know, *mor* means purple, *iz* means track. Combined it means 'purple track.' This refers to a time when we Turks were trapped in a maze of mountains in Central Asia, sir. We were facing death by hunger and thirst when out of nowhere a grey wolf appeared. It laid down a track—a phosphorescent one so that it would be visible even at night, which is why it was purple—and led us to safety. As you know, sir, today many European politicians call Atatürk the 'grey wolf.' That is because he, too, led us out of the wilderness." (2005:112)

Although this is a fictional scene, it faithfully depicts the serious play on naming that accompanied changes in the Turkish Jewish historical landscape. To his teacher's chagrin, this character's elaborate yarn creatively reinterprets the signification of "Moris" from the most foreign to the most authentically Turkish by means of referencing none other than Atatürk, the secular godhead of the republic whose name itself means "father of the Turks." If the baptismal event of naming Moris was pregnant with Jewish affectations, the moment of its interpretation as such is foiled by Moris's recasting. Moris's fictional speech epitomizes naming as a process of interpreting meaning across historically disparate milieus. Naming signals and reiterates cosmopolitan knowledge about context-bound political and cultural shifts, and the varied choices Turkish Jews made during this period of change reflect how even the most powerful state classifications do not always trump community and individual ontologies.

Although viewed by some historians as a model for minority integration (Altabé et al. 1996; Shaw 1991), the assimilation of Jews to Turkish national culture has been regarded by other scholars as imperfect (Bali 2001; Kastoryano 1992). Although minority Turkification was compelled in early republican Turkey, assimilatory gestures such as minority adoption of "Turkish" and "Muslim" names were regarded by ultranationalists as sneaky attempts by minorities to dissimulate as "real Turks" (Eissenstat 2005:253).[4] In fact, not unlike Jews elsewhere in the Diaspora (Kaganoff 1977:18–19), many Turkish Jews that I met had double names— one for the Jewish community and one for civic purposes—as a matter of security and to deal with the annoyance of all those questions about foreignness. Someone known as "Rozi" to her Jewish friends and family will use "Rûyam" at school or on her business card. Marriage forms at the rabbinate therefore ask not only for the "legal" (that is, Turkish) name of the individuals registering to marry but also for the Hebrew or Jewish names that will be used in the ceremony. In a letter sent home from a Jewish organization in Istanbul, a postscript reminds parents to "make sure your children know their *Jewish* names, too!"

Simply put, what counts today as a "Turkish," "Jewish," or "foreign" name is the product of changing political and interpretive structures that, over time, condition our understanding of what names generally mean. As has been shown through studies of Turkish debates over the politics of Kurdish names (Aslan 2009), the denaturalizing of national ideologies requires an awareness of how signs come to signify what they do (see also Inoue 2004a, 2004b). By undoing naturalized assumptions of iconicity believed to obtain between names and nations (Steedly 1996), anthropologists have found that ontologies are products of ideological processes that erase their own histories (Gal and Irvine 1995). This is particularly salient in the seemingly ahistorical process of marking a Jewish name as "Turkish" or "foreign." However, the method of Türköz's intriguing study (2007) derives from memories of Turkish name changes and suggests that not only do names change meaning in terms of their interpretations over time but also that Jews in Turkey exhibit a heightened awareness about this process and mythologize the history of changing names (or changing interpretations of names) to understand their contemporary meanings. Through participant-observation, I likewise found that Turkish Jews regularly use names to reinscribe the erased history of present-day ontologies.

Using the Moroccan Jewish example of a "Sifrou native's name, which carries the attachment *Sifroui* to his name when he is away from Sifrou, or a Jew *yahud,* who is called *yahudi,*" Clifford Geertz argued that relational processing makes us "contextualized persons" (in Cooper 1999:18). As made clear by the intense dialogues about naming that I observed in Istanbul, Turkish Jews interpret names through their ability to conjure up past contexts. But what, then, to make of name talk that points to the past as a kind of interpretive context (see Davidson 2007)? Cultural codes about names are indeed "entangled in history" (vom Bruck and Bodenhorn 2006:1–30). One way in which we might comb through these tangles is by thinking of names as "signs of history" and as "signs in history" (Parmentier 1987, 2007). In this formulation, "signs of history" are those media that represent the past, such as books, gravestones, and so forth, while "signs in history" take on heightened social meaning precisely because of their function of representing the past. For example, if a gravestone is a "sign of history," to deface a gravestone is to create a "sign in history." The act of defacing a "sign of history" necessarily seizes on the first signifier of the past to create a new meaning about the past that is usable toward present claims. Parmentier (2007:273) argues this distinction is not one of opposition but of inclusion: "signs in history" rely on an established chain of meaning but extend it for their own use.

To signify difference in the present using Parmentier's theoretical formulation, a signifier like "Lusi" must first seize on a history of French names being adopted by Ottoman minorities to signify the history of this category of names excluded from the Turkish canon. Further, "Naile" can be read as a "sign of history" in that it reflects the process of Turkification in place at the time of its giving. But the resurrection of the "Naile story" as family lore transforms the name into a "sign in history" that socializes a new generation of Turkish Jews in an awareness of the precariousness of social classifications. Naile's story also reminds us that we "must take seriously the suggestion that a person's discourse, or voice, is always already engaged in a dialogue with precedents . . . In this sense . . . the analysis of discourse is necessarily historical" (Irvine 2004:105).

Performing the Name across Time

The denotation of a name as "foreign" in and of itself is not always negative. Indeed, it can sometimes be a source of social capital (Goldberg 1997:54–55). This is partially dependent on who is classifying whom and the power relations that obtain between classifier and classified. Given that the work of reclassification often takes place at the level of connotation rather than denotation, understanding this process thus requires some probing of the different interpretive logics on which "foreigners" and "natives" draw. As Hill (1998) argues about the racist undertones of Mock Spanish, a useful distinction can be made between "direct indexicality," or what names seem to "index" in the dictionary sense, and "indirect indexicality," or what names connote by indirect association with other negatively (or positively) valued social categories ("minority," "outsider," and so on). Often non-Jewish Turks are unaware of the dangerous indirect connotations Jews read into interpretations of their names as "foreign." Although non-Jewish Turks seem oblivious to these negative connotations, Turkish Jews have been socialized, through storytelling as well as other performative genres, to know that having a "foreign" name in prior historical contexts has led to exclusion, expulsion, and death.

Some of the most productive sites of sociality—and socialization—for the Jewish community of Istanbul are its family clubs. The centers provide a "Jewish" space for boys in club uniforms to play basketball, for women to meet over coffee, and for teens to choreograph folk dances in the auditorium. While living in Istanbul, I attended community-theater productions that took place at these clubs, including the following: a cabaret of songs in French, Turkish, Greek, and Hebrew; a Judeo-Spanish and Turkish play about a Jewish neighborhood in Istanbul; and a folkloric dance performance narrating the biblical account of the Jews' escape from Egyptian slavery. In observing these performances, I found that ontological processes are not just located in the realm of bounded speech events, such as conversations between Lusi and a broker or between her and her grandmother. In Istanbul this is a dialogue that often takes place on communal stages and requires scripting, rehearsal, and public spectacle.

One of these performances was a show called "Salomons of the Dance." Its narrative chronicled Jewish history from the perspective of a series of fictional characters, all with the same name: Salomon. The Hebrew name "Shlomo"—which in its Turkish iteration becomes "Salomon" and refers to King Solomon of biblical Israel—is popular in its many local variations, pronunciations, and spellings in Jewish communities throughout the world. The show's performers enacted wandering generations of Salomons both horizontally throughout sites in the Diaspora and vertically through time. In each era presented onstage the name "Salomon" indexed a Jew, but what the play strikingly enacted was not the direct indexicality of Salomon qua Jew but rather, indirect indexicality—that is, what a man marked as a "Salomon" might say, even feel, as the bearer of such a name, given his particular cultural and historical milieu.

The actor portraying the first Salomon appeared onstage in a red and black satin costume, playing the role of a Spanish Jew from around 1490. The actor was a twenty-five-year-old community star, famous for his energetic lead singing in a popular Turkish band that plays rock versions of Judeo-Spanish songs. During this show he crooned in Spanish, girls dancing around him, swinging lacy fans to the rhythm of the canned musical soundtrack. Suddenly, the staged festivities froze as the troupe enacted the expulsion of Spanish Jewry. The scene took place in Turkish (although many in the audience still speak Judeo-Spanish, inherited from ancestors who fled a scene such as this).

The name "Salomon" iconically represents Jewishness in the community's imagination and in Turkish society more generally. The anti-Semitic *Salomon Fıkraları* (Salomon's Tales), a popular cartoon series in the 1930s Turkish press, portrayed a Jewish man named Salomon as foolish, money hungry, and unattractive (Bali 1999; Bayraktar 2006). Although the performance piece played out some of those stereotypes, given the *longue durée* offered by the show's narrative, the name "Salomon" indexed Jewish men in a wide range of social and historical contexts. By "telescoping" (Cooper 1999:16) across time and space in such a dramatic fashion, the show rehearsed, literally and figuratively, how the rights and responsibilities of one with such a name shift, depending on where a particular Salomon falls in the ever-changing Jewish historical and geographic landscape (what has been called a "chronotope").[5]

The narrative of Jewish names in Istanbul has traversed time and demands a multi-sited reading. Turkish Jews demonstrate awareness that being a "Salomon" meant different things at different times and to different audiences. The "Salomons of the Dance" performers enacted settings in which the name indexes, on the one hand, an idyllic situation (the pre-Inquisition era of the "golden age" of Spain) and on the other hand, a nightmare (transport to Auschwitz). A Salomon who found himself a Jewish subject of the Spanish Inquisition would be expected to wear clothes that distinguish him from non-Jews, would be engaged in certain trades, speak certain languages, and eventually convert or flee the territory. The configuration of multiple semiotic spheres would build a set of meanings making him who he was then.[6] Another Salomon, living in German-occupied Thessalonica during World War II, would learn that his name created a deadly subjectivity.

Defining Salomon as "a Jewish man's name" offered no interpretive context, either vertically through time or horizontally across continents (not to mention with respect to class, religion, race, and so on). The performance insisted on the name "Salomon" as a "rigid designator" (Kripke 1981), a sign that appears to designate the same thing across contexts. Indeed, it would appear that "the generalizing effect of time ultimately works in favor of category over individual" (Herzfeld 1982:300), and here the name "Salomon" indexed an unchanging, even essential, identity. As Ann Stoler suggests, "The claim that there are essences that distinguish social kinds is very different than positing that these essences are unchanging and stable in time" (2008:4). This claim is evidenced by the performance of centuries of Salomons acting out an essentialized identity against shifting backdrops: a court doctor called Salomon performed his royal duties to the Ottoman Sultan as a harem of dancers seductively gyrated; the menacing gates of Auschwitz framed the end of life for a young Greek Jew named Salomon; and a Sabbath meal in Istanbul awaited Salomon, the father of the house and a businessman in charge of a wholesale fabric store, Salomon's Silks, that was much like those still in operation in Şişli, an area of Istanbul where many Jews own small clothing shops and the streets of which swim in discarded material at day's end. Viewing the spectacle of one name attached to characters in multiple historical contexts highlighted the tension of a symbol whose meanings change yet somehow continue to index "Jewishness."[7]

Unlike findings about how Chinese language ideologies define naming as a system of meaning in which "signifiers and their homophones are seen as somehow inseparable from the signifieds" (Blum 1997:357), the Turkish Jewish ideology made explicit by this performance is one that understands naming as against the philosophy of naming as rigid designator popularized by Paul Kripke. Instead, Turkish Jews see naming as a model in which names mark people in a relatively arbitrary and certainly malleable sign relationship. Through linguistic (and perilinguistic) clues, publicly performed events such as "Salomons of the Dance" reiterate the community-wide understanding of how a chain of meanings can attach to one name over time.

Onomast-Icons and Historicizing Reclassifications

In 2003, I accompanied a Turkish Jewish friend, Rahel, on a research trip to Istanbul's Atatürk Library. As a Turk, she officially had access to a subsection of archives not open to non-Turkish citizens, yet the librarians eyed her name on the request form with suspicion. Part of the librarian's job description at the national library includes deciding who has access (based on Turkish citizenship) to the archives and who needs special permission to access these sources. When asked for additional identification, my friend became indignant, protesting, "I am a [Turkish] citizen and that is my name." Still unsure, they then asked, "Are you Armenian?" Annoyed, albeit not surprised, to have her citizenship in question yet once again, Rahel sighed, "No, I am Jewish."

It may not be surprising, perhaps, that most of my Turkish Jewish friends' names are not found in popular reference books, such as the book of Turkish personal names entitled *Türkiye'de Kadın—Erkek Adları Sözlüğü* (A Dictionary of Women's and Men's Personal Names in Turkey) (Adviye and Tuncay 1992). Although reference books such as these seem authoritative, they are themselves the artifacts of human reclassifications (not unlike those made by the librarian) in which certain names deemed outside of the collective simply do not appear. I first encountered this dictionary in 2000 in the office of Baruh Pinto, whose interest in onomastics—the study of names and their meanings—offered me a look at the processes through which Turkish Jews understand their names. Baruh, then a ninety-year-old Turkish Jewish man, was hard at work writing his own book about Turkish Jewish family names. The walls of his home office were lined with reference books: nearly fifty dictionaries occupied a central throne above an old desktop computer, sets of encyclopedias filled the shelves, and the remaining spaces were covered by maps of the Ottoman Empire, the Turkish Republic, biblical Israel, and the Iberian Peninsula.

Among all those reference books was Baruh's own contribution to the world of onomastic knowledge, a five-hundred-page tome called *What's Behind a Name?* (Pinto 1997). The book includes an elaborate compilation of family names and a Turkish Jewish community history from the Spanish Inquisition to the present. His project was based on the premise that throughout time, Jews have adapted to new circumstances by changing their names to become modern, while trying when possible to preserve something of the previous name's spirit. When I met Baruh, he had just begun a new project, a Sephardic onomasticon (a book of his community's surnames; see Pinto 2004), analyzing the layers of meaning attributable to Turkish Jewish family names found on a list of community members given him by the office of the chief rabbi of Istanbul.

I became Baruh's volunteer assistant, typing for him and enjoying his company and coffee. I loved watching him bent over the list of names at his desk, painstakingly searching for meaning, flipping alphabetically through his vast collection of dictionaries and checking for references in biblical translations. His method for solving etymological mysteries was to classify names according to their posited origin as biblical, cultural, theophoric, or toponymic. When confronted with an ambiguous name (which happened more often than not), Baruh searched for the name's origins in the Bible as well as in any atlas and any dictionary in Hebrew, Spanish, Arabic, Persian, Turkish, Italian, Greek, or Latin, in which he sought references to professional, physical, or moral particularities, animals, plants, and precious stones or metals (Pinto 2004:6). After exhausting the possibility of finding onomastic meaning in dictionaries, he moved on to his favorite reference tool, the *Encyclopedia Judaica* (1972). Baruh was a consummate *bricoleur,* which anthropologist Claude Lévi-Strauss defined as "someone who uses the 'means at hand' . . . to index the possible answers which the whole set can offer to his problem" (1966:18). He pieced together information from various frames through which he experienced the world, calling his project "a patchwork." He drew from many sources and fragments in Turkish Jewish history, literally cutting out pieces of paper with different sources of etymologies and pasting them into other chapters. When I checked if a name made more sense if it was written with a soft G (in Turkish, Ğ) or a hard G, he complained that the rabbinate's list didn't distinguish between Latin letters and those with Turkish diacritics: "to them it doesn't matter if they spell a Jewish person's name with an S or an Ş, as long as they pay their dues on time; to me it matters tremendously!"

A typical entry looked like this:

Table 2.1. Entry in the Sephardic onomasticon

Family Name	Etymology in 1. English, 2. French, 3. Hebrew, 4. Judeo-Espanyol, 5. Spanish, 6. Turkish	Notes
Bevnakil	1. Long distance story 2. Histoire relevant 3. Divre mi Mirhak 4. Estoria de un pasado leşano 5. Historia de un pasado lejano 6. Uzak bir maziye, bağlı bir hikaye	Does not appear in Kaganoff, Enc. Jud., BBL concordance, Develloğlu, etc. BEVN = distance, distance, merhak, distaniye, distancia, maziye NAKIL= history, histoire, divre, Estoria, Historia, Hikaye Com. It probably refers to the long past of the Jewish people.

Source: Pinto (2004:91)

Rather than defining Jewish names through one dictionary, Baruh's work parsed meaning intertextually across reference works. This is evident in the example cited here in which, under the notes section, he explains that he cannot find the name "Bevnakil" in reference books such as a book of Jewish names (Kaganoff 1977), the *Ottoman-Turkish Encyclopedic Glossaries* (Develloğlu 1999), the *Encyclopedia Judaica* (1972), or biblical concordances. Seeking meaning intertextually across reference books signals how the selection above—and other entries in Baruh's onomasticon—can be read as a map of the process through which Baruh analyzes each name. I selected the name above from hundreds of entries because it nicely illustrates an idea Baruh conveys throughout his work:

each name is a story and at times, one that moves across time and space. In his first book, *What's Behind a Name* (1997), Baruh argues that names serve as indexes for change and continuity, sometimes traveling long distances with their owners, other times remaining true to a baptismal meaning, and still other times shifting with fashion and the political demands of time and place.

Although Baruh's research began as a post-retirement hobby, classifying information was a task familiar to him from his first career operating a Kardex file system. Baruh described his first profession to me in the context of a story of a reunion with his estranged sister that itself points to his awareness of the importance of understanding the material consequences of reclassifications across time:

> In 1942, finding work (in Turkey) was impossible. I would arrive at an interview and find the post filled. My name sounded foreign and people were very nationalistic at the time. Unable to find work in Istanbul, I left for British Palestine. There I found a job working as a Kardexman, filing forms by name or category. One day, working in the Kardex room, I heard that someone wanted to see me. To my surprise, in walked my sister, Rachelle, who had left Istanbul and settled in Paris.
>
> When the Nazis occupied Paris, my sister wanted to leave France. Because she was Sephardic, she turned to the Spanish Consulate which offered her protection as a descendant of Spaniards. Once she arrived in Spain, she was told, "It is true that you are a Spanish subject, but this is valid only when you are living outside of Spain." As a consequence, she had to leave Spain for Palestine. (Personal communication, April, 2003)

Paralleling the historical features of Naile's narrative, the story Baruh recounted shows how the classificatory logic of his profession as a Kardexman dovetails with the way governments, politicians, and individuals file people into changeable categories of "citizen" and "alien" (see Comaroff and Comaroff 2001), often determined exclusively by name and subject to revision and reinterpretation during times of political change. Baruh filed as a profession and as a hobby, as a way of making ends meet and as a way of sorting out his family's layers of shifting associations. Given that his own life had been influenced by the ongoing reclassifications of categories of citizenship and belonging, it seemed fitting that he would dedicate his later years to sorting out these crossed lines and transposing them into a comprehensive work outlining the effects of these larger historical processes on Jewish names. He turned to onomastics to highlight the temporal implications of the project of understanding how he himself, over time, had been made a foreigner.

Anchoring Jewish Names in Istanbul

> To take up the name one is called is no simple submission to prior authority, for the name is already unmoored from prior context, and entered into the labor of self definition.
>
> —*Butler 1997*

Pace Butler, names are not always "unmoored" from historical context, at least not for Turkish Jews forced into the labor of self-definition each time their names are considered "foreign." If names today seem obviously "Turkish" or "foreign," these classifications rely on shortcuts that are products of cultural codes, socialized and naturalized to save what semiotician Umberto Eco has called "definitional energies" (1984:84). Baruh's colossal project, *The Sephardic Onomasticon,* traces the ideological process through which things seem to mean something by themselves. By going back over the etymologic trails, by reinvesting definitional energies, Baruh resisted reclassification of Turkish Jewish names as simply "foreign." By slowly pulling apart the tangles of Ottoman and Turkish Jewish names and by exposing the history of reclassifications to which Turkish Jews have been subject, Baruh (like the performers of "Salomons of the Dance") returned reified icons to their proper place in Turkish Jewish naming ideology as shifting, fluid indexes. He denaturalized the reclassifications that Lusi, Rahel, and other Turkish Jews face on a daily basis by organizing them into time-bound and context-specific interpretations. In addition to its inherent value as a hobby, Baruh saw his onomastic research as benefiting the Turkish Jewish community, global Sephardic Jewry, and the world at large. This wide-reaching pedagogical and socializing goal was made explicit in his choice to publish the onomasticon's preface in the six languages largely used to define the names themselves (English, French, Hebrew, Judeo-Spanish, Spanish, and Turkish). He did so to reach a wide audience, especially an audience of dispersed Sephardic Jews who might be researching how their own names caused them to be "reclassified," despite the fact that this decision caused him enormous editorial complications and costs.

Baruh's research process reveals how names as markers of identity are hardened into icons (symbols that are understood through convention as identical to what they purport to represent). Such symbols become iconic by means of the historical and present-day ordering and assignment of names (and other symbols) to interpretive or mythical frames. Unlike Baruh the bibliophile, most people don't consult multiple reference books as they go about their business classifying people and things they encounter. Instead, people draw on a set of myths that shape how we classify persons, places, and things. Myth "abolishes the complexity of human acts, it gives them the simplicity of essences, it does away with all dialectics, with any going back beyond what is immediately visible" (Barthes 1987:132).[8]

Family narratives (Naile's story), a communal performance ("Salomons of the Dance"), and an individual intellectual pursuit (Baruh's onomasticon) illustrate the ongoing (although qualitatively different) labor that must take place across time for reclassification to occur and, importantly, for it to be rehistoricized and for myths of belonging to be made and undone. Attention to ontology's process—as exemplified by the cases considered in this chapter—returns a sense of chronotopic complexity to otherwise naturalized (that is, decontextualized and dehistoricized) "signs of history," making them, instead, "signs in history."

This chapter has focused on the moments of tension in which meanings about Turkish names are temporally (if only temporarily) reshuffled. Names allow Turkish Jews to understand their present classification as built on earlier ontologies, as "signs that show time" or "signs in history." Jews in Turkey perform knowledge of the way signs—in this case, names—build on previous meanings to make sense of classifications in the present.[9]

THREE

The Limits of
Cosmopolitanism

Throughout my fieldwork research, my Turkish Jewish friends advised me to follow their example and erase my own Jewishness from the public sphere, citing a list of "don'ts" that sometimes seemed endless: don't nail your *mezuzah* to the outside of the doorframe, don't wear a Jewish star necklace, and, just in case, don't tell your landlord you are Jewish. I constantly confronted the seemingly ironic claim Turkish Jews make of feeling at home in a country where Jewish difference is carefully maintained in the private domain, while public space is seen as a universal sphere in which difference must be erased. This chapter describes how the Turkish Jewish community deals with these tensions by maintaining its appearance of disappearance, particularly as this relates to expressions of difference from the Muslim majority. By focusing on cosmopolitanism's limits, I argue—following Werbner (2006) and against many popular theories of the phenomenon—that expressions of difference are not always celebratory ethical choices made by individuals faced with multiple ways of being. Indeed, the erasure of difference reveals that cosmopolitan affects are often censored when and where difference is imagined to invite danger.

Becoming Turkish, along with the fear of not being perceived as Turkish enough, has engendered a profusion of effacing social practices among Jews in Istanbul. Layered upon these assimilationist conditions, local anti-Semitism and the complicated relationship Turkish Jews have with Israel (and, perhaps more importantly, the relationship that anti-Semites and/or anti-Zionists *perceive* them as having with Israel) generate an additional set of incentives to disappear.

If we are indeed in a "cosmopolitan moment," as many have argued, the process of "'cosmopolitanization' occurs as unintended and unseen *side effects* of actions which are not intended as 'cosmopolitan' in the normative sense" (Beck and Sznaider 2006:7). The Turkish Jewish case illuminates some of these unintended side effects, including the denial and erasure of cosmopolitan affects despite their public celebration. In tension with official participation in public cosmopolitanism, Jews in Turkey regularly opt for a low profile in the public sphere, and this choice plays out recursively in architectural, bodily, and linguistic domains.

In order to develop this notion of cosmopolitanization, this chapter deals with the key symbol of *güvenlik* (security) and the role it occupies in Turkish Jewish life. In Lakoff's terms—"What type of security is meant? What are its political objectives and what are its technical methods?" (2008:402)—I outline how, in light of security concerns, Turkish Jews conform to what they perceive as the correct kinds of erasure of cosmopolitan difference from the public sphere. I then discuss sites where concerns about assimilation and security overlap in spaces where the borders between private and public are ambiguous and must be negotiated.

The dangerous—and often disavowed—cosmopolitanism I observed in Istanbul underscores Beck and Sznaider's "rejection of the claim that cosmopolitanism is a conscious and voluntary choice" (2006:7). If cosmopolitanism is not always an individual choice, what kind of "actually existing cosmopolitanisms" does ethnography reveal? Studying cosmopolitanism through the experiences of Turkish Jews allows us to focus on a number of lessons to be learned about the contours of lived cosmopolitanism, especially at a time when officials seem to embrace cosmopolitanism but when everyday practices seem like classically ethno-parochial performances.

"Security" as a Key Symbol

Getting through security at official Turkish Jewish buildings (such as the rabbinate, synagogues, or the Jewish Museum) resembles boarding a plane on an international flight since the World Trade Center attacks. From adolescence on, many young Jewish adults in Istanbul are trained to monitor and guard these passages and will say that they work for the security of the community, or simply "in security." As volunteer

security personnel, they operate the steel doors at synagogues, checking passports (of foreigners) and faces (of community members) before
allowing guests to pass through a second door that provides access to
the site itself. The system's design ensures that the two doors can never
be opened at the same time—the theory being that if an attack began,
only the few people in the liminal space between the doors would be
compromised. Since the most recent bombings, many Jewish community buildings have had their security structure redesigned. Entrances
are now surrounded by concrete walls and are accessible only through
tunnels that add an extra layer of security cushioning between the street
and the community.

If Jews feel at home in Turkey, why do they place so much emphasis
on security? As Mary Louise Pratt thoughtfully observes, "As soon as
you mention security, you suggest there's a danger . . . otherwise the
subject wouldn't be coming up" (2004:140). Turkish Jews' lives are col-
ored by questions of *güvenlik,* reflecting their palpable fear of physical
violence and community dissolution. When I ask Jews about the security
situation, they largely answer that the elaborate technical aspects of defending the community (unmarked buildings, high surrounding walls,
metal detectors, and trained personnel) are a response to the 1986 attack
on the Neve Shalom synagogue. Despite the popular argument that the
deadly violence of the mid-1980s forced a retreat, archival press coverage
of the event records Turkey's (and the world's) surprise to discover Jews
still living in Istanbul, indicating that the Jewish community's effacement from the official Turkish narrative was already happening through
ideological violence and *symbolic* omissions. The idea that the bombing
cast attention on Jews who were largely living outside of public recognition—and that this sudden attention might be dangerous—was reiterated by means of a cartoon that appeared in the pages of the Turkish
Jewish press following the 2003 bombings, in which two (Jewish) men
are discussing the latest attacks. The first comments that since the last
synagogue bombing, thanks to the general media, the broader public has
"gotten to know us better. For example, how big a population we are, how
long we have been in this territory and how cohesive a community we
are, where our synagogues are, where we live, etc." The second character
scratches his head as if mystified and worries aloud, "Do you think they
found out my home address?" (Mandel 2004:115)

As the cartoon illustrates, being a Jewish cosmopolitan means not only knowing about different ways of being, but also knowing in which contexts, for whom, and in what ways one should (and can safely) perform difference. This is nowhere more evident than in centrality of "security" as a key symbol in the Turkish Jewish community.

Tolerance: The Flip Side of Security

Because I had read so much about it, I took the tolerance trope as a starting point for understanding Turkish Jewish life. Nonetheless, through fieldwork conducted between 2000 and 2003 and during shorter research visits since then, I have observed how it does not always correspond to Turkish Jews' lived experience. Turkish Jews perform a doubled identity in light of demands for Turkish integration and out of fear of being marked as non-Turks, that is, as "different" or "foreign." Unlike rural Nigerians, for example, who are intent on performing their cosmopolitanism by exhibiting their knowledge of different languages, styles, or affects (Gable 2006), or Nepali shamans who understand modernity as defined through the demonstration of cosmopolitan knowledge (Pigg 1996:193), Turkish Jews find themselves, despite an increasingly popular public discourse of tolerance, performing an everyday anti-cosmopolitan show that insists on their patriotism.[1]

Against the public message of tolerance, this lived cosmopolitanism points to Jews' perceptions about the ultimate limits of tolerance. In Turkish Jewish collective memory, the terrorist attack at Neve Shalom (and episodic violence since) indexes the need for closure and has been transformed into an iconic symbol. Young Jews who regularly socialize with Muslim Turks analogize the community's historically insular tendencies to a prison or an island. One twenty-eight-year-old male described the issue of socially mandated attempts at closure to me:

> My [Jewish] girlfriend wishes the community were more open . . . less like the stereotypical *korkak yahudi* [fearful Jew]. But she is very naïve; she doesn't know that if you are a Jew, Muslims will never see you as a person. When my girlfriend and I go out with friends, she fits in perfectly: she doesn't have a foreign name or a Jewish accent and can pass for a Turkish girl. But because I speak [Judeo-]Spanish with my parents at home I have an accent. As a Jew you might be stereotyped as being good at business.

Or they might hate you for it. Think about Neve Shalom—they killed
them for just being Jewish.

If "the whole social structure is present in each interaction" (Bourdieu 1982:67), symbolic distinctions between self and other should reso-
nate as the same melody in different keys. The iteration of Neve Shalom
against the backdrop of assimilation through non-marked identity (lack
of a Jewish accent, a non-Jewish name) reminds us that the iconic events
of 1986 index security concerns in recursively occurring symbolic fields.
Because of its ability to stand as one part of a larger whole (that is, a
metonym), I see the 1986 attack as a metonymic device through which
Turkish Jews justify separateness and social invisibility in the face of ho-
mogenizing Turkish state ideology. The basic element of differentiation,
the physical border dividing private Jewish space from the public Turkish domain, is represented through the community's practice of *güvenlik*
and whose mechanics and personnel guard these passages. The border
between opposing domains (secure/vulnerable) refracts through a number of social practices among Jews in Istanbul, such as the concealment
of differences in physical space and body, linguistic practices, and naming strategies. Security serves as a leitmotif for Turkish Jews' ongoing negotiation of dangerous cosmopolitanism. What analogies can be drawn
between physical erasures (unmarked institutions and bodies) and symbolic ones (unmarked language and naming practices)?

Private Fear and Public Comfort in Istanbul

Recent studies dealing with the notion of public and private space emphasizes that these domains are fluid and flexible, and that "leakage"
occurs between the seemingly opposed spheres (Herzfeld 1997; Shryock
2004). Turkey has garnered special attention as a test case for the public/
private divide with the rise of political Islam in Turkey since the 1990s
(White 2002), the secular imaginary of the public domain has been
challenged and secular idols (such as the Turkish Republic's founder,
Atatürk) are increasingly domesticated in private spaces (Özyürek 2004;
Navaro-Yashin 2002). In parallel, Jewish difference in the public sphere
has begun to emerge as an object of research (Bunzl 1996; Levy 1999),
complicating and challenging the notion of a clear opposition between

public and private (Habermas 1989) by documenting moments of friction, boundary breaking, and dialogue.

Under Ottoman rule, Jews occupied a specific social position with collective rights and responsibilities. The creation of the Turkish Republic reinterpreted Jews' status as individuals with the rights and responsibility of full citizens, denying them official (read "separate") group recognition. The Jewish community in Istanbul today is not segregated legally or politically from general Turkish society or its institutions, but this juridical position of equality is imperfectly matched by widespread discrimination, social rejection, and suspicion of "foreigners." Among Turkish Jews and perhaps among Turks in general, this ambiguity has bred cautiousness about displaying difference in public. Precisely because there is today no government recognition of Jews as a collective entity with communal rights, it remains up to members and officials of the Jewish community itself to debate and negotiate their own boundaries and those of the community. Yet among Istanbul's Jews, the borders between what community members consider private and public are well known and elaborately guarded.

Turkish Jews practice a quiet cultural citizenship less threatening to a state that directly or indirectly supports a classic Turkish republican (Kemalist) ideology, in which difference is a private matter. "Jewish" Turkishness exists in small, symbolic gestures as well as in the idea that the Jews still retain a private collective that is not privy to non-Jews. Using the local vernacular, Bali (2007) describes this posture as *kayadez*, the Judeo-Spanish term for "silence" or "quiet," which he glosses in English as "low profile."

Given the lack of signage at all major Jewish community buildings in Istanbul, one has to have access to prior knowledge about the location of the space, acquire permission, and announce an arrival beforehand in order to even find those spaces where Jews congregate. This is explained in sentences such as the following, which often accompany the Jewish travel section of guidebooks: "Given security concerns, you must make prior arrangements with the Chief Rabbinate for entry to Jewish sites. Admission is by prior arrangement only."[2]

My first visit to the Jewish Museum in Istanbul took me through the back streets of Beyoğlu, trying to find the place in a tangle of old crooked streets. Before I found the museum I found myself exasperated; the lack of signs made me miss the entrance to the alley a number of times. Unlike Istanbul's other museums, whose well-marked signage encourages passing tourists to visit, the Jewish Museum is ensconced in a quiet corner without any external markings. A sign would likely encourage higher museum attendance but would also risk inviting the kind of visitors the community fears most. When I finally located the museum, a security guard sat outside the office and instructed me to push my passport through the slotted, bulletproof window. After a few minutes of waiting I was buzzed into the liminal passage. The galleries were empty that day, and the guide working at the museum began to chat with me after a few minutes. I engaged her in conversation about security, about which she explained, "You get used to it. There are certain shortcuts everyone learns. For example, when we let visitors into the gallery, it is easier if we know them before they arrive; this makes the work of security much simpler." Turkish Jews seemed to accept that the boundary between public and private would be a heavily guarded one (see also Tuval 2004).

Diners at the kosher restaurant that used to operate near one of Istanbul's smaller synagogues also needed to wait for admission through double doors. A friend working in security told me that the restaurant's doors did not actually operate like those at the synagogue; rather, they were mimetic, offering a familiar impression of secure passage between public and private domains. Inside the restaurant, tourists put on traditional Jewish head coverings and knew that this was a safe place to signify Judaism (unlike other venues in Turkey, where public displays of Judaism are discouraged by travel books, tour guides, and locals, who instead recommend wearing a baseball hat). I first noted this avoidance of distinctively Jewish marking in regards to the internal placement of the *mezuzah,* but the practice extends from religious architecture to secular venues such as museums, social clubs, and kosher restaurants. I found that this kind of unmarked identity echoed in deletions of difference not only from the collective body but also from the physical bodies of individual Jews.

Recursive Physical Erasures

For Turkish Jews, performing Jewish identity in public involves a kind of self-nomination. In the same way that Jewish men do not wear ritual head coverings in Turkish public space, the wearing of Judaica (six-pointed stars of David or other symbols) is restricted to under-sweater fashion. Some young members of the community explained to me that they wanted to wear a Jewish charm, but that their parents aggressively discouraged identifying themselves "too openly" as Jews. T-shirts from Turkish Jewish sports clubs (which are popular and well-attended) lack distinctive markings such as Hebrew writing, stars, or other symbols that might index Judaism. In private Jewish spaces such as a holiday gathering or community event, however, a Jewish charm or t-shirt is proudly displayed.

An ironic example of the imperative to hide markings of Jewish identity occurred as part of a commemoration of Holocaust Memorial Day, another way in which Turkish Jews engage with knowledge of difference and Jewish history writ large. Following their visit to Nazi death camps in Poland (see Feldman 2002), a group of Turkish Jewish high school students created a presentation to share the knowledge they gained abroad. They reenacted historical episodes characterizing wartime life and distributed yellow paper stars that resembled those the Jews were forced to wear under Nazi rule in order to prevent their "passing" as non-Jews. After the emotionally compelling commemoration ceremony was over, participants were explicitly instructed to "remember to *remove* your stars when you walk out into the streets [of Istanbul]." This interaction suggests Turkish Jews' resistance to self-nomination in public. As described by Stratton, "For a group to be named makes it possible to identify people as members of that group. The Nazis understood this politics of visibility when they made those designated as Jews wear yellow stars" (2000:103).[3] If Nazi laws attempted to make Jewish invisibility impossible by marking clothes with Jewish symbols, in Turkey, where religious garb is banned from public institutions (White 2002:146), the republic, or "fantasies of the State" (Navaro-Yashin 2002), mandates the inverse of self-nomination: outside of official ceremonies that are choreographed by the rabbinate, the Quincentennial Foundation, or other representative bodies, passing (secretly being Jewish) is often seen as the safest way to be Turkish.

As the students exited through the barbed wire fence surrounding the youth center, their parents tried to keep them quiet so that the group of Jewish children spilling onto the residential street wouldn't draw attention to itself. Such "quieting down" points to another of the Jewish community's strategies of invisibility, which involves assimilation through linguistic practices. More formally, this includes the near-total adoption of Modern Turkish, a language that Jews only began speaking in earnest after the republic was created.

Disappearing into the Turkish Language Standard

> To have a state composed of peoples who speak the same language
> or to make only those peoples who speak the same language an
> independent state seems more natural and most desirable.
>
> —*Ziya Gökalp, cited in Fishman 1988:106*

Gökalp, who was known as "Atatürk's philosopher," summed up the early republican goals of linguistic unification in the above statement. Like many other modern nation-builders (see Blommaert and Verschueren 1998), Atatürk glorified homogeneity through monolingualism. Turkey's "Vatandaş, Türkçe Konuş!" (Citizen, Speak Turkish!) language campaign forced generations of Jews to hide their linguistic difference. Interestingly, major proponents of this campaign were patriotic Turkish Jews, such as Abraham Galante and Tekin Alp (né Moiz Kohen). As an example of the reforms implemented toward the creation of the Turkish Republic, one could offer excerpts from the statutes of the Turkish Language Society as they appear in the original 1943 publication and as they were revised during the incorporation of the society into the Atatürk Supreme Council for Culture, Language, and History in 1986 (Landau 1993:136). The goals stated in this document include the "Turkification" of the lexicon and syntax (read "Turkification" as purification), the promotion of scientific studies of Turkish, and the standardization of dictionaries and spelling with a focus on etymology. A more explicit national objective of language reform appears in the revised version of the statutes: "Considering the Turkish language's vital role in unifying the nation, to take measures to cultivate language awareness among the new generation; to prepare materials with this aim in mind and make them available to public organizations, to state and private educational institutions, and to the press" (Landau 1993:137). An intense focus on language reform usually accompanies more general social reforms (Fishman 1988:130), and the Turkish case was no different.

In the early years of the republic, Jews conversed in Judeo-Spanish (as they had for hundreds of years) or French (acquired in semi-colonial schools such as the Alliance Israélite Universelle). An elderly Jewish acquaintance, Sara, described to me an episode of linguistic erasure that occurred when she and her mother visited the hot springs of Bursa in the early 1920s, the formative years of the Turkish Republic. Their playful banter in French drew the attention of a policeman passing by on horseback, who called out, "Vatandaş, Türkçe Konuş!" (Citizen, Speak Turkish!) Sara, who had begun learning Turkish when she entered school, cheekily called back, "Ben Türk değilim!" (I'm not a Turk!) The policeman then proceeded to drag the girl and her mother out of the baths and brought them to the local police station. Their papers were officially confirmed and their identity verified, but only after an uncomfortable number of hours waiting in wet clothes. These sorts of incidents recur in the stories of elderly Jews with whom I spoke in Istanbul. Retelling this story in her living room in 2007, Sara clasped her cheeks, still blushing seventy years after making an innocent child's treasonous claim. Many Turkish Jews between the ages of fifty and sixty described the shame of speaking a foreign language in the streets of Istanbul, as one interviewee recalled: "French was the language spoken in my parents' home; outside they did not want to be too conspicuous. I was always told to 'hush up' in public, lest I shouted in French and revealed our identity." The hushing-up of the Jews in her generation likely was a combination of trying to hide what might be perceived as "foreignness" with a response to a 1960 ordinance, issued by the military governor of Istanbul, "forbidding people from speaking with loud voices in public places lest this create a bad impression among Western tourists" (Kasaba 1997:25).

Nearly a century after Atatürkist language reforms were conceived and implemented, linguistic nationalism was still a topic of heated debate. In August 2002, the Turkish Parliament passed legislation allowing Kurdish-language broadcasting and instruction. The passing of this law created juridical openings and possibilities in the Turkish public sphere for the recognition of the region's historical polyglot multiplicity. Although some regard this change as lip service to European Union overtures (Spolsky 2004)—again, a question of not creating a bad impression among Westerners—the policy shift seemed to signal a new era in which Turkey could celebrate cosmopolitanism through an acknowledgement of its citizens' polyglot orientation.

Later that summer, Turkish pop star Sezen Aksu tested the new law's strength by giving a concert called "The Turkish Mosaic." Playing to a full house at the amphitheater at Ephesus, the concert opened with some local bands, one of which played Judeo-Spanish music. Aksu's performance showcased songs in Greek, Armenian, Judeo-Spanish, and Kurdish alongside popular Turkish numbers. The leftist press applauded the performance, while those on the right questioned Aksu's loyalty to Turkey (Turkish Daily News 2002). There still exists a delicate balance between memorializing the mixed heritage of Ottoman times (often imagined as a mosaic) and glorifying the "one nation, one people" movements of Atatürk and later generations of staunch republicans (see Silverstein 2008; Hart 2009). At the practical level the censure (or potential for such) of non-Turkish languages in public performances threatens the speakers who take up the mantle of freedom offered by these changing political frameworks.

Long-held stereotypes of Jewish speech as different from standard speech include talking loudly, using non-Turkish words, and in general, speaking *bozuk Türkçe* (broken Turkish). After mentioning that I was planning a trip to Büyük Ada, a Jewish acquaintance joked, "What kind of vacation is that? With all those Jews around it will be so crowded and everyone will be yelling!" Another time, when I called to my friend, Selim, who was a few rooms down, a third (also Jewish) friend mocked me, saying that I spoke Turkish just like his grandmother! Given that my interlocutors in Turkey were mostly Jews, I began to wonder if I had learned a "Jewish" Turkish, rather than some "standard" variation I might use everywhere. Would I be marked as one of "them" when talking to non-Jews? Even though official definitions of republican Turkism focus on language and "civilization" rather than on ethnicity or religion, folk definitions of authentic citizenship still endure and can be located in ethnic-religious markers such as language varieties (accents, vocabulary, and syntax) as well as in names that sound Turkish or foreign.

Today, young Jews in Istanbul profess a high competency in "standard" Turkish and elderly Jews express pride in their grandchildren's unmarked speech. Unlike the Armenians whom one of my interviewees met while performing with Aksu, most Turkish Jews now lack an intimate language to cement their sense of community and difference. Instead, they speak Turkish with the knowledge that assimilation demands other symbolic boundary work. If certain words from Judeo-Spanish, French, or Hebrew survive in Jewish speech, these can be selectively omitted from non-Jewish discourse while employed more heavily among Jewish intimates. A new generation of Turkish Jews has mastered the ability to switch codes between a marked Jewish-Turkish and a standard variety.

As more and more Jews in Turkey find themselves speaking, writing, and reading Turkish as a "mother tongue" (see Şaul 1983:345), they are losing a private language (or languages) they once used to discuss the tensions of these differences in an intimate space. For example, the Turkish Jewish press was once published in Judeo-Spanish (Ladino), addressing community affairs and internally critiquing the leadership, but now that Turkish is the dominant language of the press, its writers and editors are constantly aware that their audience may be wider than originally intended. However, speaking the same language as others does not necessarily mean that one inhabits the same socio-cultural sphere.[4]

Turkish Jewish polyglots are not cosmopolitan through an automatic understanding of different cultures as embodied in the many languages they know. Instead, their multilingualism points to a cosmopolitan engagement with difference, or with a long history of living among (or between) different symbolic systems, be they political, economic, or linguistic. Cosmopolitanism among Turkish Jews might include a kind of polyglot orientation (Şaul 1983), but perhaps more importantly, it involves a collective knowledge about what to say, how to say it, to whom, and when.

Israel as (Failed) Litmus Test for Turkish Cosmopolitanism

One of the perhaps unintended side effects of cosmopolitanization is that certain folks will be labeled cosmopolitans even against their vehement claims of patriotism.[5] I found that the Jews in Turkey keep cosmopolitanism behind closed doors not out of any conspiracy (as anti-Semites regularly claim) but because the models of citizenship for Jews and other non-Muslims *demand* their invisibility. Erasure, a studied choice resulting from the triple consciousness mentioned in earlier chapters, is a strategy used by Turkish Jews to assimilate into Turkish society. Despite Jews' long-standing efforts to assimilate, Turkish nationalists, leftists, and Islamists still seem to perceive their cosmopolitanism as dangerous (Bali 2009). Why?

One example of the weighing of different symbolic codes that characterizes cosmopolitan knowledge is the serious deliberations that occur when Turkish Jews decide to perform or erase a Turkish–Jewish–Israel connection. This kind of logical process—the careful balancing of a national or cosmopolitan attachment—has a regular history in the postrepublican Turkish scene (and many other Diaspora locales). A similar question—to be or not to be "cosmopolitan"—came to the fore in the aftermath of the 2003 synagogue bombings, when Israeli emergency workers (known as "ZAKA"; Stadler et al. 2005) volunteered in Turkey to aid in rescue and to clear the carnage. They wore Chassidic garb (black hats, coats, and untrimmed beards), attracting the kind of attention Jews in Istanbul usually avoid:

> The spectacle was too much for one . . . official, who sidled up to the spokesman with a hissed request: "Lower your profile . . . We don't want to offend the Muslims here." Such sensitivity was nothing new for Nessli Varol, a 23-year-old daughter of Turkish émigrés who flew in from Israel for the funeral of an uncle killed in the second bombing . . .
> "The Jews here have a prosperous life, but there is also fear. They stick together and avoid too much exposure. When I used to visit my grandmother as a child, she would tell her Muslim friends I was from France, rather than Israel," she said. (Schleifer 2003)

Why was a cosmopolitan connection with a French foreigner more acceptable than one with an Israeli? As succinctly documented by Oğuzlu (2010), beginning in the 1990s, Turkish–Israeli relations exhibited a rapid increase in cooperation, including more high-level state visits, the signing of a free trade agreement, the beginning of an extensive military cooperation process and a major increase in the number of Israeli tourists to Turkey. Just as quickly as they began, this relationship entered what has been called a "cooling down" period, with relations precipitously declining both in tenor and in practice. Although many have assumed that the rise of the AKP (Justice and Development Party) in Turkey influenced the turn, in fact the relations began to sour prior to the party's ascent, with former Turkish Prime Minister Ecevit publicly criticizing Israel in its approach to Yasser Arafat (Oğuzlu 2010). Further, the political relationship between Turkey and Israel that began in the 1990s was largely a discursive one, with few material supports in social or economic domains (Bengio 2009). In the decade following, major diplomatic divides have revolved around an ever-mounting Turkish political critique of Israel's treatment of Palestinians—visible in high relief during Prime Minister Erdoğan's 2009 clash with Israeli President Shimon Peres at the World Economic Forum in Davos, Switzerland—as well as in the AKP's willingness to view the Palestinian Hamas as a legitimate political force, in contrast to Israel's consideration of them as a terrorist organization.

However, charting diplomatic or economic relations is only one way to measure the relationship between Turks and Israelis. One aspect of the Turkish–Israeli relationship that is often overlooked is a private one, and this is central to an understanding of Turkish Jewish identity. Turkish Jews are aware that they are perceived (sometimes inaccurately) by Muslim Turks to be Zionists and Israel sympathizers, as well as the fact that were they to claim such an affiliation with and/or affection for Israel, it would be a widely disparaged and dangerous position to take. In the Turkish Jewish community, Israel is everywhere and nowhere at the same time. Nearly every Jewish home I visited in Istanbul had a collection of items from Israel. Dead Sea soaps and creams fill bathroom vanities, Israeli good luck charms hang on bedroom walls, and Israeli food items, such as Elite brand coffee, Wissotsky tea, or Max Brenner chocolates, are regularly served at Jewish social gatherings. These "artifacts" (usually duty-free offerings) of contact between Turkish Jews and Israelis should not be surprising given the history of such a huge out-migration of the former after the establishment of the State of Israel in 1948, during which family networks became separated (see Weiker 1988:22); an estimated one hundred thousand Jews of Turkish origin now live in Israel (Elazar and Weinfeld 2000:367).[6] Turkish Jews obtain knowledge about Israel through informal community education, reading Jewish history books, visiting the country and, perhaps most importantly, through family ties as well as television and news articles. I often entered a Turkish Jewish home to find the family watching Israeli television, in Hebrew, on satellite channels or through internet streaming.

Turkish Jews' knowledge of Israel is a part of their cosmopolitan package they generally conceal in public, and willingness to affiliate with Israel or to discuss it at all follows the broader Turkish political scene, as explained to me by a journalist for the Jewish paper, *Şalom:* "We didn't used to write about Israel, but when the Turkish general press began publishing articles about it, we were able to join in." In an interview with an ultra-Orthodox (Haredi) Israeli radio program following a 2010 Israeli raid on a Turkish flotilla that attempted to break the blockade of Gaza, the Turkish Chief Rabbi Haleva condemned Israel's actions, demonstrating the undivided loyalty Turkish Jews are supposed to demonstrate in public discussions of Turkish relations to other states. In a *Jerusalem Post* article entitled "Turkey Boosts Security for Jews," Turkish Prime Minister Erdoğan heavily condemned the Israeli government's actions during the flotilla episode. In the same breath, he warned that anti-Israel sentiments, evident in the massive street protests at the time, should not be allowed to spill over into anti-Semitism against Turkish Jews, saying, "Our Jewish citizens have, as members of the Turkish people, defended, and continue to defend, the right position of Turkey to the utmost" and insisted that "looking with hatred upon our Jewish citizens . . . is not acceptable; it cannot be and should never be" (Mandel 2010). But why should Turkish Jews be punished for the actions of a foreign government? Both Islamists and members of the political left in Turkey have long associated Jews—even those in the Diaspora—with Zionism. As reported in the press, despite Erdoğan's warnings, security at twenty sites associated with Jewish institutions in Istanbul was increased (if that were possible, at this point) (Mandel 2010). By saying that Turkish Jews should not be punished for Israel's actions, Erdoğan reinforced the seemingly natural and logical connection between Turkish Jews and Israel in the first place.

In cosmopolitanism's seemingly unlimited collections of potential identifications, what is acceptable and what is forbidden? Public support for Israel in Turkey easily falls into the category of the forbidden. Jews with whom I discussed Israel expressed a wide range of political opinions about their posited relationship to the "Jewish State." However, while opinions and emotions about Israel run deep among Jews in Turkey, I rarely observed a Turkish Jew advocating for Israel, or for that matter heavily criticizing Israel, in his or her role as a spokesperson for

Jews. The majority of North American Jewish organizations advocate for Israel in numerous public and political forums under a Zionist banner, but "notwithstanding a few businessmen and Turkish citizens of Jewish origin, there was no influential pro-Israeli lobby in Turkey" (Oğuzlu 2010:277; see also Bengio 2009). The rabbinate and other Turkish Jewish representatives are publicly committed to maintaining Turkish Jewish life in Turkey and not in Israel.

In the aftermath of the 2003 bombings a media fray erupted over the definition of the true home for Turkish Jews.[7] Ariel Sharon, then Prime Minister of Israel, asserted in a press conference that the best response to anti-Semitic attacks (such as the one in Turkey) was the immigration of Diaspora Jewry to Israel, the true home of the Jews (Lazaroff and Katz 2003:2). This drew an immediate refutation from representatives of the Turkish Jewish community, disavowing a connection to Israel and insisting that their status as Turkish citizens was not at risk and that they were indeed at home in Turkey. Many turned the event into an opportunity to boast (yet again) of the long history of exemplary relations between Muslims and Jews in Turkey. Again, the old specter of rootless cosmopolitanism raised its head, not as an individual choice or an ethical orientation but as a Diaspora "problem" to be solved. This reiterates the important corrective the Jewish case makes toward understanding the collective aspect of cosmopolitanism: those who disparage cosmopolitans don't seem particularly concerned with the free-floating individual who is at home everywhere as well as nowhere. As has been observed in the cases of Indians in Uganda, Japanese Americans, and Yemenis in the Persian Gulf, "allegations about divided loyalty—in extreme form the diaspora can serve as a fifth column—can be used as a pretext for discrimination and persecution against a diaspora community" (Sheffer 1994:72). It is only when diasporic cosmopolitans get together across borders (or are imagined to) that anti-cosmopolitans raise questions about their patriotism.

In spite of government denial that anti-Semitism is a problem, Turkey—like many countries—has an anti-foreigner element (Schleifer 2004; Bali 2009), and the Israel question can be used as an excuse to spout otherwise distasteful (and sometimes illegal) anti-Semitic views. Commentators in Turkey have made it clear that a Turkish Jewish cosmopolitanism that includes support for Israel would be a dangerous move, writing, for example, that

Turkey, despite its good relations with Israel, despite the Jewish com-
munity's general tendency to think of Turkey as a Jewish friendly place,
I believe has its share of anti-Semitism, with the anti-Semitic rhetoric
of its left and right alike, which never fail to accompany each other on
"Jewish matters." Every Friday in Beyazit after prayers an Israeli flag goes
up in flames, its warmth reaching Jews here long before it ever does the
Israeli border, the same of course happens in most leftist demonstrations.
(Sandalcı 2003)

The author of this piece, a non-Jewish human rights activist and
writer for the news journal *Turkish Daily News,* refers to the anti-Israeli
demonstrations that take place each week in Beyazit Square, home to
one of the oldest mosques in Istanbul and named for Sultan Beyazit II,
who is credited with welcoming the Jewish community into the Ottoman Empire after their expulsion from Spain (an irony likely lost on
demonstrators). Turkish (and other) anti-Zionists often imagine that all
Jews are Zionists (or vice versa). Although the Turkish Jewish community is not officially affiliated with any Zionist movement, in her op-ed
piece Sandalcı recognizes that the anti-Israel actions of some protesters
have spilled over into general Turkish anti-Semitic rhetoric and violence.
I mention that Sandalcı is not Jewish in order to emphasize the rarity
of Jewish public critique in Turkey; suffice it to say, this is a piece that
most Jewish Turks would not dare to write.[8]

Whatever knowledge Turkish Jews have about Israel via familial,
historical, or religious connections is downplayed in public, pointing to
their cosmopolitan knowledge as a kind of mediating filter. If Jews use
cosmopolitan knowledge about when to disavow knowledge of Israel,
thus maintaining the status quo, this knowledge is a reaction to both
reality and perception. For example, the practice of double naming can
be found throughout this population as a matter of security and a way
of dealing with the annoyance of all those questions about foreignness.
A man known as "Moshe" to Jewish friends and family will print "Metin" (the name used at school and on his identity card) on his business
card. Often these name-changing efforts were done in the name of "what
ifs," such as "What if my employer is anti-Semitic?" "What if the customers don't want to do business with non-Muslims?" Jewish perceptions of anti-Semitism in Turkey are, in fact, not always based on acts
of political or overt discrimination but on social exclusions, widespread

conspiracy theories, and reactions to pervasive negative media representations of Jews (Toktaş 2006b:220). This issue of mediated anti-Semitism
came to the fore again in late 2008, following Israel's invasion of the
Gaza Strip. Anti-Semitic signage appeared on a Turkish social club, reading "Dogs Welcome; No Jews or Armenians" (Teibel 2009). Although the
government condemned the act and fined the club officials, the calculus
Jews make of the official discourses, media caricatures, as well as the
intermittent attacks on the community averages out to cosmopolitan
caution, or what Marcus might deem "paranoia within reason" (1999:5).

Security, Demographics, and Assimilation: Erasure as Symptom or Cure?

In spite of all its high-tech security, the Jewish community of Turkey
is hardly closed. Jews work and play in the same venues as non-Jewish Turks, they go to the same bars and movie theaters, wear the same
clothes, speak Turkish like their compatriots and, increasingly, marry
Muslims. If prior to the 1960s intermarriage was quite rare, by 1992 marriages between Jews and non-Jews in Turkey was recorded at 42 percent,
with the rate of intermarriage nearly doubling between 1990 and 2001
(Tuval 2004:67–68). The collective is not geographically, linguistically, or
occupationally contained as it is in some other Jewish enclave societies,
such as those observed in Morocco (Levy 1997) or England (Valins 2003).
If legal distinctions, external and internal social pressures, languages,
and residential patterns once made the boundaries between Jewish and
non-Jewish Turks clear, the community certainly can now be understood as relatively porous.

In 2009 I attended a wedding in Istanbul, noting that the invitations to the ceremony, held at Neve Shalom, included a special security
pass that guests were instructed to bring with them to gain entry to the
synagogue. At the reception, I was seated next to a twenty-nine-year-old
Turkish Jewish woman, Shila, and her Muslim husband. At the reception, Shila danced ecstatically to Israeli folk tunes. She later explained to
me she had learned these dances as part of a Jewish troupe as a student
in Istanbul, memories she described with nostalgia. She told me how
when her son was born she insisted on officially listing his religion as
Jewish, because she wanted him to have access to the sociability that

Jewish community activities had offered her as a child. In early 2009, she had a change of heart. Following Israel's invasion of Gaza, a move that Turkish officials condemned in national and international forums, she found that people she once considered friends suddenly became distant. Back at work, Shila recalled, she was overwhelmed by the cold shoulder given to her by co-workers, with whom she previously had good relations: "People stopped talking to me. It was as if, by some association with Israel, I wasn't the same person anymore." Further dismayed by the rash of anti-Semitic comments reported in Turkish papers following the invasion, she decided to remove the word "Jewish" from her son's official identification.

Is the erasure of Jews from the national body politic a "symptom of modernity," as Bunzl (2004) so convincingly argues? Do Jews in Istanbul see their erasure from Turkish public life as symptomatic of a completed process of modernization or as a cure for the ills of anti-Semitism and assimilation? In 1843, Marx wrote, "The social emancipation of the Jew is the emancipation of society from Judaism." While most members of the community say that they have retreated to a more private Jewish space since the first Neve Shalom attack in the 1980s, one educator in the Turkish Jewish community explained that "the attack made us open up, we were suddenly visible." As if challenging Marx's assertion, he continued, "I am not against emancipation. I am against assimilation, disappearing." The iconicity of Neve Shalom was—and continues to be—deployed variously to encompass a shifting discourse of physical and social security, which are likely more conjoined than divisible in the first place. After the bombing of 2003, friends told me, they stopped going to synagogue as regularly as they once had. They admitted that despite the sophisticated security provided by the community, there was no way to guarantee that the synagogues were safe. They were scared. It also seemed that having a complex security apparatus didn't necessarily grow from violence alone but from perceptions of insecurity, broadly defined. For many Jews, "cosmopolitan knowledge" allowed them to maintain a delicate balance between being "too Jewish" and "too assimilated."

A member of the Judeo-Spanish musical group mentioned above once explained to me that even though Turkey's religious minorities are often lumped together, there are major differences in their levels of integration:

We gave this concert with an Armenian band that seemed so closed off from Turkish society. They even speak Armenian among themselves! It reminded me of how they say the Jewish community was at the end of the last [nineteenth] century. We Jews are paying the price of opening up in other ways: language loss, mixed marriages and community conflict. We've been debating about whether to promote openness, if it is better to be more universalistic and join general society or if it is preferable to stick with other Jews.

When it comes to physical security Jewish community buildings are protected; however, the social border between Jews and non-Jews is much less rigid than it might seem and therefore, requires constant disassembly and rebuilding. Ambiguity creates a special kind of concern, one that I heard echoed in a security speech given to participants in a conference for Jewish young adults from the Black Sea region held in Istanbul in 2003: "There is already security around the whole site. However, your name tag is your pass. Without it we can't let you in because we don't want marked and unmarked people mingling around."

A parallel rhetoric weighing assimilation and physical security was set into relief when in 2002, I joined fifty Jewish young adults on a group tour to a popular tourist venue during the Jewish holiday of Chanukah. After everyone had settled into their rooms, I overheard tour organizers debating the security risk involved with candle lighting, a traditional Chanukah ritual. At first I thought they were concerned about creating a fire hazard; however, it was soon apparent that they feared breaching cosmopolitanism's limits. They asked each other, "Should we light the candles with the hotel staff around?" "Can we get a private room so the other hotel patrons won't see us?" Given my observations of how "security" could be invoked to address a wide swath of concerns, I pressed the organizers to explain their fears. They informed me that they were concerned about Islamic fundamentalists, anti-Semites, accusations of practicing witchcraft, strange looks, even of being kicked out of the hotel!

When the time came to light the candles, I saw why the group feared that non-Jews might perceive the ritual as pagan or otherwise offensive: members of the group had brought what seemed to be the world's largest candelabra, a metal structure roughly three feet tall, whose branches' width exceeded my arm span. When I inquired about the origin of such an oversized ritual object (typical Chanukah candelabras are much

FIGURE 8
Lighting an oversized candelabra during Chanukah.
Marcy Brink-Danan, 2002.

smaller), one organizer explained that in the wake of a Turkish trend to put up "New Year trees" (resembling American Christmas trees) in the winter, a Jewish group had organized a project to distribute the oversized candelabras to Jewish homes to be decorated with tinsel and lights. Reminiscent of the discussion of the *mezuzah* being at once a promise of secure identity and one that might draw negative attention, the issue of fighting assimilation while remaining safely "invisible" constantly challenges community members. Yet again, members of the community wrestled between the dangers of assimilating and the desire to protect themselves from threats of being perceived as non-assimilated.

Pointing to the contexts and conditions in which cosmopolitanism is censored, this chapter has considered recursive erasures of cosmopoli-

tanism in Turkish Jewish architecture, bodily marking, and language
that illuminate the conditions under which people consider themselves
dangerous—or even dystopian—cosmopolitans (see Ossman 2006). If,
as some have asserted, we are living in a "cosmopolitan moment" (Beck
and Sznaider 2006:7), for some actually existing cosmopolitans the moment is fraught with danger. Who today is afraid of being called "cosmopolitan?" Unlike in many parts of the world, where seemingly paro-
chial actors feel compelled to put on an awkward-fitting cosmopolitan
costume (Ferguson 1992; Tsing 2005), against the backdrop of Turkey's
strong statist tradition (Barkey 2000; Heper 1992) Jews sometimes find
the shoe fits all too well. Cosmopolitanism among Turkish Jews involves
a much more private, practical, and protectionist way of managing difference. Rethinking cosmopolitanism along these lines suggests a shift
not only at the level of theorizing the phenomenon (away from choice
and ethics and toward a complicated knowledge of difference) but also in
method. Studying cosmopolitanism as knowledge performed and erased
from public requires attention to the semiotics of discourse, narrative,
conversation, genre, theatricality, and style, as well as to the rhetoric
of more obvious public pronouncements.

Among Istanbul's Jews, self-nomination in the public sphere is a
relatively new phenomenon. In 2003 I attended a rehearsal of Jewish
schoolchildren who were busy learning songs in Judeo-Spanish. The
children and other musicians, intellectuals, craftspeople, and volunteers
were engaged in preparations for Istanbul's first celebration of the European Day of Jewish Culture, inaugurated in Europe in 1996 and in which
twenty-one cities now participate. I followed news about the transformation of Galata and its environs into an outdoor stage that would come
alive with Jewish music, food, exhibitions, and displays with no small
amount of disbelief.

How would the community that I had found so concerned with
security open its doors wide open to the public? How would it—how
could it—perform Jewishness on the streets of Galata? Reports of the
event marked its great success, and so it came as an ironic surprise when,
just two months later, Neve Shalom synagogue was again attacked, this
time by Turkish perpetrators of Islamist orientation. Despite the bombs
that threaten to force Istanbul's Jews back in the "closet" just as they
were finally coming out, the community has celebrated the European

Day of Jewish Culture every year since its adoption in Turkey in 2003. In 2009, the celebration fell on the anniversary of the 1986 attack on Neve Shalom. Organizers of the Day of Jewish Culture acknowledged this tragic coincidence with the following text on their promotional website: "We commemorate with respect, the victims of this incident that coincides this year with European Day of Jewish Culture that is organized simultaneously all over Europe."[9] Rather than making a retreat, making alliances with the European Union and European Jewish communities has allowed Istanbul's Jews to represent themselves as counting, symbolically, beyond what their numbers might predict. Yet these representations are not part of Jews' everyday performances of self in Turkey; they are more carefully choreographed spectacles.

FOUR

Performing Difference:
Turkish Jews on the National Stage

In the early 2000s, a small group of Turkish citizens performed their civic duty as members of a secular democratic regime by going to the polls, voting by secret ballot, and inaugurating their leader in a lavish ceremony: on October 24, 2002, Jews throughout Turkey participated in a community-wide election of the Turkish chief rabbi. I observed how Turkish Jews, a minority that historically eschewed overt political participation, held this community-wide election at the same time as Turkish national elections were going forward. This parallel exercise in democracy gave the Turkish Jewish community a unique space to debate the meaning of democratic citizenship, to discuss their role as a distinct religious community in the Turkish Republic, and to perform that identity in a public, highly orchestrated event: the ritual investiture of the chief rabbi.[1]

While the institution of the chief rabbi in the Ottoman Empire and the Turkish Republic has been described through the disciplinary framework of history (Benbassa 1995; Karmi 1996; Rodrigue 1992; Shaw 1991), there has been no ethnographic analysis of the local meanings attributed to the Turkish chief rabbi. As a corrective, this chapter chronicles the evolution of the democracy discourse surrounding the investiture of a new chief rabbi by means of ethnographic observations of organizers of the event, voters, and delegates; conversations with reporters at the Turkish Jewish press who covered the event; text analysis of news articles that reported on the event itself; and speeches delivered during the inauguration. I attended the inauguration, recording not only the structure and content of the ceremony but also participants' reactions to it. I found that the democratic election of the chief rabbi served as a process whereby Turkish Jews campaigned for a politics of presence in the public sphere. I will thus argue that non-governmental rituals, such as the election of a chief rabbi, offer marginalized communities a stage upon which to perform larger discourses, such as democratization, and a political platform they might otherwise be denied (see Greenhouse and Roshanak 1998; Ignatowski 2004).

If Turkey's strong statist tradition (Barkey 2000; Heper 1992) set the national terms for early republican life, Turks increasingly question the definition of Turkishness, essentially becoming "anthropologists of themselves" (Navaro-Yashin 2002:21) and reinterpreting Turkish history (Bozdoğan and Kasaba 1997; Kandiyoti 2002; Neyzi 2002:141). European Union candidacy and an increase in Islam-infused and ethnic politics (specifically Kurdish) and a change in media practices have necessitated a critical reckoning of the definition of Turkish history, democracy (Brink-Danan 2009), politics, and culture (Kaplan 2003; İçduygu and Soner 2006). Indeed, the year of the chief rabbi's election, 2002, coincided with a general increase of intensity of the "democratization" discourse, spurred by European Union demands for Turkish political reform. At least in theory, "democratization ... gives space to voices from the margins that have the potential to provide new points of view and, thus, new styles and sets of relationships" (Tanabe 2007:561). As such, the time was ripe for a discussion of what democracy means in the Turkish setting.

In seemingly endless contexts, the term democracy is employed toward a wide range of political and social goals. The openness of "democracy" as a political signifier is one reason for its success as a rallying cry for so many seemingly distinct groups (see Gutmann 2002; Paley 2002). However, there remains a tendency among international organizations, non-government organizations, governments, and other policymakers to apply inflexible yardsticks of "real" democracy by which to measure democratization in different parts of the globe (Paley 2002:485; Schmitter and Karl 1991:76). We should not, however, assume that democracy means the same thing across different contexts (Schaffer 1997).

Anthropologists have long recognized elections as an important site of self-definition for the ritual's participants (Herzog 1987; Kertzer 1988).

As such, elections function as sites of condensed meaning, communicated through symbolic action and metaphor (Turner 1974). As a "dense transfer point" of power (Williams 1980:243), elections, installments, and coronations all constitute fertile ground for the ritualized performance of ideologies, concise political statements, and claims about the past and the future. However, beyond serving as a site for debating ideas, elections serve to perform a kind of political presence. Turkish Jews seek a representative political presence to advocate for "cultural citizenship," the right to be different while remaining part of the national community (Rosaldo 1994). However, where cultural citizenship is widely regarded as threatening, how can it be performed without alienating the Turkish government or citizens?

Political theorists have often focused on the challenge of democratic regimes to serve both individuals and collectives (especially minorities or other marginalized groups). This tension between democratic philosophy and practice is especially notable in cases where liberal democracy's focus on the individual citizen clashes with communal wishes for collective representation of difference (Benhabib 1996). Toward an analysis of this phenomenon, Phillips has distinguished between a "politics of ideas" and a "politics of presence," emphasizing how the former does not always address the needs of those marginalized from the democratic process. She argues that "political exclusion is increasingly . . . viewed in terms that can only be met by political presence, and much of this development has depended on a more complex understanding of the relationship between ideas and experience" (Phillips 1994:77–78). The tension creates a critical opening for ethnographic study, whereby the attention of anthropologists to lived experience is well suited to exploring the complexity of relationships between the politics of ideas and of presence. The value of understanding the politics of presence is especially salient in the analysis of collectives that want to claim cultural citizenship in the face of historically exclusionary hegemonic practices. Many Jews still believe that their acceptance as a minority in Turkish society is conditional upon their keeping a low profile. As Neyzi has argued, the combination of social insularity and the "oligarchic structure of community leadership, [itself a] legacy of the centralization associated with the establishment of the Chief Rabbinate," created an environment in which Turkish Jews shy away from public spectacles (2005:174).[2]

In order to contextualize the election of the chief rabbi, I first provide a brief overview of the role of the rabbinate in Turkish Jewish history. Following this, I offer a glimpse of the Turkish political scene that served as a backdrop to the 2002 ritual of investiture. I note, especially, invocations of the term "democracy" and references to the Turkish Republic generated during the election cycle. Here I pay special attention to how many Turkish Jews saw the outcome of the vote as a "democratic disappointment." Next, I detail the rabbi's investiture ceremony and consider how this performance represented Turkish Jewry in a semi-public setting. In conclusion, I analyze the election and inauguration as a "politics of presence" in which democracy is seen not only as a practice through which to debate ideas but also as an attempt to represent collective difference in the public sphere.

Chief Rabbis in the Ottoman Empire and Turkey: Why Democracy Now?

The activities of the Jewish community of Turkey are organized centrally, albeit divided into two main branches, religious and lay committees. Elites who serve in the rabbinate have a wide-reaching influence on the Jewish community, especially because the structure of the rabbinate accounts for both "religious" and "lay" activities, and the leaders of the community are drawn from the same exclusive social pool (Tuval 2004).[3] As an organization, the rabbinate controls official Jewish activities and community representations in Turkey.

The first Ottoman chief rabbi officially represented the community under the reign of Sultan Mehmet, who created the position in 1453, paralleling organizational roles played by Greek Orthodox and Armenian patriarchs (Karmi 1996). The nature of the position has shifted dramatically since its creation, falling out of power during the sixteenth century and later revived in the nineteenth (Benbassa and Rodrigue 2000; Cohen 2008; Levy 1994; Rozen 2002). Throughout the years, the responsibilities of the rabbinate have ranged from acting as community tax collectors to spiritual advisors (not necessarily in that order); it gained and lost power in relation to the needs of the community and the demands of imperial and national leadership (Barnai 1992; Bornstein-Makovetsky 1992). In the early years of the Turkish Republic, the position lost significant authority, yet the community later revived the role. In 1953 and 1967, seventy men over the age of twenty-one (over half of whom had a "religious" appointment in the communal structure) formed a committee to nominate Rav (Rabbi) Rafael Saban and Rav David Asseo, respectively, as their leaders (Kastoryano 1992). Rabbi Asseo served as *hahambaşı* (chief rabbi) until his death in 2002.

When I began ethnographic fieldwork in Istanbul in August 2002, the rabbinate was a body running without a head. Rav Asseo had recently died and a new chief rabbi had not yet been chosen. Nonetheless, given the sophisticated organization that is the rabbinate (*hahambaşılık*)— which maintains a dedicated (and largely volunteer) corps of lay and religious leadership—the passing of Rav Asseo left no apparent institutional vacuum. What was lacking, rather, was a liaison to the Turkish government and an official spokesperson to represent the community in political arenas. This was graphically portrayed in Turkey's Jewish paper, *Şalom*,[4] by showing the chief rabbi's desk framed by a large portrait of Atatürk and the Turkish flag (Hart 1999; Özyürek 2004) but without an occupant.

In the fall of 2002, this same paper announced that the chief rabbi's election would be decided by means of a community-wide representative democratic vote (in Turkish, *temsili demokrasi*). Community members would vote on an electoral college of 150 secular members, and an additional ten-person committee of religious leaders would be appointed (Ovadya 2002). Candidates for the electoral college represented the areas of Istanbul (and a few other cities, most notably, Izmir) most heavily populated by Jews and linked to synagogues operating in those areas.[5]

Notable changes in the process for 2002 included the introduction of a community-wide representational democratic process, reduction of the age of qualifying candidates from twenty-one to eighteen, and the inclusion of women in the process as voters and as delegates who would later choose the new chief rabbi. The terms of appointment had also been, in the words of the press, "modernized": the new rabbi would serve for only seven years—renewing his position through an achieved rate of success—rather than hold an ascribed lifetime appointment. Historical accounts emphasize that the selection process of the Ottoman and Turkish chief rabbi has long been a theater for political debates about modernity and tradition (see especially Benbassa 1995; Stein 2003). However, the new emphasis on democracy anchored the rabbi's role around a particular concept of the state rather than on questions of Jewish law.

Although the rabbinate seemed to have the ultimate authority over the Turkish Jewish community, it soon became clear that as an institution, it answered to a higher power. While the chief rabbi wears a royal purple gown on formal occasions, the 2002 election was distinctly cloaked in the red and white hues of the Turkish flag as well as the blue and yellow of the European Union. From the permissions requested by the community from the Ministry of Internal Affairs and the Governorship of Istanbul to the oversight of the municipal police department and Provincial Authorities of Istanbul, the community ensured that a ritual that might have been private became a public, indeed, national endeavor; the "specter" of the republic featured prominently in every step of the process of electing and investing the chief rabbi.[6]

The novelty of a democratically elected chief rabbi generated a significant buzz in community discussions. Turkish Jews might have used the democratic election as an opportunity to ask fundamental questions about the nature of the community. They might have debated the value of a patriarchal leadership role in a community whose women serve tirelessly as volunteers and organizers. Strikingly, however, the overwhelming focus of discussion was not on community visions (ideas) but on the nature of democracy itself. As I will show below, the community's discussion coalesced around two major themes: democracy as a disappointment; and democracy as political presence, or more specifically, a form of representation.

Democratic Disappointments: Reporting on Community and Nation

Şalom, the single paper dedicated to reporting on and for the Turkish Jewish population, gives voice to many of the Jewish community's hopes and fears. The pages of the Turkish Jewish press endlessly engage in a comparison of their community's status as a religious minority within a secular state with other places and times, producing what I call "cosmopolitan knowledge." They contrast their own milieu with Israel, European Union member countries (especially France), and the United States, asking questions such as "How secular [*laik*] is Israel?" or

"Why do American Jews have so many denominations?" Commenting on democracy in the Middle East, a headline in *Şalom* read: "Searching for Democracy in the Arab World" (Kasuto 2003:8). Accompanying the article was a photo of what seemed to be a political rally in an unknown location with a caption stating: "A rising voice in the Arab world: 'Freedom of Speech, Yes!'"

In October 2002, three candidates for chief rabbi were announced in the paper. Following criteria outlined in the "Chief Rabbi Election Procedure Draft" published by the rabbinate in *Şalom,* the candidates for chief rabbi were over forty years old, citizens of the Turkish Republic, and members of the religious council (*Bet-Din*) (Ovadya 2002).[7] When the rabbinate announced the election in the Jewish paper, it emphasized the importance of democratic participation as an opportunity for the community to come together in "a fitting unity of brotherhood."

Community reporters argued that participation in the process of electing a chief rabbi was not only a means to elect a new leader but also a way for the community to reaffirm core values. However, I would suggest that the process offered more than just a rich site for Jewish "identity work": it also offered a place for Turkish Jews to debate the very nature of democracy and participatory government in Turkey.

How did the Turkish Jewish community define democracy during the election of the chief rabbi? *Şalom*'s reporters framed articles about the upcoming election with photos of smiling voters and pithy quotes about democracy, such as "Democracy means not 'I am as good as you are' but 'You are as good as I am.'"[8] One reporter insisted that the Turkish Jewish community was embarking on a "test of its democratic principles," and dissected the term "democracy" for readers:

> Democracy literally means that the public itself is in power. In other words, as long as it is the public who elects candidates to serve the public, it is the public who is in power. If it is not the public who elects candidates to serve the public and instead offices are appointed or "elected" by certain people, then this system can at most be called a mild autocracy or neo-autocracy. (Molinas 2002:3)

This same reporter framed "democracy" as a populist movement in order to appeal to a broad audience, encouraging community members to vote:

Go and validate your existence by saying "I vote, therefore I am." If you are indifferent toward elections and refrain from voting, rest assured that you will only please those who say, "Democracy is too good for us." For in that case, they will be proven right.

I say: "To the polls!" and take a huge step toward democracy, the system that ensures healthy governing for all modern societies. Do not forget that democracy is the lesser of the "evils" among all governing systems. (Molinas 2002:3)

Although this reporter wrote specifically about the elections for the chief rabbi, he could as easily have been discussing Turkey's general elections that were slated to take place in the same season. To whom does this reporter refer as "those who would say that democracy is too good for us?" To Muslim Turks who stand in judgment of Jews? To Europeans who dismiss Turks as prospective members of their polity? Both interpretations might be possible, and perhaps it is worth viewing the former as framed by the ongoing debate about external judgments of what is democratic and what is not.

As such, *Şalom*'s urgent summons to participate in the representative elections (that is, to "pass" the test of democracy) is paired here with a deep skepticism about the process. This sentiment echoed throughout many conversations I heard during the election season. Even as reporters and readers supported the idea of a new rabbi being elected (rather than appointed), many were doubtful about the details. Misgivings about voters' ability to make a "good" decision factored into reporters' concerns about the outcome of the vote, as illustrated by a cartoon printed in *Şalom*. In the cartoon, when asked, "Who are you voting for?" a man answers, "I'm voting for the leader who roots for my [sports] team. That way, at least we'll have something in common." The cartoon makes fun of voters' "petty" concerns, but again, it is not clear which voters are being belittled: Jews electing their chief rabbi or Turks electing their government. The characters are unmarked as Jews; the "common man" could either be a voter in the general national election or one choosing his delegate for the nomination for the chief rabbi.

Immediately following the election of Rabbi (Rav) İsak Haleva as chief rabbi, I attended a staff meeting in the news office that shares building space with an upscale boutique and a meditation center, although the office itself is separated from the other building occupants by a rigorous security apparatus. I observed Şalom's reporters milling around, anxiously discussing how to report on the election. They were critical of the lack of disclosure about the details of the election and disappointed by low voter turnout for what was supposed to be a major step in the democratization of the Jewish community in Turkey. A twenty-five-year-old reporter cited a statistic that less than 20 percent of the community had voted, and wanted to report this as a personal disappointment. His editor, a sixty-three-year-old head writer for the paper, interpreted the results in a more positive light, saying, "Let's look at it from a different perspective; there are always two sides to a story: on one hand, it was a low turnout; on the other hand, for the first-ever election, it wasn't so bad." After debating the matter amongst themselves, the staff agreed that Şalom, as the sole mouthpiece of Jews in Turkey, had to report on the event in a way that would be meaningful to its readers as well as to the participants in the election.

In an interesting compromise, the paper reported on the election in a few different modes. As is typical in the paper, major news items recurred across columns, allowing dialogue to become text and dissonance to emerge. For example, while on the Turkish-language pages, reporters offered a description of the event including dates, procedures, and outcomes, on the Judeo-Spanish page there appeared a humorous column entitled "Letra e-mail a mi Prima Zelda" (An E-Mail Letter to My Cousin Zelda) (Anonymous 2002). A hypothetical e-mail from a Turkish Jew, "Rachel," intended for her cousin "Zelda," "mistakenly" ended up in the hands of the editors, who claimed that after contacting the author about her mistake, they received permission to reprint the letter. In the letter, "Rachel" critiques the handling of the elections, questioning whether or not they were democratic and expressing her disapproval of the delegates who would eventually elect the chief rabbi. Describing her husband's involvement as a delegate, she noted his anxiety about the process. Further, she belittles the election by complaining that she had to miss out on a boat cruise on the Bosphorus in order to vote. She continues in this vein, mocking her husband and other voters and critiquing the fuss made over "una eleksiyon ke savemos kualo va ser a la fin!" (an election whose ending we already know!) This was a common criticism of many with whom I spoke about the elections, perhaps accounting for the low voter turnout that so concerned the news staff.[9]

In an interview, a twenty-seven-year-old Turkish Jewish friend recalled why she voted in an election whose outcome was obvious:

> I voted for Haleva, knowing that even if I didn't cast my vote he would still win. It was the first time that we had an event like this in Turkey. Not to mention, this was the first time that the leaders of the Jewish community asked our opinion!

The Jewish press itself had defined the election as "a test of our democracy." Although the reporters felt depressed over the low voter turnout and overall community skepticism about the process, they were not entirely surprised. My conversations with Turkish Jews over the past decade often turned to democracy's failures. Among Turkish Jews, an oppositional reading (see Hall 1980) of their current political milieu resonates with a broader malaise about the state of Turkish democracy, a gloomy awareness that is emphasized in comments such as "We live in an Orwellian state," and "Big Brother is watching us." Once, when members of a group of Jewish adults whose interactions I had been recording for linguistic analysis demanded that I stop recording, the organizer of the group explained the problem as that of Turkey's "weak" democracy, saying, "I know that you have no intention of writing anything negative about us. I'll tell you what this is . . . it is because Turkey isn't yet democratic enough. People have no experience with free speech."

Turkish Jews had real reason to fear and, at the same time, value democracy. They had gained equal citizenship through the nondemocratic regime change that created the Turkish Republic and sustained its hegemonic dictates under decades of one-party rule. The Turkish public today democratically elects its leaders, but if political leaders or private individuals challenge the basic principles of Kemalism (or otherwise "insult Turkishness"), the generals of the secular army stand in the wings waiting for their cue to hold a coup. This became clear when, at the same time that the Jewish community was holding elections for the new chief rabbi, national elections held the media's attention. Among the 2002 candidates, AKP (Justice and Development Party) candidate Erdoğan professed an Islamist politics that Kemalists claimed ran contrary to secularist democratic principles. At the time, secular Turkish friends (Jews and Muslims alike) melodramatically predicted an Islamic takeover. Nonetheless, I was reassured that any attempts to close bars, veil women, or otherwise "bring Islam into the public sphere" would be quickly undermined by an army takeover.

As the election campaign for their local leader progressed, my Jewish friends observed the polls for national election showing an overwhelming majority in support of the AKP. A representative from the rabbinate told me that they had a "good, proactive, relationship to AKP" and that it is "wise to keep lines of communication open between us, we live in the same country and are willing to give them a chance." This political sector particularly concerned some Jews, who see their future in Turkey linked to the maintenance of secular law. In addition, AKP leaders have a clear history of anti-Semitic rhetoric. However, while AKP party leaders claimed to have changed their ways, Jews in Turkey privately confessed their overall discomfort with the idea of democracy if that meant it could be used to install politicians with avowedly anti-democratic ideals. References to Hitler's election by popular vote quietly reverberated among community members, who watched the polls predict success for Islamist parties. What kept them calm, despite what they saw as the inevitable rise to power of parties whose press and leaders consistently espoused anti-Semitic *rhetoric,* was the knowledge that the Turkish army generals (the guardians of secularism) would never allow political *activities* that challenged Kemalism. In 2002 the new national government (the majority of which represented the Islamist AKP) was installed without army intervention, but the specter of a possible coup has held parties hostage to the generals' strictly Kemalist vision of democracy.

Not long after national elections were held, another Turkish Jewish friend explicitly compared them to the community elections, claiming that she voted even though she felt the outcome was already known:

> I have to tell you, it was the same for the general elections for the government as for the chief rabbi. I knew [Rav] Haleva would win like I knew that AKP would win; everybody on television and in the papers said so. In this case, I voted for CHP [a staunchly Kemalist party], even though they are known to be corrupt. At least that way I could say I did everything I could to prevent an Islamist government from coming to power.

If Jewish community members expressed disappointment in Turkish democracy, they agreed that a "show" of democratic practices served as a powerful way to claim Jewishness in public. By describing the investiture ceremony for the chief rabbi and reactions to it, I now turn to the performance of difference claimed through a discourse of democratization.

The Investiture Ceremony

I consider the investiture of the democratically elected chief rabbi of Turkey as a performance through which Jews claimed a viable presence in Turkish affairs. Although the community continued to run smoothly in the months it was "headless," the ceremony highlighted certain themes that had emerged, among which democracy and the specter of the state featured prominently.

The ceremony to inaugurate Rav İsak Haleva incorporated old prayers and new visions. The ceremony was held at Neve Shalom synagogue, whose inconspicuous entrance, fortified with a cement wall, metal detectors, and security cameras gives way to a resplendent interior. Wooden pews line the main floor in a semicircular pattern around the ark that holds the Torah scrolls, above which an eight-ton chandelier dangles precariously. Above the main section, the women's balcony is accessible by two main stairways. The space holds one thousand people and, despite the chill in the air on the night of the investiture, it was overfull with excited community members and officials.

The men sat in the synagogue's main hall, their heads covered with blue skullcaps emblazoned with the golden image of the breastplate worn by the chief rabbi. From above in the women's section where I sat, a sea of sapphire satin seemed to cover the congregation. Male Turkish governmental leaders, lay leaders of the Jewish community, and a handful of Israeli politicians sat in the front pews, bookmarked on each end by attentive security guards.

The upper floor of the sanctuary overflowed with women, the scent of perfume overwhelming, well-coiffed hair and polished nails ubiquitous. Packed tightly together in the balcony, women angled for a better view. Because the community attendees included at least as many women as men, a projection screen was set up in the upper halls of the synagogue with a broadcast of the event. Simultaneity did not compensate for these women's distance from the main hall, about which many of them quietly grumbled.

The newly elected Turkish chief rabbi entered the hall dressed in regal purple with a silky headdress. After leading the evening prayers, Rav Haleva donned a prayer shawl brought as a gift by Rav Bakhsi-Doron, Israel's Sephardic chief rabbi at the time. Two members of Turkey's *Bet-Din* (religious council) then ceremoniously outfitted Rav Haleva with the symbol of the rabbinate, a breastplate in the shape of the Ten Commandments—the distilled essence of textual authority of religious Jewish life. The symbolism of the Ten Commandments weighed heavily during the evening, as the rabbi adjusted to the heavy pendant hanging around his neck.

However, in addition to his spiritual responsibilities, the rabbi's political obligations were equally represented that evening; namely, his relationship to Turkish law and to international Jewish leadership. In his acceptance speech, the rabbi highlighted the dual responsibilities inherent in his office, promising to "fulfill my mission with a firm adherence to our country's laws and regulations within the framework of the precepts of our holy religion."

Speeches by the chief rabbi and then Community President Bensiyon Pinto, which dwelt at length on the chief rabbi's historical relationship to the state, were sandwiched between a series of religious rites. The ceremony served, at times, as a stage from which to praise Turkey, as Rav Haleva's speech professed:

> It is my pleasure and my responsibility to announce to the world that we are indebted to the Turkish nation's dignified nobility and its government's recognition of rights for standing here today as a Jewish community with a size and a quality enough to elect a chief rabbi by free will [*özgür iradesiyle*].

Here, the new rabbi highlighted the value and "countablility" of the community. The election and investiture were invoked as impacting not only Turkish Jews but also as having potential ramifications beyond the community, as indicated in speeches given by representatives of Turkish political parties. Jewish Community President Pinto used the installation of the chief rabbi as a platform to praise the Turkish Republic and be explicit about the role of Jews as the positive face of difference.[10] His words spoke to the ritual as a politically opportune moment to represent the community as the "good minority" to an audience that included not only Turkish Jews but also diplomats and other foreigners, whom Pinto directly addressed in his speech:

> Our community has contributed generously to various stages of European Union accession processes, which the majority of Turkish people regard positively. We especially try to invite delegations who have the power to shape public opinion in their home countries so they can personally get to know our country and its people. We are happy to observe how effective and credible this strategy has proved so far. Our guests are impressed with what they see and experience. On their return they promote Turkey in various aspects. The common wish of people living in this country is to reach the level of modern civilizations as glorious Atatürk had himself signaled. I believe that cooperative efforts spent in Turkey's name toward attainment of equal member status in the European Union will be rewarded sooner than expected. We, the Turkish Jews, will continue to work towards this goal to the best of our ability.

The Jewish community here is represented, despite its marginal status, as politically aware, responsible, contributing, powerful, modern, and cooperative. In effect, Pinto champions Turkish Jews' cultural citizenship, arguing: "You need us!" And: "You need us to be different!"

The two Hebrew invocations at the ceremony's closing (the prayer for the state and its leaders, and the prayer for the community) were translated into Turkish and enclosed in the printed program. The first asks for God to bless the Turkish Republic and its tenth president, Ahmet Necdet Sezer.[11] By mixing secular and religious symbols, the ceremony created an ambiguous atmosphere in which not only were the values of the community on display but in which local officials had a platform from which to discuss national goals and visions. What better way to embody the role of the chief rabbi, in charge of religious questions for a largely secular community and an intermediary between community and state? The chief rabbi is a person, Rav İsak Haleva, whose actions, humor, and knowledge were scrutinized by voters and reporters in the pre-election period. At the same time, his enactment of the *role* of chief rabbi in performance through ritual election and investiture drew on certain signifiers to create a meaningful symbol for the Jewish community and, perhaps more importantly, for the Turkish government.

Turning to a Turkish Jewish friend at my side, I commented on the newly invested rabbi's powerful oratory skills. She laughed a bit, saying,

"Well, I guess. Although, it might be better if he could lose his Jewish accent!" This comment spoke to the performative nature of ritual, emphasizing form over content. Indeed, community members expressed one major criticism of the whole undertaking; namely, that the election and investiture were each a "show." However, as many of my Turkish Jewish acquaintances explained, using democracy as a means through which to claim political presence points to the fact that in this setting, "the play's the thing."

Despite the debate, cynicism, and doubt surrounding the chief rabbi's election, I would argue that this was not an example of "failed" ritual (cf. Chao 1999). Ritual performances may suffer from their obviously choreographed appearance as a "show," but their pomp lends a patina of authority to an otherwise unmarked change in social status. This could patently be seen when, at a community event held soon after the investiture, an audience of hundreds rose to their feet to honor the new chief rabbi as he entered the auditorium. As well, in conversation with attendees during the investiture, I noted that many swelled with pride at seeing "their" rabbi perform in such a regal way. One sixty-year-old woman beside whom I sat during the ceremony explained later, "Some people remember seeing Atatürk. I will remember being present at the investiture." Given that the well-choreographed ceremony balanced markedly Jewish frames with those linked to the state, the syncretistic pose of the rabbi as a "state Jew" resonated with another attendee, who said, "I am a Turkish nationalist. I don't know a lot about the chief rabbi. But he does a good job protecting the community and representing us as good Jews in Turkey. What is especially important is that he protects our honor." Indeed, since his election, the chief rabbi has taken on the grave responsibility of attempting to combat the increase of anti-Semitism in Turkey, for example, by holding interfaith events and public ceremonies on Muslim holidays.

Seeing community politics as a show—or sociodrama—does not discount its central symbolic function (Hill 2000; McLeod 1999), which is to represent the community to higher powers. A few weeks after the investiture, I overheard a conversation between an organizer of the event and an American rabbi who had attended it. The latter mocked the ceremony, saying, "Now the comedy is over." The organizer replied, "Oh no, it is just beginning!" According to the organizer (and many rabbinic officials outside of Turkey), "from a religious standpoint, this ceremony and this role has no meaning; it is a show, a charade. It is the closest we Jews have to a coronation." The rabbi's function in Turkish Jewish society is not to intervene between his people and God, to enforce Jewish law, or even to be a teacher (a classical definition of the term "rabbi"); rather, as the 2002 election and investiture showed, the role of chief rabbi was largely political, defined by his ability to represent the community and mediate between it and the Turkish government.

Representative Democracy and Performing the Politics of Presence

With the investiture behind them, some community leaders recalled the ceremony with criticism, saying, "Everyone knows that this was a show for the Turkish government." These remarks, coming from the very organizers of the "show," intrigued me; as Scott has argued, studying the structure of ceremonies is "a privileged pathway to the 'official mind'" (1990:58). Minority elites have the unenviable job of presenting a unified front to the majority or its officials in order to make their small voice "countable" (Herzfeld 1997:92); however, this pretend unity often discredits their authority among those who have disagreed in the first place, namely their constituents and fellow members of the community.

Why would the Jewish community invest so much time and effort in a democratic performance to please the government? When I pressed them on the issue, they explained, "We had to show that the community was unified and strong, despite our dwindling demographics." Levy (1999:633) notes that communities with declining numbers are motivated to create what he calls "cultural enclaves." Here I observed quite the opposite: the Turkish Jewish community recognized that its decreased demographics made it increasingly dependent on the government for support. Thus the show, performed for the government, attempted to claim viability despite the small community's sense of increasing irrelevance. As such, the chief rabbi's election and inauguration had to embody a meaning beyond that of a private ritual for the community alone.

As the main interlocutor between Jewish community members, the Turkish government, and international Jewish leadership, the chief rabbi's prestige is crucially determined by his ability to bridge divides—both religious–secular and national–international. Indeed, as many Turkish Jews expressed to me, his presence was valued only inasmuch as he was able to perform well as a representative for the community.

In spite of Turkish Jews' historically low-profile status and their individual gestures of assimilation, in the role as representatives of Turkey's "good minority," community officials increasingly serve in a self-conscious role as public advocates. Given that their function as political actors in the public sphere today is contingent on their being different (thus testifying to Turkish tolerance of difference as part of the regime's proof of democracy), this is a role that Turkish Jews are unable to fill except as a collective, which brings us back to the question of their ability to participate as individuals or as a group.

In this milieu, the choice of a democratic election, in which the community's leadership might come under public scrutiny, reveals a desire among (some) Turkish Jews to critically assess the society that conditions the terms of its power. As Turkey's Islamist political parties have done for pious Muslims and political Islamists, the Turkish Jewish community's elections for the chief rabbi allowed its members to question democracy on their "own terms" (Çınar 2005:20). One of the main critiques of democracy that political theory has offered us (and, therefore, leaves room for ethnographic investigation) is the inability of liberal regimes to reckon with assertions of collective identity (see for example Benhabib 1996; Kymlicka 1995; Phillips 2007; Young 1989). When Turkish Jews invoke democracy's ability to represent them, they are not just talking about the representation of individuals but also about representation as a collective. They are, indeed, vying for a politics of presence *as a group,* which current models of liberal individual Turkish citizenship denies to collectives.

By electing a religious official through a democratic process, the community found a legitimate forum to debate foundational assumptions about modern communal leadership and politics. In this light, criticisms of the community election function as a micro-critique of democracy in Turkey. These criticisms show that Jews in Turkey see the scaffolding of political power as a weakly built structure. Turkish Jews are deeply aware of the history of changing political frameworks and how, as a minority, they must constantly update their relations with the reigning power. The campaign and election of a new chief rabbi in Turkey allowed the Jewish community to participate in national debates on a local scale. Although Jews might have used the rabbi's election to express their particular concerns about the community (dwindling demographics, Jewish education, and so on), instead their concerns reflected an overall preoccupation with democratization and representation. In short, they expressed doubts about claiming cultural citizenship, not as individuals but as a collective in a Turkish democracy.

Through the spectacular performances of the election campaign and investiture ceremony, I observed how the chief rabbi was chosen for his ability to perform a model of state-approved Judaism for Turkish Jews. Calling the process of electing a chief rabbi in Turkey an example of "representative democracy" (temsili demokrasi) contains a double entendre of sorts: temsil can be parsed as "representative" (as in the delegates who, once nominated, cast their votes for the chief rabbi) but also as "show" or "spectacle."[12] The ritual election and installment of the Turkish chief rabbi in 2002 reckoned with the inherently ideological problem of representing Jews (Kirshenblatt-Gimblett 1998).

I have attempted, in this chapter, to focus attention on the importance of political performance and representation. My mapping shows that the Turkish chief rabbi represents a composite of values that Turkish Jews hold dear: secularism, tradition, modernity, tolerance, and democracy. He comes to stand for these ideas by means of what his words, dress, actions, and office index to his multiple audiences. At moments of liminality, such as the democratic election of the chief rabbi in 2002, these indexes become visible, showcasing that how the rabbi represents is more telling, at times, than what he represents.

What emerged during the election and investiture of the chief rabbi was a strong debate about Turkey's weak democracy. In this light, we might characterize Turkish Jews as ambivalent about democracy: on one hand, they embrace its equalizing power; on the other, they fear its ability to erase the difference, patriarchy, and centralized power that have been pivotal to their experience, both as Turks and as Jews. This is perhaps not surprising, given that European Union debates about Turkey's candidacy for admission currently occupy so much media time, judging Turkey against an ever-shifting democratic yardstick (Rumford 2003). That this debate should be so prominent among Turkish Jews, however, sparks certain critical questions: Who in Turkey still has a stake in the definition of democracy? Do Diaspora Jews (or other minorities) have a particular role to play in the shaping and interpreting of their countries' political systems (see Bunzl 2004)?

Jews in Istanbul used their local election to participate in a broader political debate to which they have limited access due to their small numbers and disempowered status as a Turkish minority. Through the rituals, symbols, and interpretations surrounding the election and investiture of Turkey's chief rabbi, Turkish Jews envisioned democracy as a disappointment, but at the same time remained committed to its potential to offer them collective representation. Seeing representation as a question of political presence points to performance as a critical site for anthropologists to study the way minorities (and their leadership) manage collective difference in a liberal public sphere. As such, a hypothetical *Şalom* reporter might well have argued of Turkish Jewry in 2002, "*We* vote, therefore *we* are."

FIVE

Intimate Negotiations:
Turkish Jews Between Stages

As discussed in the previous chapter in relation to the chief rabbi's election, the Turkish verb *temsil etmek* means "to represent." Self-representation, itself a kind of performance, is central to how Turkish Jews imagine their participation in public and also private spaces. Although it might come as a surprise, anthropology has been engaged with questions of Turkish Jewish performances for over a century. Employed by the Smithsonian Institution, Cyrus Adler, a Jewish American scholar of Semitic studies, organized living ethnographic dioramas—foreign villages—of world cultures in expositions held between 1888 and 1897, "in which Jews were present but not visible as such" (Kirshenblatt-Gimblett 1998:89). Expositions such as these, which enjoyed wide popular appeal in Europe and the United States, were part spectacle and part ethnography. In his organizational role as the exposition's commissioner, Adler traveled to Turkey, Persia, Egypt, Tunis, and Morocco (99), visiting local Jewish communities in cities along the way and cultivating his Jewish ties. Adler arranged and organized the performance of hundreds of people as part of the Turkish Village in the World's Columbian Exposition (known more colloquially as the "World's Fair"); an estimated four-fifths of Adler's performers were Jews, which drew concerns from some attendees about how authentically the villages represented Turkey. In the minds of some spectators, Jews (even "Oriental" ones) were not real Turks, but rather were engaging in the *performance* of Turkishness: "Some have said that all this does not represent Turkey, and that the Turkish village is purely a speculative enterprise of some Oriental

Jews," though this observer did concede that "the originators, whoever they may be, are seeking to represent Turkey . . . and have given the village a distinctive Turkish meaning" (100). Adler himself was unable to distinguish between Muslim and Turkish Jews during his trip to Constantinople. As such, "Jews could therefore live and work in the Turkish Village at the Chicago fair *in their capacity as Turks*" (emphasis in original). Indeed, performers acted as "Moorish, Tunisian, or Egyptian and assumed to be Muslim, but many were actually Jewish" (Kirshenblatt-Gimblett 1998:100; see also Cohen 2008).

It has been argued that Turkish identity is expressed as a zero-sum game: "One may speak of Christian Arabs, but a Christian Turk is an absurdity and a contradiction in terms . . . a non-Muslim in Turkey may be called a Turkish citizen, but never a Turk" (Lewis 2001:15). During ethnographic research in Turkey in 2002–2003, I found this to be sometimes true and sometimes not. Examples of syncretism abound in public Jewish events in Istanbul; since his election, the chief rabbi and his officers have prioritized this role by holding interfaith events, especially on Muslim holidays. For at least the past decade the Jewish community has regularly hosted an *iftar*, the break-fast meal held during Ramazan (Turkish: Ramadan); in 2009 this was held in tandem with Istanbul's European Day of Jewish Culture. I attended a Jewish community *iftar* held in Neve Shalom synagogue in 2002. The main hall was converted into a dining room, filled with 300 attendees (many of whom were also present at the investiture) seated at tables set with a typical Turkish *iftar sofrası*, including the Ramazan staple—fresh *pide* (flatbread)—prepared in the kosher kitchen of the Jewish home for the aged. Speeches given by rabbis, imams, community leaders, and the head of the municipality focused on the history of multi-religious neighborhoods, the similarities in Judaism's and Islam's fasting traditions, and the "universal brotherhood and friendship" between Muslims and Jews, emphasizing the role of religion in bringing peace and prosperity to Turkey. The "bride's room" in the synagogue hall was converted into a *mescit* (or prayer space) to which observant Muslims retired after the meal to pray.

Turkish Jews have some habits that are unlike those of their Muslim neighbors and others that reveal their integration into the national Turkish fabric. When I began my research, a frequent saying was quoted to me that revealed the dual face of Turkish Jewish alienation from and assimilation within the broader Turkish scene, in a sentence that neatly combined Turkish and Judeo-Spanish: "No mos karişeyamos münço a las meseles de hükümet" (We don't get involved much in government affairs). If the chief rabbi's election and his subsequent performances in the Turkish arena are one kind of show, the dress rehearsals and actors' workshops that take place in Turkish Jewish homes, schools, and social clubs are equally informative for an understanding of how Turkish Jews understand their social position and what it means to "act Turkish" or "act Jewish," especially when the stage upon which one is performing is not as grandiose as that set for the chief rabbi or other officials. Private discussions, such as those I recorded at Turkish Jewish adult study groups and parent-teacher association meetings, expressed a clearer opposition between Jewishness and Turkishness that necessarily hinged on other entrenched binaries, such as private versus public and religious versus secular. Attention to performance deepens our understanding of the logic of group classifications by thinking of it as a show conditioned by its theater, its audiences, and its players.

This chapter is organized to give the reader a taste of the range of performative spaces in which Turkish Jews find themselves today. I present a selection of scenes, from displays geared entirely inward (toward an exclusively Jewish audience) to those staged largely for an external, non-Jewish gaze, as described in the preceding chapter. These include concerts, adult study groups, parent-teacher association meetings, and pre-marital consultations—in the form of "lessons"—for those about to get married by the rabbinate. I show how these ritualized spaces offer the community a variety of stages upon which to perform cosmopolitan knowledge. As the chapter comes to an end, I compare the modes of display involved in creating a contextually successful cosmopolitan performance. This chapter therefore brings together anthropologically informed theories of performance with my observations of enactments—as well as evasions—of cosmopolitan knowledge.

Representing Turkish Jewish Culture in Istanbul and Abroad

In the fall of 2002, in a small, well-secured cultural center in Istanbul, a dozen or so Jewish "young adults" (read: unmarried) lounged on oversized pillows and couches, discussing the plans for a meeting of Jewish peers from the Black Sea region for spring of 2003. The meeting, which the Turkish Jewish community was slated to host, would bring over one hundred Jewish young adults from Bulgaria, Georgia, Romania, Turkey, and Ukraine together at a country club near Istanbul for a long weekend of Jewish and general activities to "promote the survival of the Jewish people in the Black Sea region." As indicated by the material produced by previous year's organizers for the meeting in Bulgaria, this second meeting was envisioned as a way to continue building bridges among Jews from the region, with an explicit statement of internationalism: "In this world of disappearing borders . . . we strengthen the connection between young Jews from this region . . . who are facing common problems and fears. Beyond that, we share the experience of being together and the joy of being part of one whole piece—the Jewish people." The cosmopolitan–national tensions of such a meeting revolved around plans to make participants aware of their national Jewish cultures while at the same time, enforcing the idea that there was an overarching commonality among participants. As such, each group of participants was invited to perform a "country presentation" on the first night of the event. During the organizational meeting in January, a debate ensued about the best way to represent Turkey. One volunteer offered: "We are in Turkey and we want to show that we still exist here, as Turks. What is the best kind of representation of Turkey that we can offer our guests?" To which some proposed a menu of typical Turkish tourist fare: Turkish folk songs, Turkish coffee, *nargile* (water pipes), and belly dancing. This suggestion drew some skepticism from others in the room, with one attendee crying out, "These are Turkish cultural things, not Jewish ones!" Another suggested that there could be a presentation of Ladino songs, but nobody in the room really knew enough material to stage a whole concert. One solution was to bring in Shira,[1] an Israeli ethnomusicologist doing research in Istanbul on Sephardic music, to teach the Turkish participants Ladino songs in order to perform them during the country presentation. A third suggestion, and one that seemed to draw the most support, was that a group of folk dancers from one of the youth clubs come to the event and perform two Turkish dances and two Israeli ones, as the latter are the most popular kind of Turkish Jewish entertainment. When one asks about Jewish culture in Turkey, people often invoke the popular dance groups called *folklor* that perform Israeli folk dances. The rebuttal to this idea was that it would not be particular to the Turkish Jewish community, as Israeli dance is studied and performed around the world. In the end, the conference organizers did not manage to learn Ladino songs, nor did they opt to perform Israeli folk dances; instead, a professional belly dancer arrived in a sparkly and revealing costume to entertain the guests from around the region while an Israeli beverage company, Elite, sponsored the Turkish coffee reception.

In early November 2002, the ethnomusicologist gave a performance at a small concert hall in Istanbul. She had released a recording of Judeo-Spanish songs based on interviews and samples taken from the musical repertoire of elderly Turkish Jews. As I observed during the planning meeting for the Black Sea event, members of the Jewish community regularly contacted her rather than their local experts for authoritative information on Judeo-Spanish music. Before singing a favorite Judeo-Spanish song, she made a confession about the supposedly traditional sources of her music:

> I have a secret, but don't let it leave this room. When I started to sing these songs I assumed that they were part of the Sephardic tradition, carried on the lips of singers expelled from Spain 500 years ago. But then I noticed something strange: many of the songs had a musical structure that didn't exist in Spain. So, I did some research and found that the songs aren't that old. We found a copy of a Salonikan newspaper whose writers popularized these songs by writing Judeo-Spanish poems and instructing their readership to sing along to the tune of a Greek or Turkish song which was in fashion at the time. So, as you can imagine, the song isn't really a traditional Jewish song, but it is beautiful nonetheless.

By calling the song "non-traditional," Shira professed an ideology of linguistic and musical purism. But why is syncretism a dirty little secret? If a Spanish song can be Jewish, why can't a Turkish one?

The audience at the ethnomusicologist's concert included many from the Jewish community, including the members of a popular music group, Sefarad, who rose to some celebrity in Turkey in the mid-2000s. When I was living in Istanbul in 2002–2003, Sefarad had just begun to gain a foothold in the wider Turkish music scene, and still performed regularly for Jewish community events. Jewish music enthusiast Joel Bresler's website, "Sephardic Music: A Century of Recordings," describes the "crossover" success of this group:

By far the most unusual example of Sephardic music in Turkey comes from a group named Sefarad. Fronted by three young Jewish musicians, Sefarad has sold hundreds of thousands of copies of recordings containing Sephardic music, and even hit the Turkish pop charts—unheard of anywhere else. In the double CD *Sefarad, Volume 2* songs are presented twice on different CDs, once in Turkish and once in Ladino. (The arrangements, backbeats, running times, etc. are all the same.) Quite simply, these are the best selling Sephardic recordings in the world.[2]

The group took a Ladino song called "Avram Avinu" or sometimes "Kuando el Rey Nimrod," invoking the biblical patriarch, Abraham (Avram), and changed the lyrics completely to an unrelated theme celebrating the sun-drenched club scene of Bodrum, a popular vacation spot on Turkey's Aegean coast. As such, the song "Bodrum" is imminently "Turkish," performed by Turks (who happen to be Jews) who have transformed this Sephardic tune—a standard in Jewish music circles—into a widely popular version with the possibility of many meanings attaching to it at once. By beginning their career with a double billing of Ladino and Turkish songs, the group members capitalized on their difference as Jews (participating in a rising music scene with a sound they call "ethno-pop") but performed a special kind of Turkishness. One only needs to glance at the cover of one of their albums, *Evvel Zaman* (Once upon a Time), in which band members pose in front of a silhouette of the Galata Tower, to situate their style against a backdrop of historical performances of difference. If Sefarad enjoys a special following in the Turkish Jewish community, however, their ability to perform "as Turks" is unquestioned among their many non-Jewish fans throughout Turkey.

With respect to the question of representation, Sefarad's members once provided an interesting inversion of the usual claims to Turkishness that exclude non-Muslims by critiquing the performances of Turkish stars in the Eurovision international music contest, long a theater for "public representation of the nation" (Baker 2008:173). In a 2004 newspaper interview with the Turkish newspaper *Zaman*, Sefarad claimed a more authentic Turkishness vis-à-vis Sephardic culture than that of some of the reigning stars in Turkish music, such as Sertab Erener, who represented Turkey's first win in the 2003 Eurovision contest with an English-language song called "Everyway That I Can," or Athena, another Turkish group who performed an English-language song with a ska beat in the following year's competition. In the article, a member of Sefarad argued, "I don't see anything Turkish about these songs. They don't represent Turkey . . . They might as well be representing England!" ("bu parçalar Türkiye'yi temsil etmiyor . . . ").[3]

Described as a bland synthesis of pop and Turkish music, or "the musical version of an EU summit: state Orientalism, offensive to no one" (Gumpert 2007:151), Erener's song signified, at least to the band members of Sefarad, an inauthentic representation of Turkishness on an international stage. In the same article, the interviewer asked the performers if one could call Sefarad's music "Jewish." Cem, the band's bassist, replied by reiterating the history of the expulsion and the idea that Jews found refuge in the Ottoman Empire, explaining that "Sephardic music was shaped by the synthesis of Ottoman and Spanish melodies, therefore to call it 'Jewish' would be wrong."

Another concert of Judeo-Spanish song took place in 2003 in the basement of a trendy Spanish *tapas* restaurant near Taksim, one of Istanbul's centers of nightlife. In this context, the old (or not-so-old) Spanish songs seamlessly fit the overall theme and atmosphere of the place. Most diners at the candlelit restaurant would hardly recognize that the Spanish sung by the performers was a variety brought to the Ottoman Empire by Jewish exiles of the Iberian Peninsula over five hundred years ago. The performers were Jewish Turks who had grown up singing and dancing in the shows regularly held at Jewish community social clubs. After going to a dozen of these kinds of shows, I had become familiar with the standard repertoire. One such standard is "Avram Avinu," the tune popularized by Sefarad in Turkey under the name "Bodrum." Most traditional Ladino versions of the song describe the patriarch Abraham by calling him *luz de Yisrael* (Judeo-Spanish; light of Israel). When I heard the song being played in the Spanish restaurant, I noted that the small group of talented cabaret performers had altered the lyrics from "light of Israel" to "light of the nation." Historically, Jews have been called "the people of Israel," "the Jewish people," "the Jewish nation," and "the Hebrew nation," as well as other monikers. When I mentioned to the performers that I had never heard a version of the song in which Jews were called "the nation," they explained that saying the word "Israel" was too political these days and they preferred to keep politics out of their music. I realized then that all the concerts I had seen previously had been performed for exclusively Jewish audiences; this was the first in which the audience's religious affiliation was unknown, ambiguous, and most likely not Jewish. They came to eat *tapas,* not to celebrate Jewish heritage. This collection of anecdotes highlights how in music, among other genres, being a Jew in Istanbul involves defining oneself in light of what others may think of one's performance. But this definition is likewise performed in more intimate spaces.

Marriage Lessons: People, Purity, and Pride

In the past few decades, leaders of the Jewish community in Istanbul have entered a survival mode that borders on a kind of panic. An informal study conducted in the 1980s (Tuval 2004:xxxiii) confirmed what many instinctively felt: the community was shrinking, and fast. Community officials organized a series of new activities to promote more education, community cohesion, and Jewish knowledge among the Jews still left in Istanbul. Among the new activities was a course for couples about to marry. Each couple that wants to be married in a Jewish ceremony must now register with the rabbinate, and there are no alternative Jewish ceremonies performed outside its auspices. Every Turkish Jewish wedding ceremony I attended looked more or less the same, save a changed cast of characters, hairdos, and dresses. The pre-marriage seminar, conducted by the three rabbis and lay educator, was yet another mandatory step in the highly ritualized Turkish Jewish marriage process.

The seminars I attended between 2002 and 2003 were held in the auditorium of the Jewish School, a space in which rows of seats with folding desks descended from the auditorium entrance to the front of the room, where a table was covered with bulging manila envelopes. On the desk was a projector beaming a presentation onto a white screen. The leaders of the seminar included two local rabbis and a lay leader in their mid-thirties, wearing their dark hair short. They were clean-shaven and clothed in dark suits and ties. A third rabbi in charge of the seminar came from the ultra-Orthodox Chabad sect. Although this man enjoyed no official status in Turkey (as compared to the chief rabbi and other local leaders) he was often brought in to signify "real" Judaism. Raised in Istanbul, the lay leader was a volunteer who conducted the meetings and was responsible for their organization and for introducing the three rabbis. He also wore a suit. Filling the first three rows of the auditorium were recently engaged couples. Although they would all be married in a state-recognized civil ceremony, they were required to attend this event in order to have a ceremony with a rabbi in a synagogue. Most women were dressed smartly in slacks and blouses. Some men wore suits, although most had button-down shirts tucked into their pants.

The seminar consisted of pre-marriage counseling, a how-to for starting an "authentic" Jewish family, and an overall emphasis on Jewish continuity. Even though I was still single, the course leader let me observe the lectures on several occasions. Given the scope of the course, I shouldn't have been offended when the rabbis leading the lecture asked me why I was wasting my time on research. They suggested I devote my time to better pursuits, namely, finding a husband. "Hadi, evlen artık ya!" (Come on, get married already!), they chided, warning me that after age thirty it gets much harder to find a mate.

In each session I attended, the pre-marriage lectures began with an introduction by a lay leader in the community. He congratulated all the couples and handed out a gift package that included a Turkish-language book called *Yahudi Evine İlk Adım* (First Steps to a Jewish Home). The package also included a translation of *The Waters of Eden* (*Eden Suları*), a book about menstrual purity written by an Orthodox American rabbi, which explains the history and meaning of immersing in a *mikveh* (ritual bath) after menstruation. The couples were also given a *mezuzah*, a pamphlet about the Neve Shalom synagogue (where most weddings are held), and a certificate of attendance at the seminar.

The first rabbi praised the contents of the gift package to the seminar participants, blushing at mention of the *mikveh* book. The next section of the seminar discussed what makes someone Jewish. This section was led in English by the Chabad rabbi I have called "Dov" (he did not know much Turkish at the time of the seminars, but has since learned it).

RABBI DOV: If you were born in Japan are you a part of the Japanese people? You are all getting married to Jews, but why? What makes you Jewish? Is it family or culture? Maybe you are getting married to Jews because your ancestors left Spain to maintain Jewish life. If we had stayed in Spain, perhaps we would have had European Union citizenship today . . . but would we be Jewish?

The European Union joke got a big laugh, but few audience members dared to provide a concise answer to the question of what made them Jewish. The talks went on for a long time without becoming any more specific about what answers would satisfy the "What is a Jew?" query Rabbi Dov posed. Is being a Jew reckoning with a historical legacy that dictates present behavior? Is it keeping kosher, observing the Sabbath, and following the laws of ritual purity? The rabbis argued that they weren't police; they could only suggest that community members follow these practices. During the seminar, the definition of a Jewish family was assigned to the group, with some give-and-take but few voiced opinions from the participants. The lecture continued along these lines of questioning:

> RABBI DOV: Today, we are not going to talk about practice or philosophy. What is "Jewish?"
>
> AUDIENCE: "Man," "human," "system of beliefs," "community," "business!"
>
> RABBI DOV: There are many definitions of "Jewish," apparently. Some people say they are atheists and that they are still Jewish.
>
> AUDIENCE: (*laughter*)
>
> RABBI DOV: Okay, a little Jewish. Being Jewish is a connection; Jewish means being a family? But some Jews don't have a family. There are many answers to this question, but not one true definition. Maybe the definition is a combination of family, history, belief, practice, business, survival. I think there is something a little deeper, a key to all other things: the Jewish soul. The most practical definition is someone who has a Jewish soul. When you are Jewish, you are not Muslim or Christian, but this is deductive. Being Jewish is, in essence, having a Jewish psyche, a Jewish subconscious. Sometimes we ignore it. But what happens in Venice when we see a *magen David* [a six-pointed star]? Why do we feel happy? If a bomb explodes at a Jewish center in Argentina, why do we feel sad? You guys are getting married. In a few years you will have kids. How will we transmit this feeling to another generation? Children learn from their parents, they watch them and imitate their ways. The most important question for this generation is not, "Will your kids be Jewish?" It is, "Will your grandchildren be Jews?" It isn't enough to be Jewish in your heart . . . you should go to synagogue, say prayers and blessings, put up *mezuzot*, these little things ensure our survival as Jews.

The following lecture, by another local rabbi, involved an overhead presentation that used a specific set of symbols to frame the ambiguously floating signifier that the Chabad rabbi had left hanging in the air. How could one make the Jewish soul something materially accessible to these young couples? The presentation used clip art images of a *mezuzah*, Jewish stars, a *chupah* (the wedding canopy), a *ketubah* (the marriage contract), *kippot* (skullcaps), and Sabbath candles. The all-male speakers discussed at length the woman's role in maintaining the Jewish home: among other things, she was hypothetically responsible for the level of *kashrut* (Jewish dietary laws) observance and for instilling in her children the essence of Judaism.

The lecture series was a dangerous gamble. By ritualizing the marriage lessons and inviting their audience to be a partner in the "What is a Jew?" show, the rabbis risked "the possibility that [they would] encounter [themselves] making up [their] conceptions of the world, society, [their] very selves. [They] may slip in that fatal perspective of recognizing culture as construct, arbitrary, conventional, invented by mortals" (Moore and Myerhoff 1977:18). The performance of marriage lessons by community leaders for an audience made up of the next generation of Jewish couples in Istanbul was a form of "restored behavior," a type of salvage performance aimed at resurrecting a lost cultural form:

> Just as physical well-being depends on a varied gene pool, so social well-being depends of a varied "culture-pool." Restored behavior is one way of preserving a varied culture pool. It is a strategy which fits into, and yet opposes, world monoculture. It is an artificial means of preserving the wild. (Schechner 1985:114)

I experienced a similar restored behavior, except this time it was for my benefit—a show that anthropologists have come to expect of those they observe but which never fails to remind us of the performative nature of culture. A twenty-five-year-old friend invited me to his parents' home for a Sabbath meal. The table was abundantly set with a variety of homemade foods and the necessary accoutrements for the ritual blessings of the candles, wine, and bread. When it came time to perform the rituals, my friend's brother-in-law recited the requisite blessings. I overheard my host and another friend chatting in Turkish following the rituals, in which the other guest asked, "Do you guys do this every Friday night?" to which he replied, "No, never!" Turkish Jews have cosmopolitan knowledge about which kinds of performances are appropriate for certain stages. In the case of the Sabbath dinner, the show they thought I would expect was the one to which I was privy.

Given the cosmopolitan frames historically available to the Jewish community, the roles performed by a member of the community (and claiming to be a member entails already adopting a set role) change depending upon what stage they are acting. Are they giving a speech to the Jewish women's volunteer group? Speaking to a group of tourists? Welcoming imams and priests as guests to a Jewish community event (such as the community *iftar*)? The notion of "framing" imagines individuals as communicatively oriented toward the given context, or frame, in which they perceive themselves to be at a certain time (Goffman 1981).

How Jewish Is Our School?

Lectures over the undefinable essence of Judaism are a locus for intense debate in Istanbul and abroad, reckoned less through certificates and lectures and more through an ongoing dialogue. Reminiscent of the way in which names in Turkey index belonging or exclusion, the definitions of Jewishness, Turkishness, and/or Turkish Jewishness are not self-evident categories but are naturalized through ongoing debates and discussions, that is, performances. In many settings I would hear the question, "Is *this* Jewish?" bantered about. "This" might be music, philosophy, language, or a profession. Likewise, the question might be asked, "Is *this* Turkish?" However, the parent-teacher committee meeting at the Jewish school was the last place I expected to hear the "What is a Jew?" question. After all, it was the only *Jewish* School in Istanbul. But as I learned from a debate one night, not only is the question "How Jewish is our school?" fraught with problems, it is also difficult to get everyone to agree that all the students are Jews.

Arriving at a consensus on the definition of a "Jewish" student is a bit tricky. As Turkish secular law recognizes the father as the "source" of the child's religious affiliation (Delaney 1995, 1998), in order to attend the school only the father of the student has to be Jewish. In Orthodox Jewish practice (nominally the only form of Jewish practice accepted in Turkey), however, the mother's genealogical line determines her child's religious status. Thus, the dual frames of Orthodox Jewish religion and the Turkish Republic create a certain friction. This friction was played out on the school committee "stage" around two sets of characters: Jewish religious authorities, who have no real jurisdiction over the school, and secular parents who are willing to accept the children of Jewish fathers as Jews.

The school's library shelves are well stocked with stories and parables of Atatürk; the Jewish curriculum, however, occupies but one hour of class time per week. The school's educational goals remained fixed by their adherence to the national curriculum (a decidedly republican-focused narrative; see Kaplan 2003), which operates as the primary organizing principle for all schools in Turkey.

Even if certain Jews in Turkey strive to frame their lives through Jewish texts, they largely rely on mediating translations to access them. Biblical or liturgical Hebrew (as well as Modern Hebrew) remains a largely ignored subject among Jews in Istanbul. When I began my investigation into different languages being used in the community, I interviewed the Hebrew teacher at the Jewish school, asking him why Jews study Hebrew. He quickly corrected my assumption, telling me that the proper question was, "Why *don't* Jews in Istanbul care about learning Hebrew?" He elaborated on his inability to convince the Turkish Jews he taught of the use-value for studying Hebrew; students expressed far greater interest in English, which would gain them entrance to prestigious university programs and higher-paying jobs (or both). The same teacher offered small private courses to community members, who enjoyed the meetings, which gave them the chance to socialize with other Jews, but didn't seem to learn much Hebrew in the end. During a car ride home from one of these meetings, I discussed this situation with a man who had offered me a lift. I told him that at first I was surprised at how secular the community seemed, and he said quite simply, as if it should be obvious to me, "It's because of Atatürk!" "Jews don't know how to pray because of Atatürk?" I wondered aloud. "The secularist movement was so strong that it was almost shameful to know how to pray. Besides the fact that nobody really learns Hebrew much. There's no real framework for it. So, unless your father really takes an interest in bringing you to synagogue, you can't expect to pick up that knowledge from your peers or the community itself; they want us to be good Turks, not pious Jews."

While some educators in the community try to convince children—and others—of the inherent value of liturgical Hebrew, they often protest, saying, "Why should we spend hours reciting prayers that we don't understand? Hebrew has no meaning for us Turkish speakers." I once had a funny conversation with a five-year-old who got distracted during a Hebrew lesson; when I asked him what language was on the worksheet, he shrugged his shoulders, "Bilmem. İspanyolca?" (I don't know. Spanish?) At five, he knew that there were Jewish languages that grown-ups spoke (including Judeo-Spanish), but to him it didn't matter which one he faced, as all were equally unintelligible and equally Jewish.

In this way, Jews in Istanbul resemble their Muslim neighbors: due to the government's control of Arabic and Islamic education, Muslims interested in reading the Quran or praying have long learned the requisite texts by rote memorization:

> Turkey's experience is exceptional in that education does not grant direct access to the theological literature, which is still memorized and recited in Arabic, since the Quran was dictated to the Prophet Muhammed in that language. Translated, the Quran would no longer be "the word of God." Most Turks have no knowledge of the Arabic language and rely for Quranic interpretation on the sermons, lessons, or published Turkish-language works of their religious teachers. There are lively debates among Islamist intellectuals who either are able to read and understand the Quran or have access to internationally circulated interpretations. (White 2002:24)

During an interview with me, a Jewish linguist at a prestigious Turkish university commended Atatürk on adapting Modern Turkish to the roman alphabet (in lieu of the Ottoman script formerly used), calling him a genius: "If only we Jews could pray in Romanized Hebrew, or even in Turkish, perhaps we would be still praying today!" In a separate meeting with a teacher at the Jewish School, I was reminded that the school isn't a religious school; it is a secular school of Jews. Because the school bases itself on a secular Turkish curriculum and the budget and curriculum is set by the state, there is an Atatürk corner in the library, but educators struggle with how to incorporate the history of Israel, the Holocaust, and even local Jewish history.

A student at the Jewish School complained that even the principal was a Muslim and that Turkish officials were always coming around to check that school functions were being "properly acted out." According to him, during Chanukah, a state inspector was due to come for a visit and the school's teachers took down the candelabra in order to "avoid trouble." The student recounted to me that on Turkish Independence Day the students were reciting the national student oath when the inspector entered the hall. My own first exposure to the oath—and to the everyday rhetoric of Turkish state love—began quite literally with a rude awakening. It was the fall of 2002 and I had just moved to Istanbul to conduct research. I was staying on a small street in an area of Istanbul called Fulya which shared a corner with an elementary school. The warm weather obliged me to sleep with all the apartment windows open. The summer exhaled its last humid breath and with it, early each morning, an unfamiliar sound punctured the stagnant air: the voices of schoolchildren chanting in unison. This collective gesture is a secular ritual in which Turkish children declare how happy they are to be Turks ("Ne Mutlu Türküm Diyene!") each morning before their school lessons begin:

> I am Turkish, I am honest, I am industrious.
> My principle: to protect the young, to respect the elderly,
> To love my country and my nation more than myself.
> My ideal: to rise up, to go forward.
> Hey, Great Atatürk! I pledge to walk without stopping
> to the goal you showed us, along the path which you cleared.
> My existence (identity) is an endowment to Turkish existence.
> What happiness for one who says "I am a Turk"!

As the student at the Jewish School recalled, the stern inspector observed the recitation of the oath and proceeded to march around, barking criticism: "Aren't you proud of being Turkish? Why don't you say it more loudly? More proudly?" While the student claimed that the inspector was a local leader of an ultra-nationalist political party (suggesting this reason for his zeal), this story speaks more generally to the kind of performances expected of students and teachers at the Jewish School.

I attended a number of parent-teacher meetings, held in the conference room of the recently built school. The room is sparse, save a rug decorated with six-pointed stars, a table surrounded by black swivel chairs, a bookshelf with some pristine volumes of the *Encyclopedia Britannica*, and a few medals and awards. From his painted portrait on the wall, a larger-than life image of Atatürk surveyed the meeting of educators and parents. Fifteen or so educators and parents sat around the oblong table, swiveling in their chairs, taking notes, and drinking tea out of plastic cups. At one meeting, during which I sat with the math teacher, the "What is a Jew?" question was reawakened. Certain parents wanted to organize after-school events around Jewish holiday celebrations, but the meeting's script began with a sword fight. (*Stage direction: Jewish teacher aims her lance at a parent*): Which of the Jewish children will be celebrating the holiday? (*Stage direction: A parent retaliates*): What about the case of the child who comes from divorced parents?

One educator asked about a woman whose child attended the school and who wanted to get more involved with planning committees. The woman's name was Fatma (a Turkish name marked as non-Jewish), and the educator asked in Judeo-Spanish, "Es vedre mi?" (Is she a "green?"—a pejorative word for Muslim) clearly rejecting syncretism (or a joint Jewish-Muslim identity) as a possibility. In contrast to the official events that celebrate syncretism, everyday performances of Turkish Jewishness support assertions of Turkish (and Jewish) zero-sum identity. By switching to Judeo-Spanish, the educator claimed authority by performing in the language of "real Jews" and as one entitled to inspect others' credentials. Some parents argued that it was the responsibility of the only Jewish school to take care of the children of mixed marriages, collecting them together "like lost sheep; it wasn't their fault that their fathers strayed from the herd." The invocation of the herd here implies that a fence needs to be constructed around Jewishness in order to keep it intact. One of the more religiously observant women I had met in the community raised her voice during one of these meetings, saying, "Our school isn't a *real* Jewish school. We only have a few hours of Jewish education each week, how can we expect them to know anything?" A secular man in attendance mocked her, "What do you expect? It isn't a *yeshiva* [Hebrew; a religious Jewish seminary]! It is a TURKISH-Jewish school. We are in Turkey; don't forget! Anyways, our school isn't a conversion center!" Pointing to Atatürk's portrait, this man put on the costume of a nationalist in order to argue for a secular framework in which to imagine the Jewish school's purpose.

However, challenges to the proper performance of "Jewishness" at the school don't only come from political figures and officials. One student I knew decided to become religiously observant during his sophomore year of high school. He began to grow sidelocks, in conformity with the Orthodox Jewish tradition of not trimming the sides of one's beard. He knew he was not conforming to the overwhelmingly secularist model of Turkish Judaism. Despite his aberrant performance, his family was still surprised when teachers called home to let them know that their son was being harassed by the other children, who said his sidelocks "stank," and had been calling him anti-Jewish slurs and other general insults.

The more I observed the Jewish School, the more it became clear that the performance of Judaism in that setting was always conditioned by the expectations of Turkish secularism: guarded by Atatürk's eyes in the teachers' lounge, the state-appointed principal, the teachers, and even the majority of secularist Jewish students.

Behind and Betwixt the Scenes

Jews in Istanbul are privy to multiple sources of knowledge for identity building. In order to reckon with these sources, Jews sit, talk, and argue together in "interpretive communities" (see Fish 1980). By taking up a role in an interpretive community, Jews dialogically make sense of these options, collectively deciding which sources will be authoritatively "Jewish," "Turkish," "Sephardic," "modern," "traditional," and so on. Some Jews come to the stage in a leading role, such as that of chief rabbi, lay leader, or other political figure. These characters ultimately garner the most authority in community knowledge work. Nonetheless, their opinions are formed in conversation with others in supporting roles acting as teachers, tailors, doctors, or lawyers. In the theater of a community, there are few soliloquies.

In a community as well organized as the Turkish Jewish one, there was always some meeting going on. I often joined in to observe people gathered together to make sense of the kinds of sources relevant to their lives (as well as to filter out those that did not), including marriage seminars, parent-teacher associations, adult study groups, the office of the rabbinate, and other venues where Jews met. I wanted to understand how individuals negotiate available frames and yet remain on balanced footing as those frames shift (Goffman 1981). Each of the scenes—the big stages and little everyday theaters—described above invoke the question: How do Turkish Jews draw on their cosmopolitan collection of knowledge to decide which performances of self are appropriate? What I found was a contingent cosmopolitanism whose performance depended on Turkish Jews' mastery of various knowledges, familiarity with the cast of characters and, most importantly, understanding of their audiences' expectations. By observing performances, for example, of different music groups in Istanbul, I understood that the enactment of different strands of cosmopolitan knowledge depended largely on the way the performers imagined their audience might interpret a given display.

This chapter's examples further reveal that the stage itself does not necessarily frame the actors; actors bring other stages, and even imagined audiences, to their performances. For example, after attending nearly half a year of sessions with my notebook and recorder in hand, I was asked by an organizer to stop recording the sessions of a Torah study group. Each meeting took place at a private home of one of the group members. As such, the houses that hosted the study group were, in theory, intimate space. Nonetheless, by bringing different actors together, the home was made public. The group members became suspicious that I might bring their discussions to light and decided it would be better if I ceased recording. Thoughts of neighbors, future conversations, and other repercussions of the performance outside of the cozy living rooms of group members brought an imaginary audience into the seemingly private space.

Each of the scenes described in this chapter engages with the problem of performing culture (see Kirshenblatt-Gimblett 1998). One reason to examine cosmopolitanism in light of performance theory is that although social scientists are well aware that the distinction between the cosmopolitan and the local is a largely false binary, it becomes imminently clear through observations of "actually existing cosmopolitanisms" (Calhoun 1998) that there are times and places when cosmopolitanism is valued and other times when it is to be repudiated. I have here tried to challenge notions of cosmopolitanism as either inherently hidden or public, hegemonic or subversive, and elaborate a more complicated theme of knowledge as being communicated not only in context but, rather, *in performance*. In this sense, a song, such as that sung by the musicians discussed above, can be Turkish, Jewish, or both, but will be assigned a relational ontological status through performance. These performances include those staged in theaters, but also the kinds of shows that people put on during interviews with reporters (in the case of Sefarad) or around the table at a parent-teacher meeting. Like the Ottoman Jews who performed as Turks at the World's Fair in late nineteenth century while in Chicago and as Jews at home in the empire, different possibilities for "acting like" Jews or Turks (or both) in twenty-first-century Istanbul are relational and contextual. Imagining cosmopolitanism as something performative enables us to interpret it in context and consider it in relation to acts that have come before as well as those yet to come (see Phelan and Lane 1998:188).

By looking at socio-cultural phenomena with an eye to the performative nature of identity work, certain patterns begin to emerge about the role of ritual, face-work, and communication in the negotiation of complex identities. Rather than imagining cosmopolitanism as a powerful idea coming from nowhere, cosmopolitanism qua performance focuses our attention on its enacted negotiations, the chorus of voices who promote it, and those for whom it strikes a dissonant chord.

SIX

The One Who Writes
Difference: Inside Secrecy

"In retrospect, it appears that the ability to encourage the voluntarily mute to speak, and the talent to open the innermost thoughts and interpret the secrets of hundreds of interviewees, was a basic condition in writing this study" (Tuval 2004:lxvii).[1] So concludes the author of a study of modern Turkish Jewry who describes his work as a "picture of a community that had lain shrouded in thick fog for many years" (lxvii). This scholar was not the first—nor the last—to describe the difficulty in gaining access to Turkish Jewish life. Elazar and others, in a footnote to their demographic description of the Jews of Turkey, likewise assert that the community is "extremely reluctant to have its activities publicized in any way at all, on the grounds that if neither the Turkish government nor the Turkish people are antagonized, the Turkish [Jewish] community might be able to be permitted to continue functioning. The consensus is that the slightest publicity might endanger the status quo" (1984:128). Similarly, Mills writes, "In spite of the fact that, compared with Greeks, Jews were far more open to my research . . . I had a great deal of difficulty using a snowball effect to gain increasing numbers of interviews through primary contacts" (2010:173).

After some months of fieldwork, and with the help of some friends, I was able to make significant inroads into Istanbul's Jewish communal networks. I found Turkish Jews willing to talk with me, but this agreement came with an omnipresent cautionary tone. "Your work sounds interesting, but, due to security, there is one thing about which you must never write," insisted a reporter at the Jewish paper in Istanbul. We were chatting over glasses of Turkish tea in her smoky office when she put down her cigarette, took the field notebook from my hands and wrote, in capital letters, the following word: XXXXXXX.[2] She deliberated a moment then scratched it violently off the page: X̶X̶X̶X̶X̶X̶X̶.

The editor's was only one of many warnings I received while conducting fieldwork with the Jewish community of Turkey. Throughout my research, I observed that Turkish Jews justified censorship by invoking *güvenlik* (security). Anti-Semitism, periodic attacks on Jewish individuals, and ongoing threats on Jewish institutions (see Mallet 2008:456) create a paranoid worldview for many Turkish Jews: displaying difference is a dangerous game few wish to play.

Jews in Turkey consider self-censorship a way of protecting themselves from both social discrimination and physical harm. Accordingly, everyone seemed to have an opinion about what I should (and should not) publish. Each time I took out my notebook at a community event, a local rabbi insisted on playing censor, delivering a humorless imperative couched in a question: "You'll make sure to give me a copy of your articles before you publish them, right?" The repetition of episodes in which Turkish Jews warned against the sharing of community secrets left me with a sinking feeling that in such a self-censoring milieu, I would be left without a story; unless, perhaps, *silence itself* was a story worth telling.

I understand silence as a strategy through which private and public domains are constituted and guarded (see Bauman 1983 and Gal 2002). This chapter considers silence through an interpretation of Barbara Kirshenblatt-Gimblett's suggestive notion of a "semiotics of secrecy" (1998). Kirshenblatt-Gimblett offers three useful suggestions for a semiotics of secrecy that I adopt in my representations of Jews in Istanbul. First, a semiotics of secrecy offers itself as a "meta-sign" in that it proclaims that signifieds are not to be demanded; readers of my ethnographic accounts will have to be satisfied with the knowledge that secrets are an integral part of community relations, and that they will not be privy to particular hidden meanings (although this is unusual in a field—anthropology— historically known for parsing out exotic meanings for its audience). Second, by focusing on the signifier, a semiotics of secrecy diminishes the need to represent what is actually being signified. Third, it creates a power imbalance by splitting signifier from signified: "The signified may indeed turn out to be trivial, or it may take a lifetime to fully discover and understand what the hidden terms mean" (1998:255).

I build upon these concepts in order to discuss the representational quandaries of writing about a community that intensely guards its privacy. To this theoretical scaffolding, I contribute a critical suggestion: our subjects' semiotic strategies of secrecy offer models for ethical anthropological representations.

Turkish Public Secrets

The category "Turk" (commonly used synonymously with "Muslim") disguises the diversity of linguistic, ethnic, and religious origins of Turkey's "majority" population. Due to the performance of a singular identity in the public sphere, however, these alternative histories remain unacknowledged, and may even be suppressed at the level of the individual psyche. (Neyzi 2002:141; see also Baer 2010)

This description of Turkish public secrecy supports my assertion that Jews erase difference in their everyday Turkish lives not out of conspiracy but out of a deep knowledge about the acceptable limits, and stages, for the performance of cosmopolitanism and difference. Especially during the early years of the Turkish Republic, becoming Turkish, especially for Turkey's minorities, was a process of absorbing this knowledge about "what not to know," what Taussig calls "the most powerful form of social knowledge" (1999:2). Taussig's sensitive attention to the politics of secrecy takes for granted that this is a politics of power; here, I take a different tack, showing that the form of public secrecy takes on a particular expressive form in various local contexts (that is, public secrecy might not look the same everywhere). In documenting a particularly Turkish semiotics of secrecy, I explore silence and irony as strategies that allow the Jewish community its secrets and the ethnographer her representations beyond the intimacy of the field. Toward an ethnographic ethics, I have taken cues from the community itself about Turkish Jewish representational norms for private and public display. This ethics includes the reckoning of local taboos in content and, perhaps more importantly, in form.

If they once had a set of private languages in which to discuss community affairs and personal concerns out of earshot of non-Jewish neighbors, today Jews in Istanbul consider an unmarked Turkish to be their mother tongue. This new linguistic situation attests to a deep familiarity with the broader Turkish society, but also to the loss of an intimate register in which to communicate fears, concerns, or hopes particular to the Jewish community. Navigating through these taboos without an intimate language demands verbal dexterity. As shown in the case of Sabbateans in Turkey, who "remember to forget" their difference, especially in the public sphere (Neyzi 2002), Jews in Turkey are accustomed to finding alternate ways to speak about things that, for reasons of physical security, social fear, or community cohesion are forbidden from public (that is, non-Jewish) discourse. By necessity, Jews have found creative ways to speak and write about taboo topics while speaking Modern Turkish.

Turkish Jews are secular and traditional, rich and poor, nationalist and diasporic, but what ultimately unites them is fluency in a language of invisibility. In order to describe the grammar of a language of invisibility, I offer examples of the creative and playful ways Turkish Jews maintain linguistic taboos.

Playing with Taboos

While the study of taboo has enjoyed wide popularity in general anthropology (see Lévi-Strauss 1963; Douglas 1966; Harris 1982; Favret-Saada 1980), Neyzi comments on taboos specific to Turkish public culture:

> Facing the experienced past, rather than a constructed nostalgia, means facing up to the violence experienced in this society during this century—whether between the state and particular communities, between communities, between generations, or within the individual psyche itself. It means confronting the exclusionary aspects of national identity, and its high cost for individuals. For taboos about the past perhaps do most violence in ways not easily visible or voiced: through the secrecy and fear that works silently within the psyche. (2002:142)

While living in Istanbul in 2002, I noted that a board game called ASUR circulated through the community. ASUR, the Hebrew word for "forbidden," took its inspiration from Taboo, a board game in which

Table 6.1. Indexing the taboo

"Taboo" Term	Indexes
BISKOÇOS DE RAKI	ANASON (anisette)
(Judeo-Spanish; cookies made with anisette liqueur)	BISKUVI (cookie)
	CENAZE (funeral)
	UEVO (egg)
	SINAGOG (synagogue)

players must describe given words without referencing others or risk losing to the opposing team. One look at the design of the game board, shaped along the contours of a map of Israel, underscores my earlier assertion about relations between Turkish Jews and the Jewish State being one of the ultimate taboos among Turkish Jews. But beyond the question of content, I want to describe the game's rules in order to highlight the importance of form in how taboos are maintained. Observing ASUR at play offers insights into some of the community's taboo lexical items and themes; more importantly, however, the rules of the game offer a salient example of disemia at work, a play of opposition that allows Turkish Jews to communicate safely in private and public spheres.

The terms to be defined in this game include Jewish and Sephardic foods, rituals, and sites, as well as historic figures from Jewish, Turkish, and general history. Each card in ASUR presents one of these terms, bolded at the head of the card, and five non-utterable indexes that would potentially define the word at play (like the items in parentheses after an academic abstract).

The term (and list of non-utterable indexes) on one ASUR playing card, BISKOÇOS DE RAKI (table 6.1), refers to a dry anisette cookie baked in many Sephardic homes to accompany afternoon tea and gossip. This cookie may also accompany a traditional mourner's meal or a Sabbath luncheon held at the synagogue. A list of attributes doesn't do justice to the uniquely delectable smell of these cookies wafting out the door of the last kosher bakery in Istanbul. One day, a friend who grew up near the unassuming storefront venue pointed it out to me, murmuring, "That's a *Jewish* bakery" into my ear. "Jewish" was hushed, as if uttering the word might draw unwanted attention. Had this site not been pointed out to me, I could have easily mistaken it for any number of other bak-

Table 6.2. ASUR in play (recreated from the Turkish/Judeo-Spanish)

DAVIT: My mother makes them . . . (*hesitates*) they are a special food, special smell . . .

SARA: (*interrupts*) Chicken, *bumuelos* . . .

DAVIT: Small and round and baked . . .

SARA: Crackers

LISYA: (*on the same team*) Cookies, biscuits!

DAVIT: Mothers say this: If you go to synagogue you might . . . they want you to eat, they say it like this . .

ALL: (*cheers, laughter*) You're out! You said "synagogue!"

eries in Istanbul. When I later interviewed the owner of the bakery, who himself used three variations of the same name (Alper [Turkish], Alberto [Judeo-Spanish] and Avram [Hebrew]), I learned that he had "Turkified" the storefront over time, removing Jewish symbols and changing the name in order to avoid negative reactions from non-Jewish customers.

The game of ASUR offers the ethnographer more than a collection of culturally significant terms; watching it in play allows us to explore the process of semiosis through which meaning is dialogically made and intimacy guarded. Play operates much like an inverted dictionary: instead of defining a key term through its hyponyms as one might expect, the hyponyms themselves become the ultimate taboo and players must seek other means of communicating the unspeakable. Taking BISKOÇOS DE RAKI as an example, a typical round of play sounds something like the recreated dialogue in table 6.2.

In the course of the game, Davit's "mothers say this" soon became its own conventionalized sign. After a few rounds, even mentioning "mother" would index that the term being hinted at was one in Judeo-Spanish. The participants created an apparent iconic fitness between the Judeo-Spanish language and elderly women in the community. *Orada* (over there) eventually became "Israel." *Biz* or *bizimkiler*, literally "ours" or "us," became "the Jews." In moods of high creativity during play, it is not unusual for new indexes to spring up, showcasing the rapidity with which language change can happen and how quickly meaning hardens in a given context through repetition.

The game cards themselves comprise a fascinating dictionary of culturally salient terms in a Jewish Turk's cultural repertoire. Nonetheless, most terms in the game did not necessarily denote the community's actual taboo terms, which, like those of any community, are not fixed but ever shifting.[3] Indeed, it would be hard to impute danger to a delicious cookie. Instead of taking the taboo words out of their context and making them into a frozen dictionary, I chose to focus on the praxis of their use, as terms that come alive with each utterance, in new contexts, sometimes censored, sometimes silent, and sometimes even ironic. As the transcription in Figure 11 shows, taboo meaning is co-narrated through collaboration, correction, and interruption; and so it is with secrets.

Perhaps because play resonated with the community's contemporary practices and concerns, the board game sold well; I observed it being played at a number of community events. On a number of occasions, I recorded groups of friends playing the game with great enthusiasm. Talking around the taboo words clearly contained a charge of excitement. Players reveled in the tension of almost letting the words spill off their tongues and then holding back. I had noted the same productive power at work in everyday conversations between Turkish Jews, especially in public. I felt that the game was an incarnation of the linguistic attempts at secrecy that I had noticed earlier in my fieldwork, and I often come back to it as a metaphor for the effacing social practices of the community.

Although my research in Turkey has dealt with serious questions about assimilation, security, cultural survival, and change, imagining these negotiations as games at play captures the cultural scene of Istanbul's Jews at the turn of the twenty-first century. As evidenced by watching ASUR in play, the central survival tactic of Turkish Jews is a semiotic one: the ability to recognize, avoid, and substitute terms or themes deemed taboo and to find alternative ways of communicating the forbidden in changing contexts. Beyond the texts themselves, the vehicles through which meaning is made (practices of dissembling, secrecy, euphemism, gaming) speak not only to official expectations of minorities in Turkey but also to their dialectical role in perpetuating an ideology of effaced difference.

Winners of ASUR, those who "got" the game, preferred the protean potential of inferential to denotative speech, the loose indexes of metaphor over the tight bonds of metonymy. One of the stars of the game once gave me a tour of his home, culminating with a peek at his secret library. His impressive collection of books on Jewish themes was protected from both dust and non-Jewish observers: "I keep it behind these heavy cabinet doors so when my Muslim friends come over they don't ask me bothersome questions about Judaism. Nobody has to be reminded that I am a Jew, even though I love these books and am proud to have so many." His mother joked that if someone discovered his collection, she would pretend not to know him.

Another player who excelled at the "game" was an eighteen-year-old organizer of a popular Jewish folkloric dance troupe. She dedicated herself to the troupe's development, at times rehearsing daily in anticipation of a performance. Despite the central place this activity occupied in her life, her closest non-Jewish school friends (indeed, those she called her "best friends") had no knowledge of the group. The fear that Jewish folklore could be perceived as anti-Turkish caused it to be a non-subject for public (that is, non-Jewish) consumption.[4]

The fact that this girl's non-Jewish friends never thought to ask about her Jewish dance club points to a distinction between majority and minority perceptions of the codes of acceptable sociability. Jewish Turks must necessarily balance the mainstream culture—in this case a Turkish one—with their different experiences of Jewish sociability, culinary traditions, holidays, names, and other rituals and signifying practices. Similar to the Rum Polites, who considered "knowledge about special days of other religions . . . to be another sign of cosmopolitanism" (Örs 2006:89), Turkish Jews are constantly working to manage this difference—in this case, pertaining to folk dancing, but there are many other examples, ranging from particular Jewish celebrations (even secularized ones that correspond to the Jewish calendar but not the Turkish one) to social events such as sports, which fits neither into the category of acceptable secular public culture nor private religious practice. A wealthy homemaker explained the tensions of intimacy as having both positive and negative implications for her relationships with Jews and Muslims, saying, "I like my Muslim friends better. They are more modern and worldly, less gossipy. But I don't tell them about Jewish activities or holidays. The Jewish friends can know everything, but because of that there is a lot of pressure and talking about other people all the time." This balancing of various codes breeds a sense of cosmopolitan knowledge in which experience is mediated through a lens of general and Jewish knowledge that may be variously public, private, or something in between.

Umberto Eco has called secret knowledge "deep knowledge" in which "truth becomes identified with what is not said or what is said obscurely and must be understood beyond or beneath the surface" (1992:30). It wasn't exactly that my subjects were silent, but they were successful in being perceived as silent by non-intimates who were unable to see beneath the surface, behind the doors of the bookshelf, or behind the curtain at the rehearsal hall (see also Scott 1990). Perhaps non-intimates are unaware that there is something beyond or beneath the surface in the first place. As a way of managing the cosmopolitan tensions of citizenship and difference, Turkish Jews play a game of "hide and seek" between their intimate discourses and those they put on display.

Intimacy

> What of anthropologists? Do we not follow a similar quest for enlightenment? I, the anthropologist, have my own hubris. Like many other foreigners, I love this magnificent system, because of its seductive nature and mysterious intellectual power, and because I am often exempt from the taboos and rules that surround its secrets.
>
> —Losche 2001:114

How was I, the anthropologist, to represent deep knowledge? After I had spent a year or so in Istanbul, Jewish friends joked that I suddenly knew the best gossip.[5] Gaining access to community secrets is a two-way negotiation: on one hand, you have to be familiar enough with the community to know what kinds of questions to ask; on the other, they have to be familiar enough with you to answer. This whole process could be summed up in one word: intimacy (see Herzfeld 1997; Shryock 2004).[6] However, even if after all the border negotiations I had become privy to intimate secrets, with whom could I share them once I went back "home?" If I couldn't publish my material in journals and discuss it at conferences, then what was the purpose of coming to Istanbul in the first place?

Although I had completed a human subjects protocol, gained permission for every interview, and explained my research goals in detail to everyone with whom I worked, I often heard stories that I didn't dare write in my field notes; just because someone had agreed to be interviewed did not mean I was exempt from using editorial judgment when it came to printing her story.[7]

I once paid a visit to Turkey's National Press Museum to research the Neve Shalom massacre. However, when I opened the national paper, *Milliyet*, to the day in 1986 following the first terrorist attack against the Jewish community in Turkey, I found that day's front page missing. An anonymous knife had excised the cancerous page from an otherwise healthy body of Turkish history. This was repeated in a second paper, *Hurriyet*; this time the page was ripped with less finesse but its bloody images were as thoroughly removed from the record. When I tried to imagine who might have silenced the historical record in the archives of the Press Museum, I came up with a number of plausible suspects: Was it a Turkish ultra-nationalist who wished to deny that things like this could happen in Turkey? A leftist who burned flags at anti-Israel rallies? A Jew who believed that the blood-soaked chronicle would attract negative attention to a minority community that wished only to maintain *kayadez*—Judeo-Spanish for "silence" or "quiet," glossed in English as "low profile" (Bali 2007)—yet kept getting dragged out into public? I even suspected the friend who had escorted me to the museum, whose grandmother had been at Neve Shalom that day but survived the attack. Realizing that so many people might have such a variety of reasons to silence the representation of negative (or even diverse) images of Turkish Jewry made me panic. I found myself, like my Turkish Jewish friends, in a situation that can only be described as paranoid. Marcus understands paranoia not as a crisis of interpretation but one of representation: "So in this version of the crisis of representation the plausibility of the paranoid style is not so much its reasonableness, but rather the revitalization of the romantic, the ability to tell an appealing, wondrous story found in the real" (1999:5). In writing about the Jewish community of Istanbul, my paranoia centered on a desire to communicate an interesting tale as well as to describe the playful rules that govern secrecy in Istanbul.

In desperation, I turned to a local historian whom community leadership had ostracized for writing about the complexities of living as a minority in Turkey. His public commentary, printed in newspapers and in multiple books, included critiques of the promises made to all Turkish citizens that fell short when measured against the Jewish experience. He promptly sat me down in his living room for a lecture:

> Marcy, you are letting them get to you. Don't just become another official mouthpiece for the elite of this community. All this being nice and polite all the time, all this silence, never thinking critically . . . I tell you, it will all fall on their heads one day!

For all his outrage and bravado, this same man who chided me for becoming a mouthpiece once showed me a dissertation someone had written about the community, saying, "I can't believe he wrote *that!*" I recall reacting similarly to an online article by an American who volunteered as an educator in the Turkish Jewish community in 2003. Rather than repeating the common local cliché about Turkish tolerance and Jews as beloved minority, her article perfectly captured the idea that Jewish Turks share "common knowledge" of how to actively be Jewish without attracting attention, describing the word-of-mouth way events are publicized, their lack of overtly Jewish markings, as well as the contradiction of being a Jew in Turkey, a place where "everything is common knowledge yet nothing can be acknowledged" (Liss 2004). It is obvious that she got to know the community intimately, but she seemed to me to have missed out on a few lessons about what constitutes proper public discourse (as opposed to intimate knowledge). Although, like my historian friend, I quietly applauded her critical voice, I felt that her short article had betrayed the confidence of those community members who allowed her access to their lives and homes.

I had a similarly disquieting feeling after reading one of the few detailed studies of the Turkish Jewish community (Tuval 2004). This work offers a rich chronicle of Jewish life in Turkey in the last century, providing demographic and statistical information upon which I have drawn at length and much of which confirms my understandings of the community. However, the author of the study, who did not train in an anthropology department, was under lighter pressures to undergo self-examination about the ethical considerations in representing the community and its secrets. Part of my apprehension was borne out of my ethnographic training, as "the work of anthropology demands an explicit ethical orientation to 'the other' (Scheper-Hughes 1995:418). My discipline, for better or worse, has nearly torn itself apart at the seams over questions of how best to represent those people we study. To my anthropological ears, the tone and the contents of his work felt like a betrayal. Unlike Tuval, who seemed proud of his access to the community, I felt remarkably uneasy about getting "the voluntarily mute to speak" and my apparent "talent to open the innermost thoughts and interpret the secrets of hundreds of interviewees." Like Mills, a geographer who studied nostalgia in a once-cosmopolitan neighborhood in Istanbul, I felt wary of betraying my interlocutors' confidence and worried that my revelations could threaten them somehow, while at the same time recognizing that "this pressure to conform, and to keep secrets, lies at the core of the larger issue of exerting power through discourses of silence and codes of proper behavior, and protecting the ideals of the state and society. This is the same propriety that protects the . . . cultural memory of the tolerant cosmopolitan past" (2010:147).

If my Turkish Jewish subjects made it clear to me that their modus operandi as a minority in the Turkish Republic was to be silent, what right did I have to share even the most benign secrets with the academic community? Even if, as an outsider, I was exempt from many of the linguistic taboos that bound my friends in Istanbul, did I have an obligation to keep their secrets?

Behar comments on the moment in which anthropologists recognize that their enterprise revolves around issues of intimate knowledge: "With stark clarity, they realize that they are seeking intimacy and friendship with subjects on whose backs, ultimately, the books will be written upon which their productivity as scholars in the academic marketplace will be assessed" (1993:298–299). What magic would allow me to render secrets into a publishable, anthropological tale?[8]

Self-Display

In search of a model for my own ethnographic writing, I turned to a site where Turkish Jews exhibit heightened awareness about the rules of censorship and representation: the Turkish Jewish newspaper office. During the Ottoman era, Jewish journalism had exhibited a florescence of papers written in multiple languages (Stein 2003). Today, only one paper remains in Turkey, the former Ottoman heartland. Nonetheless, during ethnographic fieldwork among Jews in Istanbul, I found the news office of *Şalom,* to which an estimated 75 percent of the community subscribes, to be a lively center of cultural interpretation, production, and dissemination. Dedicated to reporting on and for Turkish Jews, *Şalom* gives voice to many of the Jewish community's hopes and fears.

I observed that reporters for the Turkish Jewish press endlessly engage in a comparison of their community's status as a religious minority within a secular state with other places and times, producing what I earlier called "cosmopolitan knowledge." The Jewish newspaper in Turkey operates as a central site where competing ideologies get arranged in a weekly textual dialogue. One evening the staff at the newspaper office was working on a translation of an article from the French newspaper *Le Figaro,* which asked, "Les Juifs sont-ils divisés?" (Are the Jews Divided?) The article opens with a resounding "yes" and a humorous quote with which I identified: "Two Jews, three opinions," a play on an American Jewish joke about the stereotypically fragmented organization of Jewish communities.

When translating the article for a Turkish audience, the reporters at the office thought it would be an intriguing piece for publication based on how bizarre the phrase seemed, and on the article's insistence that Jews were no strangers to debate and self-critique. Looking at me, an editor explained, "We don't have any experience with this phenomenon. It must be an Ashkenazi thing!" Surprised, I asked, "Don't Sephardim have different opinions about Judaism?" To which he replied "Two Jews, one chief rabbi!"

The use of irony and humor in the paper to soften a real critique of the rabbinate in the face of censorship has historical precedents: nineteenth-century Judeo-Spanish periodicals found in Ottoman lands likewise offered criticism and commentary of rabbinate practices and policies, even given the risk to publishers and reporters for publishing such material (Loewenthal 1996). Translations (mostly from English and French newspapers) constitute a large portion of *Şalom's* articles on international and Jewish topics; I was told by a reporter at the paper, "We don't always give sources because Turkish readers are sensitive; they will think everything is biased just based on the source from which it was translated by staff at our office." Many reporters admit they probably should give all the sources, but this doesn't happen in practice. Despite their mediating role between opposing frames, reporters are inevitably seen as mouthpieces of the community. As such, the paper often prints even original articles without an author's byline, meaning that the articles can't be traced to an original source or reporter. According to local legend, a Jewish reporter in Turkey (who now serves as a "foreign" correspondent to the paper) was quietly kicked out of the country for not revealing a source he considered confidential. Although he had been a major reporter for the mainstream Turkish press, after decades of his living abroad the editors at *Şalom* jest that they have to translate his writing "from Turkish to Turkish."

Şalom's journalists write about the community with the knowledge that their representations are being scrutinized by critical eyes. Based on distribution statistics, one assumes that the newspaper has two main readerships: members of the Jewish community (who have a real stake in how they are portrayed), and non-Jews (some of whom are obsessively curious about the Jewish community). A *Şalom* journalist once wondered aloud, "What are all those women in headscarves doing with our paper in Fatih [a conservative Muslim area of Istanbul]? I can only imagine that they are searching for conspiracy, scanning our innocent pages, ready to pounce like lions on any seemingly offensive statement" (see Henkel 2007). Concern about the best way to represent the Jews to the general public is particularly acute at the community newspaper office. Self-regulating fears instill in the editors a constant concern that bad judgment about article content might endanger the community.

Indeed, there is a troubling history of Islamist and/or ultra-nationalist presses citing the Jewish community paper's articles out of context. I came to see this kind of citational practice as an injurious intertextuality in which text is lifted directly, giving it a high modality, as in "If the Jews said it, it must be true." But the framing context guides interpretations for the new audience in a detrimental manner. For example, in 2002 a Turkish Islamist paper printed a feature on the funeral of Turkey's former Chief Rabbi, Rav Asseo. The article selected a minor government official whose presence at the funeral had been reported by the Jewish newspaper and, on a front-page spread, interrogated his motives for attending the funeral. A clichéd anti-Semitic cartoon, in which

KİTER

ahudi Hahambaşı Asseo için açılan 'Taziye defteri'ne; "Elini
dığım, hayır duasına nail olduğum, Yüce Varlık Hahambaşı-
ı satırlar 24 Temmuz tarihli Musevi yayın organı Şalom'da ya-
onra, **A.Merih Kiter**, İstihbarat Daire Başkanlığı'na atandı!

rilmedi ama sırtı sıvazlandı

alma sekeri

KADIKÖY İHL'DE HUKUKSUZLUK

Sırf çocuklarına destek vermek için okul önünde bulunan Makbule
İbrahimoğlu, hâlâ tutuklu bulunurken, kızı Selma İbrahimoğlu da
Kadıköy İHL'den, hem de savunması bile alınmadan uzaklaştırıldı.

Savunma bile almadan okuldan uzaklaştırdılar!

Ölen Hahambaşı David Asseo'dan ilim aldığını söy-
leyen bir Emniyet mensubunun İstihbarat Daire
Başkanlığı'na getirildiği Türkiye'de, Kadıköy Ana-
dolu İmam Hatip Lisesi önünde çocuklarına destek
olan Makbule İbrahimoğlu'nun tutuklanmasının
ardından kızı Selma İbrahimoğlu da okuldan uzaklaştırıldı. Ahmet Ziya İbrahimoğlu, "Eşimle ilgili
rapor niye açıklanmıyor?" diye sordu. **10'DA**

FIGURE 9
Vakit newspaper report (October 7, 2002),
with caricature of the Jew as octopus.

the Jew is portrayed as an octopus, greedily grasping for power in every part of society, accompanied the article (see figure 9).

As a newcomer, I found the image and article astonishing in their blaring anti-Semitism and disturbing assumptions about Jewish power. However, when I shared it with friends in the Turkish Jewish community, none were surprised. They had grown accustomed to being represented as octopi, snakes, devils, and other such scoundrels. To add insult to injury, the most anti-Semitic publications in Turkey regularly use the community's own publications as primary sources for apocryphal stories about Jewish pseudo-conspiracies and plots to undermine Turkey, Islam, and the world at large (Bali 2001). When, one cold night in 2002, members of Turkey's Islamist party visited the offices of the Jewish paper to seek votes for the general election, the community only had one request: stop publishing anti-Semitic treatises in the Islamic-leaning Turkish press.

Working under this atmosphere of surveillance and fear, an editor once shared with me her subtle technique of writing under the radar of antipathetic readers: use terms that only intimates will recognize, such as neighborhood names instead of cities, foreign terms, or other subtle indexicals. Accustomed to issues of writing and representation, the newspaper's editors offered me firsthand knowledge of how to select stories and images that would not endanger Jews in Turkey.

Attempted control of representation is centralized, not only through the editors of the Jewish newspaper but also at the level of the rabbinate, where I once heard an official complaining about the ethics of the paper's staff: "They don't know how to do journalism; they never check with us before they print their articles!" Although this seemed a laughable power grab at the time, I later came to understand that as the official representative body for all of Turkish Jewry, the rabbinate has a particular concern with how members of the Jewish community are portrayed. The rabbinate itself maintains a full-time staff member who scans the Turkish press daily for mention, especially negative portrayals, of the Jewish community.

Considerations about representations of Turkish Jews are not limited to newspaper editors, rabbis, or other community officials. During a planning meeting, I observed the organizers of the Black Sea conference debating how they might mark the different conference rooms for various program activities. They decided that posting placards with names such as "Jerusalem" and "Tel Aviv" would invite too much negative attention; in their understanding, even non-Jews would be able to recognize these names as cities in Israel. When jokingly considering marking the event venues with signs reading "Dimona" or "Bat Yam," they assumed that unlike Muslims at the country club where the event was scheduled to be held, who might not recognize these places, Jewish participants in the conference would know that they were Israeli cities. However, they would also recognize them as lower-class or peripheral Israeli towns. That is, the semiotics of secrecy here assumed that Muslim Turks wouldn't even be able to recognize what a sign such as "Dimona" denotes, whereas Jewish Turks (or those attending the conference from around the region) would not only understand the denotation but possess the knowledge to impute a negative connotation to the sign, undermining the positive goals of the conference itself (strengthening Jewish identity).

Of course, there are few episodes in which readers of a given sign cannot impute (or invent) the sense they think should be given to a signifier, even if their interpretation differs greatly from that which its creator (or disseminator) intends. Another example in which Turkish Jews became aware of the ways in which different actors were unable to impute meaning (or a particular meaning) to a Jewish signifier occurred when the leaders of a Jewish summer program in Istanbul decided to get t-shirts printed for their campers; their t-shirt design incorporated the name of the club and an iconic drawing of the Torah (the Pentateuch).

When the camp leaders brought the image to the (non-Jewish) printer, the owner tried to make sense of it, asking, "Are you opening a pizza shop?" This man had no Jewish reference point for the long wooden handles of the Torah scroll around which parchment is wrapped with sacred text. He saw two wooden bars and guessed that these would be used to roll out pizza dough, not biblical stories. This interaction was recalled among the counselors with great amusement. However, while the printer lacked the semiotic resources to identify a Torah scroll as a particularly Jewish symbol, the fear that others might make the indexical connection kept the t-shirts from being worn on the streets of Istanbul; the children only wore them in private spaces and the group's leaders collected them from the campers after each meeting.

These examples reinforce the centrality of a Turkish Jewish semiotics of secrecy in which the secret is maintained (or assumed to be so) by disengaging signifiers from their signifieds. As Turkish Jews contemplate this process, they become sensitive to the fact that the interpretation of signs is not a uniform process; it is, rather, a process that depends on—and socializes them into—a cosmopolitan knowledge of various and competing symbolic codes.

In another example of how Turkish Jews think about writing their community into existence, a twenty-year-old university student, a member of the Jewish community, once asked me to proofread her English composition. Under the title of "Turkey's Cultural Mosaic" she had written a short piece about Jews, Armenians, Greeks, and Kurds. However, when organizing the essay's structure, she deliberately sandwiched the Jewish section between the other groups in order to not draw attention to that particular case. I asked my friend what she feared might happen if the teacher felt that she was highlighting the Jewish case. A bright-eyed girl, known throughout the community for dramatic flair, she cried out sarcastically, "Disaster!" She quickly became serious, however, explaining her editorial choice: "Turks [i.e., Muslims] are not ready to accept non-Muslims as their equals, even today. The way I am writing the essay, I can incorporate the Jews into the story, but in a sensitive manner." The student understood that censorship was not the only way to tell a story and that other modes might offer creative strategies.

Irony

By spending time with newspaper editors, rabbinate officials, and student essayists, I learned how Turkish Jews engage with the semiotics of secrecy in life and text. Nonetheless, the first time I wrote about Turkish Jews for a public presentation, I was wracked with doubt, fear, and dread. I had recently returned from a year of fieldwork in Istanbul and was scheduled to present a paper at the 2003 American Anthropological Association meetings. The night I submitted my paper to the panel discussants, I couldn't sleep. As I lay awake in bed, I worried. Just as the newspaper editors can't totally control how their texts and images will be interpreted, neither can scholars control how their presentations will be received. Where might my words travel? What if I wasn't being careful enough about my representation? What if I hadn't disguised peoples' identities thoroughly? What business did I have presenting Turkish Jewish secrets to strangers in Chicago anyway? As I fitfully slept, explosions simultaneously ripped through the walls of two of Istanbul's most highly attended synagogues, killing twenty-three people and injuring over three hundred. The worst had happened, but it was not my taboo violation that had again brought violence to the doorstep of the most tolerated minority in Istanbul.

At the same time, I recognize that my representations of Turkish Jews have various audiences, some sympathetic and others antipathetic. The constant recognition of multiple audiences keeps me on my toes and creates an ongoing sense of paranoia. If my representations have a certain power to conceal and reveal information about Turkish Jews, my Turkish Jewish subjects themselves likewise are aware of and exercise a great deal of control in deciding which secrets to share with outsiders and which to conceal. The internal restraints placed on authorized and forbidden speech keep most members from speaking out about things deemed dangerous for public consumption. Once, after a threat to the community had been detected, a participant in a study group I had been attending exclaimed in frustration, "What can we do? We could go to Israel!" Others in the group jokingly chided him, "Hey! Be quiet, kid! Can't you see that the window's open?" I began to realize that silence wasn't the only strategy in a semiotics of secrecy. Perhaps irony and joking also balance the power disparity between intimates and non-intimates (or minorities and majorities), allowing a safe space for critique, as Bhabha suggests:

> Read as a minority speech-act the joke circulates around a doubly-articulated subject: the negatively marked subject, singled out, at first, as a figure of fun or abuse, is turned through the joke-act into an inclusive yet agonistic form of self-critical identification for which the community takes responsibility. (1998:xvii)

The "kid" who dares suggest that in the face of a security threat Jews might leave Turkey is at first negatively marked, told to "Be quiet!" At the same time, the group laughter signals a collective sigh of relief—someone finally uttered the unspeakable—and all present could take responsibility for putting him in his place while enjoying the linguistic breach for what it was worth, a self-conscious critique of the great fear of expressing difference in dangerous times (see also Scott 1990:66).

I found irony to be a powerful strategy that Turkish Jews adopted to talk about themselves. Earlier I coined Turkish Jews' existence an "ironic doubling," an outward performance of sameness and inward maintenance of difference.[9] The definition of irony as a "special kind of silence" has been attributed to Bakhtin (Fernandez and Huber 2001:5), who recognized that to non-intimates, irony passes in total silence. Its ambiguity allows it to signify privately, quietly, and sometimes, through humor.

Over a Sabbath lunch at the home of Yosi, a twenty-three-year-old Turkish Jew, the family sang a traditional Judeo-Spanish song, "Ir me kero a Yerushalayim." A souvenir from a recent trip to see relatives in Bat Yam, Israel, sat tucked into a side cabinet in the dining room. Hearing the word "Yerushalayim," the family's seven-year-old daughter grabbed the small plastic blue-and-white flag; the song prompted an association and she began to wave it vigorously. Her mother worried aloud that the Muslim maid might come in from the kitchen and see her waving the flag of another country; her father made light of the situation by joking, "You better watch out or the police will arrest you." The whole family got in on the act as the eldest son, a normally serious and shy student, muttered under his breath, "Don't worry, if the police come we'll tell them we were just about to burn it!" While foreign flag-waving in Turkey is punishable by arrest, the burning of certain countries' flags is commonplace. Guests around the table roared with laughter.

In order to balance intimate and non-intimate knowledge, Turkish Jews translate cosmopolitan knowledge into irony as a way to make intersubjective sense of it all. When something must be said, how can one still keep a secret? Irony can be a subtle tool for social critique, as outlined by Rosaldo: "In many cases, the oppressed fail to talk straight.[10] Precisely because of their oppression, subordinate people often avoid unambiguous, literal speech. They take up more oblique modes of address laced with double meanings, metaphor, irony, and humor" (1989:190).

Minorities forced to make their difference a secret indeed employ irony, as did the young student who joked that the flag was an object to be burned. Ethnographers must remain attentive not only to the ironies of those whose lives they chronicle but also to the ironies of descriptive writing itself. Perhaps social scientists avoid labeling certain discourses "ironic" for a number of reasons: command of their informants' language(s) is too weak to do anything but translate literally (denotatively); they fear discrediting informants by describing them as "saying one thing and doing another"; they don't want to make claims about their informants' inner thoughts; or, as Rosaldo argues, they take themselves (or their subjects) too seriously to entertain the notion that word-play and double entendres occur constantly among their informants and in their own writing.[11]

In an interview, a community official once offered me a history of the community's security apparatus. An engineer, he had developed the system of double doors, alarms, and wires himself, believing that the community shouldn't entrust its security to non-Jews who ran the alarm companies in Turkey. The security system became so successful that it was eventually marketed for sale outside the community. Soon, the highest-level Turkish jail adopted it for an island prison holding political detainees such as (Kurdish leader) Abdullah Öcalan. This story shed light on common references to Jewish institutions as "prisons" and "fortresses," yet if misinterpreted, it could reinforce the pernicious and widespread myth of disproportionate Jewish power that pollutes large segments of the Turkish press (see again, Bali 2001 and Schleifer 2004). During the conversation, I promised the official that I wouldn't print anything that might endanger the community. He replied, smugly, "I wouldn't tell you anything that would endanger us anyway!" Humbled, I noted the ironic position of an anthropologist who obsesses about protecting the "weak" only to find that others (more powerful than she) are already protecting themselves.

Truth Telling and Ethnography

Friendship does not keep silence, it is preserved by silence. From its first word to itself, friendship inverts itself . . . Friendship tells the truth, and this is always better left unknown.

—Derrida 1997:53

Dizir la verdad, perder l'amistad (Ladino;
Tell the truth, lose friendship).

—American Association of Jewish Friends of
Turkey Newsletter, Fall 2002

Which silences must the ethnographer maintain in order to preserve friendship with those she studies? If silence lacks overtly critical power, and if I remain committed to social criticism as part of ethnographic description, how do I intend to keep friends among those Turkish Jews who insist on keeping secrets? How do I write about the importance of secrets, their place in the local culture, and their meanings without revealing them?

It is through recognizing my own silences and ironies, as well as those of others, (especially those others that I purport to represent) that I acknowledge the different, yet perhaps equally powerful, positions of "holder" and "revealer" of secret knowledge. Secrecy, silence, and irony are not only observable from without: they are self-conscious tools that allow Turkish Jews to imagine their relationship to real conditions in a critical light.

Transposed into the terms of my own representations here, you may not know what word the newspaper editor forbid me from writing (and why), which rabbi insisted on playing censor, or which local historian chided me for playing to elite paranoid fantasies. Other readers, however, will immediately recognize the game I have played as their own. By following the strategies of representation I learned from Turkish Jews, I am able to write about their secrets without fearing that I will lose their friendship. In a paranoid milieu, secrecy, silence, and irony were tools through which the community offered a nearly invisible critique of real conditions, tools that I as an ethnographer adopt in my representations of Turkish Jews.

Conclusion

I spent some time in Istanbul surveying a private collection of community calendars and magazines from the past half-century produced by the rabbinate, Jewish charitable organizations, and local clubs. In this survey, I noted the tradition of reproducing proverbs drawn from many sources on the pages of these ephemera. Quotes are drawn (and translated) from a range of traditions, but largely fall into three categories: Atatürk's and Turkish folk sayings; quotes from philosophers (mainly from French- and German-language sources but also, more recently, English ones); and from Jewish historical or intellectual figures. Generally, the first quote in a given compilation is one attributable to Atatürk, expressing the politically correct appreciation for the father of Turkish independence by placing him on the opening page.

Collecting philosophical quotes is a popular construct in Turkish Jewish community publications; the format repeats itself in pages of the community magazine, calendars, and the Jewish paper, specifically on the one page written in Judeo-Spanish, whose authors are among the elderly who still speak that language and are also fluent in French, English, and German. Like the community calendars that sample philosophical quotes from various sources, one page of Şalom might place a quote by Yehudi Menuhin, a Jewish violinist, next to a citation from Lao Tsu or one from a disciple of the Ramakrishna.

In the community calendar from 2002–2003, the columns marking days and dates themselves take up very few pages of the booklet,

Güzel Sözler

ÖzlüSözlerRiketPinhas

FIGURE 10

Collected quotes in a community magazine.

Collection of the Author.

the rest of which are dedicated to a reference guide to Jewish holidays, prayers, and rituals, and phone numbers for synagogues, hospitals, and general municipal offices (such as the post office and electric company). The calendar is peppered with notes throughout about the importance of donating *kisba* to the communal chest. The "head tax" once collected by heads of the Jewish community under Ottoman rule now functions on a donation-only basis, with contributors becoming officially registered with the rabbinate as well as receiving calendars and invitations to events. In addition to transliterated prayers and indications when to say them, the calendar also includes a chronological account of Jewish history, beginning with the "creation of the world" (5,763 years ago), the flood of Noah's ark (4,107 years ago), the destructions of the temples in Jerusalem, and the expulsion from Spain. Next come dates for the *Fyestas Cudias* (Judeo-Spanish; Jewish holidays) as well as official vacation days such as Independence Day, Ramadan observance, and *Kurban Bayramı*, an Islamic holiday (with its slaughtering of the sacrificial sheep in the streets). The calendar also includes a *mini sözlük* (mini dictionary) of Jewish terms.

Despite the calendar's obvious borrowing from multiple sources to entertain and educate the reader, the idea that all knowledge counts as equally "Jewish" appears to be contested when knowledge and practice come into contrast. An ordinance, printed three times throughout the text (in Turkish and Ladino), urges community members to abandon the practice of serving non-kosher food at weddings and other celebrations, the bold letters chiding the community for indulging in the "strange contrast" between a rabbinate-officiated wedding in synagogue and a dinner of shellfish and other non-kosher delicacies at the hotel banquet following. In fact, Jewish weddings in Turkey are normally layered with contrasts; multiple ceremonies (one each for the engagement, the legal [government] marriage, and the religious ritual) do not negate the authenticity of one or the other. Modest dress in the receiving line in synagogue is replaced by fashionably revealing outfits for the party after. If on the one hand, a cosmopolitan array of choices are available to the Jew according to the authors of the rabbinate's calendar, on the other hand, some are beyond the scope of "Jewish" practice and not open to syncretistic adaptation.

Similarly, if definitions of Turkishness are increasingly tied, at least in some circles, to nostalgia for Ottoman cosmopolitanism, to Islam, to Europeanness, or to secularism, these categorizations are not open-ended or infinite. Jews are still regularly considered "foreign" to many a Turk (including to Jewish Turks), in spite of their history, service, assimilatory gestures, and public pronouncements. A multiplicity of sources does not erase the real and powerful organizational principles that give authority to some texts and reject others.

I learned a great deal from Baruh, the elderly man with whom I spent so much time, and other Turkish Jews about the changing, encyclopedic definition of Turkish Jewry. Baruh himself is (or was) a Judeo-Spanish-, Hebrew-, Turkish-, French-, and English-speaking Ottoman subject, Turkish citizen, Frenchman "by culture" (as he put it), pre-State Palestinian, businessman, author, minority, and autodidact. His library, insulated by walls of books and maps, is a record of cosmopolitanism's shifting signifiers. Whenever Baruh has a personal identity question, he has a profusion of reference material through which to define himself. One dictionary would never be enough to hold the definitions of a life like this. But this does not mean that some definitions don't hold more authority than others. Once, while working with Baruh on his book project about Sephardic names in Turkey, I asked him, "Which name is your favorite?" He slyly responded, "Mine." But, he says, he really likes all of them—especially the ones for which he feels certain he has made the *right* interpretation; those ones please him the most. For all the possible interpretations Baruh might make of names in Turkey, certain ideologies nonetheless guide him to ones that seem right. These ideologies are what situate knowledge in a useful, meaningful context.

As I wrote this book, I felt a deep kinship with Baruh's self-description of his work in the Kardex file system in a windowless room: in a world where a surplus of information demanded sorting, someone had to do the job. I now saw why Baruh had considered the indexing of names for his book an unending task. Depending on which categories seemed most relevant, the material could come together in a seemingly endless combination of ways. In fact, after I began writing and rewriting chapters, I found myself constantly cutting and pasting text between them. If I had a cosmopolitan set of knowledges through which

I could analyze the material collected in Istanbul, I needed to choose from among them in order to represent the community in book form.

This book has described the tensions Jews in Istanbul today face as they negotiate life as a tolerated minority and Turkish citizens. Jews have long been described as living between two worlds (see Kugelmass 1988) and as cosmopolitans and parochials (see Heilman and Cohen 1989), therefore exhibiting a doubled structure: "Roles played in public settings, and the behavior on display there, are often regarded as just that: roles and displays that do not reveal, and certainly do not constitute, their true selves, the essence of who they are" (Eisen 2000:2).

Throughout this work, I have explored the tension between backstage and public presentations (see Scott 1990; Shryock 2004) of Turkish Jewish culture. However, while I recognize the importance of distinguishing between various kinds of platforms and stages for roles Jews play in Turkey, as the epigraph for this book asserts, both public and private performances identity are sites for meaning-making; both tell us something about the lived experience of Turkish Jews.

Anthropology stresses the basic opposition between, at minimum, two ways of thinking about the world: "mine" and "yours." Anthropologists have been long aware of the negotiation between various ideologies (sometimes called "worldviews," "perspectives," or even "cultures"); we increasingly reckon with the understanding that between observer and observed, there will always be situated knowledges at work (Haraway 1988). Thus, anthropologists' own intimate experiences of disemia, heteroglossia, and interpretation are critical to their ability to make sense of all the contrasts encountered in every field (even their "own"). The explosion of writing about flexibility, diaspora, and transnationalism speaks to the increased attention given to our cosmopolitan subjects' ability to manage these tensions as well as our theoretical and methodological reckonings of them. What I hope this book has contributed, in addition to painting an impression of a community that has been little studied, is a sense of the interpretive processes all humans, but especially those cosmopolitans living "between worlds," undertake to make meaning in their lives. If the notion of a double identity, or double consciousness, implies that people must negotiate between different symbolic systems, my concept of cosmopolitan knowledge (or triple consciousness) has inevitably drawn on an understanding how things come to stand for other things. In this sense, I have described the process of how Jews deal with the issue of representation, and how this kind of knowledge is interpreted and mediated by different actors and audiences as well as through the prism of what these various participants think is expected of them.

By observing this particular ethnographic case, I have necessarily been drawn into questions of "thirdness, the ontological character of the symbol," or the nature of representation of the self and other (Keane 2003b:414). As a survival skill, Turkish Jews have become attuned to the value of understanding the subjective nature of the interpretant and how its instability makes mastery of it all the more critical. "Thirdness" is not, of course, observable only among Turkish Jews. Most self-aware people know (or can learn) that the way one experiences reality and the way others do so are often imperfectly matched, and psychological anthropology has long studied this phenomenon. Nonetheless, after observing patterns of interpretation among Jews in Turkey (rather than wide variations in their semiotic processes), the Kantian definition of the cosmopolitan as a "transcendent individual" (Rapport 1997) seemed increasingly untenable. Instead, I was more inclined to consider, following a Peircean model, that for cosmopolitans, "the self is thus both a product and an agent of semiotic communication, and therefore social and public" (Singer 1980:489). I have therefore treated the question of interpreting different ways of being at a collective level, showing how those living outside of the majority, the mainstream, or the center may be overwhelmingly compelled to become sensitive to the competing (and changing) codes that cosmopolitanization engenders. Through ethnography of the way minorities experience semiosis (that is, the interaction between the representamen, the object, and the interpretant), we observe, in high relief, how knowledge of different cultural and social codes is socialized, challenged, and organized.

Long ago, anthropologist Clifford Geertz raised the question of the "movement . . . between . . . the small imaginings of local knowledge and the large ones of cosmopolitan intent" (1973:15–16). This work has reversed Geertz's terms, investigating the tensions between local intentions and cosmopolitan knowledge, detailing the cosmopolitan knowledge that allows Jewish Turks to construct their identities from among the profusion of "worlds" (often more than two) into which they are classified or in which they consider themselves to take part. What cultural logic drives negotiations for meaningful alliances and divisions? For deciding what is Jewish, what is Turkish, and what is cosmopolitan? As I argued in the preface to this book, *pace* Pollock and others (2002), cosmopolitanism is not, in fact, "infinite ways of being," for this would be utter chaos; rather, it is a chaotic collection of knowledges and practices that are ordered and reordered into concrete "chaorders" (Werbner 2006). The power of ethnography lies not only in the description of social categories, class structures, and ethnic boundaries, but also in the detailed accounts of where these seemingly natural divisions are negotiated. Taking the Jews of Turkey as an example, this book has shown the semiotic principles around which ideologies of cosmopolitan citizenship are formed. Jews in Istanbul epitomize cosmopolitan knowledge; years of education in multiple languages, movement between cultural and economic frames, and the constant negotiation between religious laws and secular citizenship, between public and private culture, and between foreignness and citizenship have created a true semiotic awareness—that is, a knowledge of the functions of signs and representations—with which they are capable of reading meaning at many levels. My interest in this community lies in the examination of how we create ideologies of belonging and exclusion and how these ideologies make and break people into religious, linguistic, and social groups. I have explored how knowledge about difference shapes the lives of Jews in Istanbul. Each chapter took up an aspect of cosmopolitanism to show not only how ethnography of this community benefits from such a theoretical frame but also how the community's practices illuminate something about cosmopolitanism.

Chapter 1 argued that discourse analysis illustrates the political and interpretive contexts that condition cosmopolitan lives. However, this chapter also pointed to the importance of understanding discourse in light of ethnographic evidence that can contradict and/or complicate the weight of discursive realities. In light of the popularized tolerance narrative, a seemingly central element of Turkish cosmopolitanism can be seen as a discursive collaboration between Turkish Jews, their government, and foreign Jewish communities. Turkish Jews use international connections to enact their role as a tolerated minority: at the same time cosmopolitan and nationalist, to a fault.

Chapter 2 described the practices of naming and classification among Turkish Jews. This chapter offered a lens through which to study how (and when) other subjects sometimes marked as "foreign"—such as minorities, immigrants, laborers, corporations, and even plants (see Comaroff and Comaroff 2001)—are deemed a "stranger" (or "alien," "other," and so on). Such an approach also allows us to consider the implications these processes have for the "strangers" themselves as well for those who claim to not be strange—that is, "natives" or "locals." What names once meant is not necessarily what they mean today, but neither is the past absent in current readings of their signification. In the Turkish Jewish view, names are consolidations of old meanings and new ones that come together to reveal something about the "contemporary" (Rabinow et al. 2008). As this case study shows, new political systems and the symbolic systems that accompany them engender reclassifications that rely on the ability of old signifiers to signify something new or new signifiers to signify something old. Although episodes of reclassifying—such as those that take place between Muslim Turks and Jews—seem to be simple denotative moves, they are themselves the effects of a labor-intensive socializing process that builds meaning across time. By documenting cases of everyday dialogues in which names are marked as "strange," I show how questions of ontology are omnipresent, which, as Michael Herzfeld argues, "often reduces them to a banal and unthinking obviousness: the relationship between experienced reality and the discourses that render it palpable have often—like gossip—escaped critical attention, filtered out of anthropologists' awareness" (2002:186).

Chapter 3 focused on how an iconic fear of violence is expressed across multiple symbolic landscapes, resulting in Jewish invisibility, revealing the limits of tolerance, and exposing cosmopolitanism's dangers. The descriptions of Turkish Jewish life in this chapter allow us to better understand the sources (perceived and real) of the tensions minorities in Istanbul experience.

Chapter 4 provided an overview of the election and inauguration of Turkey's chief rabbi in 2002. I analyzed this process as a show of democracy, underscoring the role Turkish Jews enact on a national stage and showing how minorities, in spite of their small numbers, are able to represent more than their actual votes might count.

Chapter 5 highlighted the importance of understanding cosmopolitanism as the performance of multiple knowledges as they are displayed in various contexts. The context question for anthropologists is as old as the discipline itself; this book, however, reengages the issue of context in order to show how performance highlights the process of *bricolage* that transforms cosmopolitan knowledge into viable representations. As such, I proposed an attempt to understand collectives by studying how they classify the universe of available symbols into meaningful narratives; it is through the performance of these meaningful narratives (as representations) that we belong and disassociate, cherish and reject.

Finally, chapter 6 offered a description of the challenge of writing about people who would rather not be written about. It is no wonder that a fuller ethnographic picture of Turkish Jewry has not been available up until this point, given the limitations on researcher access as well as the taboos about representation that surround the community. Although I often felt stymied by an ethical imperative to self-censor when reporting on the Jews of Turkey, the lessons I learned about the aesthetics of representation heightened my awareness of the importance of understanding the tensions inherent in Turkish Jewish life.

The dissonance between rhetorical cosmopolitanisms and lived ones is not a peculiarly Turkish problem,[1] but one that opens the door for more ethnography of the limits of various lived cosmopolitanisms rooted firmly, if not dangerously, within their local contexts. Through fieldwork and archival research, I have attempted to understand, from the inside, what tolerance means for today's cosmopolitan Jewish citizens of Turkey. In sum, I have told a tale of the multiple ways of seeing, hearing, and speaking that fit together—both awkwardly and artfully—in a kaleidoscopic view of today's Turkish Jewish cosmopolis.

NOTES

Preface

1. GCI Group "General Agenda" press release, 1991, The Records of the Quincentennial Foundation, Box 1, American Sephardi Federation at the Center for Jewish History.

2. See Bali (1999, 2001); Beinart (1992); Benbassa (1995); Güleryüz (1992); Levy (1992, 1994); Rodrigue (1990, 1993); Rodrigue (1992); Rozen (1996); Shaw (1991); and Weiker (1988, 1992).

3. See Bali (2007).

4. In their landmark collection on Sephardi and Mizrahi history and society, Deshen and Zenner offer seven "Jewish culture areas," delimited by language, religion, political structure and "natural," i.e., physical, boundaries. However, their book lacks any essays on the Eastern Sephardi heartland of Turkey and the Balkans. Further, in their "recommended readings" section, they note the paucity of research done on Jews in these regions (1996:278).

Introduction

1. "Israel" here refers to the Jewish people, not the modern State of Israel.

2. Translations from the Turkish, Judeo-Spanish, French, and Hebrew by the author unless otherwise noted. Yağmur Nuhrat kindly assisted with Turkish translations.

3. Although Judeo-Spanish once enjoyed wide vernacular use as a primary language of Sephardic Jews (Jews who claim ancestral links to the Iberian peninsula), it is estimated that today approximately 300,000 people worldwide know it (Alexander, 2007:191). "Ladino" is the glottonym most often used to cite the text-based transliterations and translations of classical Jewish texts. Linguists sometimes refer to the spoken language of the Sephardic Jews of the Balkans as "Judezmo," while Hispanists call it "Judeo-Spanish" (Baker 1994/1995:50); North African Sephardim speak a regional variant called "Haketia."

4. In Asad's terms, "What are the discursive definitions of authorized space" (1993:8–9)?

5. "Kamondo" is the Turkish spelling; the name is also frequently cited as "Camondo."

6. For further comments on the term "community" as applied collectively to the Jews of Turkey, see Kastoryano (1992).

7. Given that the Eastern European (Ashkenazi) Jewish population in Istanbul currently numbers around 1 percent of the total Jewish population, I was taken aback when I started to hear Turkish Jews with Sephardic surnames wish me a "Gut Shabbos," Yiddish for "Good Sabbath." Nearly all of my contacts in Turkey spent Saturdays in disregard of the Jewish Sabbath, thus the acknowledgment of a Jewish day of rest among Turkish Jews was itself unusual. Stranger, however, was the use of Yiddish among Sephardim. It soon became clear that a Chabad rabbi in his early twenties (I'll call him "Dov") was the source of this neologism among Turkish Jews. Soon after I arrived in Istanbul I attended a Sabbath service at a synagogue not far from my apartment. I had visited Istanbul's synagogues before, noting the use of balconies for women when the men's section was full. I had also observed men and women seated side by side when fewer Jews were in attendance and when the numbers weren't large enough to have women seated separately in balconies. On a Sabbath morning in early September 2002, I found myself behind a newly installed wooden barrier, seated behind the only Jewish woman in synagogue with a wig (often worn instead of a hat among ultra-Orthodox Jews) rather than a lacy scarf to cover her hair. Some of the women were grumbling about the new barrier, and across it I noted a man with a full beard and black hat, the typical garb of members of the Chabad-Lubavitch sect of Judaism.

Chabadniks, as members of this sect are known, were familiar to me as a regular feature on American campuses and in the parks of major cities, appearing each holiday to engage with non-practicing Jews and encourage them (especially the men) to observe the commandments linked to those holidays. When I heard Dov and his wife speaking English after services, I politely introduced myself, upon which they promptly invited me to their home nearby for lunch. A group of Turkish Jews, around twenty to thirty years old, walked together with the couple through the streets of Istanbul, defiantly retaining their *kippot* (Hebrew; skullcaps) atop their heads, protected, seemingly, by the uncommon apparition of a man with a beard cloaked in black.

After meeting Dov, Turkish Jews I knew began searching for Jewish sites on the internet. These sites most often draw from traditional Ashkenazi Orthodox and ultra-Orthodox groups instead of seeking out knowledge from local Turkish rabbis. In addition to the influence of the Chabad rabbi, the general availability of books and internet sites in English made Anglophone materials, which are most often Ashkenazic, dominant influences on the definition of cultural Jewishness, even in the "Sephardic heart" of Turkey. Not many of the Jews I met during my time in Istanbul kept kosher or followed the strictures of the Sabbath or other holidays. However, a small yet devout group strictly observed the Torah laws, circling around the dogmatic Chabadnik and his wife and often answering with "Baruh Ha-Shem" (May God's name be blessed) when asked how they were.

Once, while walking with a particularly observant high school girl, I found myself at a loss for words when asked, "So, when is he coming?" At first I didn't know who she was referring to, then she clarified: "Moshiach" (the Messiah). The messianic obsession among some Chabadniks defines their philosophy and practice, with many anticipating that the recently deceased Rabbi Menachem M. Schneerson will again rise to claim his title as Messiah. The rabbi's image was displayed in a number of households I visited. I found the influence of the proselytizing Chabadniks most prominent among the lower-middle-class Jews whom I met; Chabad's seemingly endless resources (many of their yeshivas and other programs are free of charge) contrast with the high tuition demanded by the Jewish school. Chabad's sophisticated practice of publicizing their views via new technologies also makes their ideas about Judaism increasingly available to those with access to the internet. Once, I visited a young Jewish businessman in the office where he sells wholesale fabrics. After his business transaction ended, he showed me around. We were talking about new technologies for voice communication (i.e., internet telephone) because I had been speaking to family members that way and he wanted to start chatting with his sister, who had recently moved to Israel. While sitting at the computer, he brought out a plastic bag filled with video games in English; upon further examination, it became clear that the "games" were educational software produced by ultra-Orthodox Jews and distributed freely to those who requested them.

When I asked a local Turkish Jewish educator if he was worried about the power of Chabad to change the community, he replied: "If one person can change our community, maybe the community needs changing." I would argue that the Chabad rabbi in Istanbul, far from being "one person," is an emissary of one of the most powerful Jewish organizations in the world, one that sees as its purpose the imposition of its particular values and interpretations of Jewish law on all Jews worldwide. Every year Chabad holds a telethon, celebrity guests included, raising millions of dollars. Their youth movement, Tzivos HaShem (Hebrew; Army of God) imagines Jewish children as "God's little soldiers." A Purim (holiday) party held in 2011 hosted by the Chabad rabbi in Istanbul in association with other community members attracted an estimated 2,000 attendees (personal communication). As such, the appearance and impact of the Chabad movement in Istanbul in the twenty-first century likely deserves a book of its own, but is largely beyond the purview of this work. From links on Turkish Jewish websites to rabbinic emissaries in Istanbul, it is clear that the kinds of conversations Turkish Jews are having about Judaism today—as in the past—extend far beyond their local municipality.

8. Armenians comprise another large population among residents on the island.

9. See El-Or (2004) on English as a "must" language.

10. W. E. B. Du Bois coined the term "double consciousness" with reference to the way black folks felt in America in 1903; Boyarin argues that for Jews, "double consciousness" arises in the Jewish texts with Abraham's abandoning of his father's religion, calling this tradition "an elaborately inscribed identity constructed in the awareness of difference" (1992:66).

11. This idea resonates with Briggs's understanding of W. E. B. Du Bois' and Franz Boaz's cosmopolitanism, in which he suggests that both of these thinkers were attracted to the idea that "without rational self-consciousness, unconscious categories join disparate entities so powerfully that we fail to perceive the arbitrariness of their connections" (2005:82).

1. Tolerance, Difference, and Citizenship

1. In fact, a leader of the Quincentennial Foundation and a Turkish Jewish industrialist, Jak Kamhi, also led a Turkish public relations commission to the European Union (Elazar and Weinfeld 2000:368).

2. These include the Jewish Theological Seminary, American Friends of Hebrew University, American Friends of the Alliance Israélite Universelle, Yeshiva University, Sephardic Hebrew Academy, and Gratz College.

3. These include the National Jewish Community Relations Advisory Council, Anti-Defamation League, American Jewish Congress, American Jewish Committee, Joint Distribution Committee, and Council of Jewish Federations.

4. These include the American Friends of Israel Museum, Judah Magnes Museum (Berkeley, California), and The Jewish Museum (New York).

5. Correspondence with NJCRAC (National Jewish Community Relations Advisory Council) chair, June 7, 1991, The Records of the Quincentennial Foundation, Box 1, American Sephardi Federation at the Center for Jewish History.

6. Letter to QF/US, May 31, 1991, The Records of the Quincentennial Foundation, Box 1, American Sephardi Federation at the Center for Jewish History.

7. Status Reports by GCI for QF, March 1990–May 1992, The Records of the Quincentennial Foundation, Box 1, American Sephardi Federation at the Center for Jewish History.

8. The QF's public relations group successfully engages this network in disseminating their story beyond an elite sphere through the distribution of educational curricula, traveling exhibitions for the public, and "piggyback mailings" in which major Jewish organizations agree to distribute the QF story as a supplement to their normal programmatic mailings. The reach of these mailing lists to a wider scope of Jews or those with Jewish interest (in travel, policy, etc.) is vast: if one small organization has 1000 subscribers (Alliance Israélite Universelle), another has 15,000 (American Sephardi Federation), and yet another boasts 60,000 (Council of Jewish Federations). Soon after the beginning of the campaign, 300,000 readers of *Reform Judaism* (who may or may not have thought that Turkey was what one had for Thanksgiving) would read an article on the QF story and its goals.

9. "Education Curriculum on the Jewish Experience in the Ottoman Empire and Modern Day Turkey," General Agenda, 1989–June 1991, The Records of the Quincentennial Foundation, Box 1, American Sephardi Federation at the Center for Jewish History.

10. Letter to Haham Dr. Solomon Gaon, October 10, 1991, The Records of the Quincentennial Foundation, Box 1, American Sephardi Federation at the Center for Jewish History.

11. GCI Group Correspondence, May 17, 1991, The Records of the Quincentennial Foundation, Box 1, American Sephardi Federation at the Center for Jewish History.

12. David Fintz Altabé (Altabé, Atay, and Katz 1996:193–194).

13. The UJA (United Jewish Appeal)-Federation's missions are, according to their promotional material, "journeys—voyages to see firsthand the history, the status, and the future of the Jewish people. It's an opportunity to make new friends, explore your roots, and learn about one of the most remarkable cultures in history. And it's an occasion to travel to a myriad of fascinating locales, such as Israel, the former

Soviet Union, Poland, the Czech Republic, Hungary, and Latin America—wherever Jewish communities live today or have made their mark in history." See http://www .ujafedny.org/.

14. UJA letter to GCI Group, May 24, 1991, The Records of the Quincentennial Foundation, Box 1, American Sephardi Federation at the Center for Jewish History.

15. See http://www.turkeytravelplanner.com/special/jewish/index.html, accessed August 6, 2010.

16. ASF (American Sephardi Federation)-QF/US correspondence, May 24, 1991, The Records of the Quincentennial Foundation, Box 1, American Sephardi Federation at the Center for Jewish History.

17. GCI memo, August 29, 1991, The Records of the Quincentennial Foundation, Box 1, American Sephardi Federation at the Center for Jewish History.

18. Rabbi Howard Siegel, "Turkish 'Welcome' Not All It's Cracked Up to Be," American Jewish World, Minneapolis, Minn., April 10, 1992.

19. Personal communication (2007).

20. For a comprehensive review of the history and more recent debates in Turkey about the Capital Tax (*Varlık Vergisi*), see Bali (2005). This detailed analysis not only collects evidence about the affair from historical documents but also discusses its legacy and the resurgence of memories about it—in the form of a novel, a controversial popular film shown by the Turkish national broadcasting service (see also Eissenstat 2003), and general media—in the 1990s in Turkey. Bali's description of the relationship between those who critique the Capital Tax and the overwhelming tendency of Turkish Jewish officials to downplay its importance underscores what I have argued here about the importance of erasure of the improper element as a central strategy at play in building and disseminating the tolerance trope. In a telling anecdote, Bali recalls a Turkish Jewish student who asserted that he lacked knowledge about the Capital Tax as a direct result of the QF's "efforts to 'clean up' the country's and his community's history and who suddenly 'discovered' the event by means of the film" (Bali 2005:169).

21. Personal communication (2003).

22. See http://www.muze500.com/content/view/283/250/lang,tr/, accessed March 16, 2011.

23. A panel at the Jewish Museum in Istanbul contains press documentation of the previous century's celebration (see also Cohen 2008), which invoked the story of Passover, when the Jews are exiled from Egypt, to describe their exodus from Spain and consequent arrival in Ottoman lands. Psalm 124:2–3, which in the Hebrew original lauds God for helping the Jews to escape, is transformed into a paean to the current government in which the term "God" is replaced by "the Ottomans," and the latter are praised for their support of the Jews.

24. Speech given on December 19, 2002.

25. Naim Güleryüz, in GCI Press Release for Magnes Museum Opening, October 8, 1991, The Records of the Quincentennial Foundation, Box 1, American Sephardi Federation at the Center for Jewish History.

26. Seymour Fromer.

27. Note that the Turkish Republic, established in 1923, was founded in principled opposition to the Ottoman Empire to which the Jews came in 1492. Nonetheless, QF

members often conflate the two regimes in order to claim that tolerance is an iconic value in both. It isn't clear to which "Turkey" the ambassador here refers—the Ottoman Empire or the Republic—as he envisions the two as seamlessly intertwined.

28. Correspondence from Mustafa Akşin, Ambassador and Permanent Representative to the United Nations, to Jak Kamhi, Chairman of QF, Istanbul, New York, April 7, 1992, The Records of the Quincentennial Foundation, Box 1, American Sephardi Federation at the Center for Jewish History.

29. Newsletter of the Jewish Community of Turkey, Hanukah, 2007.

30. For a comparative account of Jews and Armenians in France, see Mandel (2003).

31. See Walzer's comment to this effect regarding immigrants in present-day France: "Perhaps what they are looking for is something like the millet system—the overseas empire established at home" (1997:40).

32. Personal communication (2007).

33. See Walzer (1997:xi–xii): "Even the most grudging forms and precarious arrangements are very good things, sufficiently rare in human history that they require not only practical but also theoretical appreciation."

2. Cosmopolitan Signs

1. See Levy (1999:635) for similar experiences among indigenous Jews in Morocco, who, through migration and changing political theaters, have been categorized as and have adopted social structures paralleling those typically occupied by "foreigners."

2. See Bering (1992) for a detailed account of the dramatic politics of Jewish naming in Germany before and during the rise of National Socialism.

3. As noted by Paméla Dorn Sezgin (personal communication, November 18, 2009), this naming choice may reflect the special relationship that this sultan maintained with Ottoman Jews: when he was ousted from power, he resided with a Jewish family in Salonika. Nonetheless, in Naile's account, the "Turkishness" of the name rather than its possible indirect "Jewish" referent was the stated rationale behind her mother's choice.

4. Sutherland (1994) explores similar bureaucratic suspicion of Gypsy name changes in the U.S. context.

5. Anthropologists increasingly pay attention to "signs that show time," a phrase coined by French literary critic Mikhail Bakhtin (1986:25); that is, we focus more and more on linguistic and other symbolic practices that anchor, contest, or otherwise signal moves across the "chronotope," the time-space matrix (Basso 1984; Bauman 2005; Agha 2007; Lempert and Perrino 2007).

6. This is what Hanks (1986) calls an "intertextual series," in which texts point back to prior contexts. Knowledge of what constitutes a proper intertextual series allows Turkish Jews to perform a world in which the name "Salomon" today is identifiable as "Jewish," although what "Jewish" itself signifies is explicitly shown here to be unstable.

7. Carucci's analysis of Marshallese names recuperates a semiotic model that does not assume meaning is stable: "Changes in signifiers, or changes in rules of

use, alter the types of realities which can result from new combinations of the code" (1984:154). As David Sutton writes, "The fact that naming practices are seen as 'custom' does not mean that we should assume that they are static" (1997:428).

8. Stoler considers these "epistemic habits . . . steeped in history and historical practices, ways of knowing that are available and 'easy to think,' called upon temporarily settled dispositions that can be challenged and that change" (2008:39).

9. In their theory of the "contemporary," Rabinow and colleagues explore meaning in the present by using the example of DNA as a key symbol that seems new but in fact builds on previous ones such as race, blood, and so forth (2008:3).

3. The Limits of Cosmopolitanism

1. Although much scholarly literature has insisted on the compatibility of a cosmopolitan patriotism (or a patriotic cosmopolitanism) (see especially Appiah 2006), anti-cosmopolitans, or cosmopolitanism's "enemies" (Beck 2002), those for whom the word remains an epithet, see the two ideologies as mutually exclusive.

2. See also the visitor page on Neve Shalom synagogue's website, at http://www .nevesalom.org/?module=modul_tek&modul=60, accessed March 16, 2011.

3. Stratton (2000) draws parallels between the Jewish experience of "self-nomination" and the gay liberation movement's emphasis on proclaiming a public gay identity. Bunzl has also documented the phenomenon of Jewish and gay visibility in comparative perspective (2004). Binnie and Skeggs (2004) likewise draw attention to gay visibility and the management of difference, which they see as an example of "cosmopolitan knowledge."

4. Inversely, speaking different languages sometimes masquerades as alterity when shared social structures are in fact observable across speakers of disparate tongues. This brings us to a larger question: is multilingualism a symptom of or a prerequisite for cosmopolitanism? Lay and scholarly definitions of cosmopolitanism seem to assert that speaking many languages "makes" one a cosmopolitan. The imagined relationship between polyglots and their cosmopolitanism has long ridden on Whorfian assumptions that knowing another language is equivalent to knowing another culture. I find that discussions of cosmopolitanism express an oversimplified understanding of how polyglots understand their worlds as multiply experienced through language. As anthropologists engage with cosmopolitan subjects, we might think more critically about what knowledge of multiple languages means for the way people understand difference.

5. Beck cites Popper on this not-so-new phenomenon of Jews being called cosmopolitan against their will: "Indeed, to feel oneself as part of a cosmopolitan community and to declare one's position publicly can be turned into its opposite by others' violent ethnic definitions of what is alien. Popper writes in his diary: 'I do not see myself as an assimilated German Jew. That is precisely how "the Führer" would have labelled me'" (Beck 2002:36).

6. For commentary on the effects and statistics around the out-migration of Turkish Jews to Israel, see Toktaş (2006a and 2006c).

7. For an anthropological discussion of this topic, see especially André Levy and Alex Weingrod (2005).

8. A rare exception to this rule is the indefatigable Turkish Jewish independent scholar Rıfat Bali. His vocal expressions and publications that expose Turkish anti-Semitism to critique are largely seen as "embarrassing" to many community members and officials, earning him a kind of "trouble-maker" status among those who would like to remain a quiet and good minority.

9. See http://www.yahudikulturuavrupagunu.com/content/view/324/lang,en/, accessed March 16, 2011.

4. Performing Difference

1. I use lowercase letters in my own translation of *hahambaşı* as "chief rabbi," unless the honorific title precedes a particular figure. Academic writing is inconsistent on this and thus I retain Neyzi's choice within the quoted text.

2. This chapter responds, in part, to Neyzi's call for "further research . . . on the public and private discourses and experience of Turkish Jews" (2005:186).

3. For a historical review of the structure of Jewish lay authority in the Ottoman Empire, see for example Bornstein-Makovetsky (1992).

4. Tuval (2004) estimates that 75 percent of Turkey's Jews subscribe to *Şalom*.

5. Specifically, the following neighborhoods of Istanbul: Neve-Şalom–Şişli, Haydarpaşa-Caddebostan, Ortaköy, Kuzguncuk, Balat, Hasköy, Yeniköy, and Bakırköy. For an overview of the changing demographics and geography of Turkish Jewry, see Varol (1989).

6. See Aretxaga (1997) and Navaro-Yashin (2002) for a discussion of the state as a spectral element in everyday social practices.

7. While Turkish citizenship might seem an obvious qualification, other chief rabbis have not had to meet this criterion for candidacy. This qualification, reminiscent of Turkish laws mandating that nominations of Greek Orthodox patriarchs in Turkey be drawn only from those Armenians with Turkish citizenship, has another serious consequence: given the demographic decline, the lack of local rabbinic seminaries, and the overwhelmingly secular outlook of Turkish Jewry, the stipulation creates a practical dilemma for future generations of Turkish Jews.

8. This quote, attributed to Theodore Parker, was translated into Turkish as "Demokrasi, 'Ben de senin kadar iyiyim' değil, 'Sen de benim kadar iyisin' demektir."

9. In part, Rabbi İsak Haleva's success was predicted because in an election season so focused on democracy as representation, he had acquired a patina of modernity and cosmopolitanism that many assumed would allow him to speak to a large variety of audiences. He studied rabbinics in Israel and now teaches Jewish thought to Islamic theology students at a university in Istanbul. His son, also a rabbi in Turkey, trained in a rabbinical seminary in New York and studied sociology.

10. Difference in the Turkish political setting does not rely on minority status based on numerical counts, but rather on definitions of communal and ethnic distinction that have been carried over from the Ottoman regime. At the same time, it behooves us to note that the Jewish case has differed from nearly all other religious and ethnic groups that have been increasingly vying for collective recognition in the public sphere.

11. The name of whoever the sitting president of the republic was at the time would have been inserted into the prayer.

12. Although the chief rabbi performed the ultimate show as political representative to the community, his performance was not a monologue. Rather, the voices of a "religious council" of five local rabbis, fifty lay officers, and fourteen volunteers tirelessly dealt with community matters. Power, in the role of the chief rabbi, seemed to be magically created, but in actuality it required the efforts of a dedicated public relations team and staff, an interpretive cadre of reporters, and thousands of community members, all of whom participated in an extended ritual performance that continued over several months in the fall of 2002.

5. Intimate Negotiations

1. A pseudonym.
2. See Sephardic Music: A Century of Recordings, at http://www.sephardicmusic .org/second_halfc_survey.htm, accessed August 5, 2010.
3. See http://www.zaman.com.tr/haber.do;jsessionid=0DCFB9CBC2395A50A6C 6448EFBCB0DA0?haberno=14653, accessed August 5, 2010.

6. The One Who Writes Difference

1. The title of this chapter is borrowed from the title of Lavie's essay (1993), in which the anthropologist is called "The One Who Writes Us."
2. As promised, I did not write the taboo lexical item.
3. If I had been working with a theoretical model of Turkish Jewish culture as a big dictionary that one had to study carefully to "know," I might have considered reproducing a dictionary of the two hundred or so ASUR cards, discussing their significance for the community and the categories into which one could meaningfully organize them. It would be an interesting project and probably suit many anthropologists and others interested in reading about another exotic (if not quite dying) culture. Instead, I follow Agha (1999) in his critique of the anthropological tendency to collect key words, noting two insufficiencies in theory and method: First, how does one go about amassing a collection of such words, and then claim that those very words are the keys to a culture? And second, how does one translate them meaningfully, given that no universal meaning could be attributed to any word taken out of context?
4. For the nationalistic significance of folkloric dancing in Turkey, see Öztürkmen (2001).
5. On joking and the anthropologist–subject relationship, see Rasmussen (1993).
6. Thanks to Michael Herzfeld and Andrew Shryock for discussions in a panel at the 2005 American Ethnological Society meetings under the title "Intimacy."
7. For a discussion of the thorny relationship between anthropologists and the bureaucratic norms of IRBs (institutional review boards) in university research, see Lederman (2006).
8. For writing on secrecy and magic, see Luhrmann (1989).
9. Butler's (1997) and Kirshenblatt-Gimblett's (1998) theories of performance and identity are particularly useful here.
10. As a counterpoint to Rosaldo's note about the "crooked" talking of the minority, Katriel offers an account of the "straight" speech where Jews are a majority (1986).

11. In this vein, Rosaldo analyzes Marx's "On the Jewish Question" in light of what Rosaldo claims is an intended ironic tenor (1989). Rather than reading Marx's call for the erasure of Jews from society literally, he asserts that our reverence for Marx (and many other theorists) has led modern readers to bypass his ironic moments in lieu of a seemingly denotative meaning.

Conclusion

1. To paraphrase Herzfeld's assertion of intimacy not being "a particularly Greek problem" (1997:xi).

REFERENCES

Abu-Lughod, Lila
1989 Zones of Theory in the Anthropology of the Arab World. Annual Reviews in Anthropology 18(1):267–306.
Adler, Frank H.
2005 Jews in Contemporary Turkey. Macalester International 15(1):127–134.
Agha, Asif
1999 *Review of* Understanding Cultures through Their Key Words: English, Russian, Polish, German, and Japanese, by Anna Wierzbicka. *In* American Anthropologist 101(4): 860–861.
———. 2005a Introduction: Semiosis across Encounters. Journal of Linguistic Anthropology 15(1):1–5.
———. 2005b Voice, Footing, Enregisterment. Journal of Linguistic Anthropology 15(1):38–59.
———. 2007 Recombinant Selves in Mass Mediated Spacetime. Language and Communication 27(3):320–335.
Alexander, Tamar
2007 *Review* of Sephardic Identity: Essays on a Vanishing Jewish Culture, ed. George K. Zucker. In Shofar: An Interdisciplinary Journal of Jewish Studies 25(4):189–191.
Altabé, David, Erhan Atay, and Israel Katz, eds.
1996 Studies on Turkish-Jewish History: Political and Social Relations, Literature, and Linguistics: The Quincentennial Papers. Brooklyn, N.Y.: Sefer-Hermon Press.
Altabev, Mary
2003 Judeo-Spanish in the Turkish Social Context. Istanbul: Isis Press.
Anonymous
2002 Letra e-Mail a Mi Prima Zelda [An E-Mail Letter to My Cousin Zelda]. Şalom.
Appadurai, Arjun
1996 Modernity at Large: Cultural Dimensions of Globalization. Minneapolis: University of Minnesota Press.

Appiah, Kwame
2006 Cosmopolitanism: Ethics in a World of Strangers. New York: W. W. Norton.
Aretxaga, Begonia
1997 Shattering Silence: Women, Nationalism, and Political Subjectivity in Northern Ireland. Princeton, N.J.: Princeton University Press.
Asad, Talal
1993 Genealogies of Religion: Discipline and Reasons of Power in Christianity and Islam. Baltimore: Johns Hopkins University Press.
Asad, Talal, Wendy Brown, Judith Butler, and Saba Mahmood
2009 Is Critique Secular? Blasphemy, Injury, and Free Speech. Berkeley, Calif.: Townsend Center for the Humanities.
Aslan, Senem
2009 Incoherent State: The Controversy over Kurdish Naming in Turkey. European Journal of Turkish Studies 10. http://ejts.revues.org/index4142.html, accessed March 20, 2011.
Aysan, Adviye, and Selma Tuncay
1992 Türkiye'de Kadın-Erkek Adları Sözlüğü [A Dictionary of Women's and Men's Personal Names in Turkey]. Istanbul: Doruk Yayıncılık.
Baer, Marc
———. 2000 Turkish Jews Rethink "500 Years of Brotherhood and Friendship." Turkish Studies Association Bulletin 24(2):63–73.
———. 2007 Globalization, Cosmopolitanism, and the Dönme in Ottoman Salonica and Turkish Istanbul. Journal of World History 18(2):141–170.
2010 The Dönme. Stanford, Calif.: Stanford University Press.
Baer, Marc, Ussama Makdisi, and Andrew Shryock
2009 Tolerance and Conversion in the Ottoman Empire: A Conversation. Comparative Studies in Society and History 51(4):927–940.
Baker, Catherine
2008 Wild Dances and Dying Wolves: Simulation, Essentialization, and National Identity at the Eurovision Song Contest. Popular Communication 6(3):173–189.
Baker, Zachary
1994/1995. Some Problems of Ladino/Judezmo Romanization. Judaica Librarianship 9 (1–2):48–56.
Bakhtin, Mikhail
1986 Speech Genres and Other Late Essays. Caryl Emerson and Michael Holquist, eds. Vern W. McGhee, trans. Austin: University of Texas Press.
Bali, Rıfat
———. 1999 Cumhuriyet Yıllarında Türkiye Yahudileri: Bir Türkleştirme Serüveni (1923–1945). Istanbul: İletişim Yayınları.
———. 2001 Les Relations entre Turcs et Juifs dans la Turquie Moderne. Istanbul: Isis Press.
———. 2003 Antisemitizmi hoşgör(me)mek [(Not) Tolerating Anti-Semitism]. Radikal, November 23. http://www.radikal.com.tr/ek_haber.php?ek=r2&haberno=2766, accessed March 21, 2011.
———. 2005 The "Varlık Vergisi" Affair: A Study of Its Legacy—Selected Documents. Istanbul: Isis Press.
———. 2007 The Alternative Way to Come to Terms with the Past/Those Who Try to Forget: Turkey's Jewish Minority. Unpublished paper.

————. 2009 Present-Day Anti-Semitism in Turkey. Bulletin of The Stephen Roth Institute for the Study of Contemporary Antisemitism and Racism 84 (16 August). Jerusalem: Jerusalem Center for Public Affairs.

————.2010 Küçük Türkiye Kozmopolit Mi? Memleket, Ülkeler Ve Kentler Dergisi: 82–85.

Barkey, Henri
2000 The Struggles of a "Strong" State. Journal of International Affairs 54(1):87–105.

Barkey, Karen
2008 Empire of Difference: The Ottomans in Comparative Perspective. Cambridge, New York: Cambridge University Press.

Barnai, Jacob
1990 On the History of the Jews in the Ottoman Empire. In Sephardi Jews in the Ottoman Empire. Esther Juhasz, ed. Pp. 19–36. Jerusalem: The Israel Museum.

————.1992 Messianism and Leadership: The Sabbatean Movement and the Leadership of the Jewish Communities in the Ottoman Empire. In Ottoman and Turkish Jewry: Community and Leadership. Aron Rodrigue, ed. Pp. 167–182. Bloomington: Indiana University.

Baron, Salo
1928 Ghetto and Emancipation. Menorah Journal 14:515–526.

Barthes, Roland
1987[1957] Mythologies. New York: Hill and Wang.

Bartu, Ayfer
1999 Who Owns the Old Quarters? Rewriting Histories of the Global Era. In Istanbul: Between the Global and the Local. Çağlar Keyder, ed. Pp. 31–46. Boulder, Colo.: Rowman and Littlefield.

Başgöz, İlhan
1999 The Meaning and Dimension of Change of Personal Names in Turkey. In Turkish Folklore and Oral Literature: Selected Essays of İlhan Başgöz. Kemal Silay, ed. Bloomington: Indiana University.

Basso, Keith
1984 Stalking with Stories: Names, Places, and Moral Narratives among the Western Apache. In Text, Play and Story. Edward Bruner, ed. Pp. 19–55. Prospect Heights, Ill.: Waveland Press.

Bat Ye'or
1985 The Dhimmi: Jews and Christians Under Islam. Madison, N.J.: Fairleigh Dickinson University Press.

————.2002 Islam and Dhimmitude: Where Civilizations Collide. Miriam Kochan and David Littman, trans. Madison, N.J.: Fairleigh Dickinson University Press.

Bauman, Richard
1983 Let Your Words Be Few: Symbolism of Speaking and Silence among Seventeenth-Century Quakers. Cambridge, New York: Cambridge University Press.

————.2005 Commentary: Indirect Indexicality, Identity, Performance Dialogic Observations. Journal of Linguistic Anthropology 15(1):145–150.

Bayraktar, Hatice
2006 Salamon und Rabeka: Judenstereotype in Karikaturen der türkischen Zeitschriften "Akbaba," "Karikatür" und "Milli İnkılap," 1933–1945. Berlin: Klaus Schwarz Verlag.

Beck, Ulrich
    2002 The Cosmopolitan Society and Its Enemies. Theory, Culture & Society 19(1/2):
    17–44.
——.2006 The Cosmopolitan Vision. Cambridge, UK and Malden, Mass.: Polity.
Beck, Ulrich, and Edgar Grande
    2007 Cosmopolitan Europe. Cambridge, UK and Malden, Mass.: Polity.
Beck, Ulrich, and Nathan Sznaider
    2006 Unpacking Cosmopolitanism for the Social Sciences: A Research Agenda.
    British Journal of Sociology 57(1):1–23.
Behar, Ruth
    1993 Translated Woman: Crossing the Border with Esperanza's Story. Boston:
    Beacon Press.
Beinart, Haim
    1992 The Sephardi Legacy. Jerusalem: Magnes Press.
Benbassa, Esther
    1995 Haim Nahum: A Sephardic Chief Rabbi in Politics, 1892–1923. Tuscaloosa:
    University of Alabama Press.
——, ed. 2010 Itinéraires sépharades: Complexité et diversité des identités. Paris:
    Presses de l'Université Paris-Sorbonne.
Benbassa, Esther, and Aron Rodrigue
    2000 Sephardi Jewry: A History of the Judeo-Spanish Community, 14th–20th
    Centuries. Berkeley: University of California Press.
Bengio, Ofra
    2009 The Turkish–Israeli Relationship: Changing Ties of Middle Eastern Out-
    siders. New York: Palgrave Macmillan.
Benhabib, Seyla
    1996 Democracy and Difference: Contesting the Boundaries of the Political.
    Princeton, N.J.: Princeton University Press.
——.2003 In Turkey, a History Lesson in Peace. New York Times, November 18.
    http://www.nytimes.com/2003/11/18/opinion/in-turkey-a-history-lesson-in-peace
    .html, accessed March 20, 2011.
——.2004 Philosophic Iterations: Cosmopolitanism and the "Right to Rights."
    http://globetrotter.berkeley.edu/people4/Benhabib/, accessed October 11, 2008.
——.2006 Another Cosmopolitanism. Oxford: Oxford University Press.
Bering, Dietz
    1992 The Stigma of Names: Antisemitism in German Daily Life, 1812–1933. Ann
    Arbor: University of Michigan Press.
Beyoğlu Jewish Rabbinate Foundation, and European Commission
    2009 Research on Perception of Different Identities and Jews. Unpublished
    document. Beyoğlu Musevi Hahamhanesi Vakfı [The Beyoğlu Jewish Rabbinate
    Foundation].
Bhabha, Homi
    1998 Foreword. In Modernity, Culture and "the Jew." Bryan Cheyette and Laura
    Marcus, eds. Pp. xv–xx. Stanford, Calif.: Stanford University Press.
Binnie, Jon, and Beverly Skeggs
    2004 Cosmopolitan Knowledge and the Production and Consumption of
    Sexualized Space: Manchester's Gay Village. The Sociological Review 52(1):39–
    61.

Blommaert, Jan, and Jef Verschueren
1998 Debating Diversity. New Brunswick, N.J.: Routledge.
Blum, Susan
1997 Naming Practices and the Power of Words in China. Language in Society 26(3):357–379.
Bornstein-Makovetsky, Leah
1992 Jewish Lay Leadership and Ottoman Authorities during the Sixteenth and Seventeenth Centuries. *In* Ottoman and Turkish Jewry: Community and Leadership. Aron Rodrigue, ed. Pp. 87–121. Bloomington: Indiana University.
———.1997 Jewish Names in Istanbul in the 18th and 19th Centuries, a Study Based on Bills of Divorce. *In* These Are the Names: Studies in Jewish Onomastics, vol. 1. Aaron Demsky, Joseph Tabory Raif, and Edwin Lawson, eds. Pp. 13–26. Ramat Gan: Bar-Ilan University Press.
Bourdieu, Pierre
1982 Language and Symbolic Power. Cambridge, Mass.: Harvard University Press.
Bowen, John R.
2007 Why the French Don't Like Headscarves: Islam, the State, and Public Space. Princeton, N.J.: Princeton University Press.
Boyarin, Daniel, and Jonathan Boyarin
1993 Diaspora: Generation and the Ground of Jewish Identity. Critical Inquiry 19(4):693–725.
Boyarin, Jonathan
1992 Storm from Paradise: The Politics of Jewish Memory. Minneapolis: University of Minnesota Press.
Boyer, Dominic
2005 AE Forum: Exclusionary Projects and Anthropological Analysis—Commentaries—Welcome to the New Europe. American Ethnologist 32(4):521–523.
Boym, Svetlana
2001 The Future of Nostalgia. New York: Basic Books.
Bozdoğan, Sibel, and Reşat Kasaba, eds.
1997 Rethinking Modernity and National Identity in Turkey. Seattle: University of Washington Press.
Braude, Benjamin, and Bernard Lewis
1982 Christians and Jews in the Ottoman Empire: The Functioning of a Plural Society. Teaneck, N.J.: Holmes and Meier.
Briggs, Charles
2005 Geneologies of Race and Culture and the Failure of Vernacular Cosmopolitanisms: Rereading Franz Boas and W. E. B. Du Bois. Public Culture 17(1): 75–100.
Brink-Danan, Marcy
2009 "I Vote, Therefore I Am": Rituals of Democracy and the Turkish Chief Rabbi. PoLAR: Political and Legal Anthropology Review 32(1):5–27.
———.2010 Counting as European: Jews and the Politics of Presence in Istanbul. *In* Orienting Istanbul: Cultural Capital of Europe? Deniz Göktürk, Levent Soysal, and İpek Türeli, eds. Pp. 279–295. London: Routledge.
———.2011 Dangerous Cosmopolitanism: Erasing Difference in Istanbul. Anthropological Quarterly 84(2) 1:439–47.

Brown, Wendy
  2006 Regulating Aversion: Tolerance in the Age of Identity and Empire. Princeton,
  N.J.: Princeton University Press.
Bunzl, Matti
  1996 The City and the Self: Narratives of Spatial Belonging among Austrian Jews.
  City and Society 8(1):50–81.
———.2003 Austrian Zionism and the Jews of the New Europe. Jewish Social Studies
  9(2):154–173.
———.2004 Symptoms of Modernity: Jews and Queers in Late-Twentieth-Century
  Vienna. Berkeley: University of California Press.
———.2005 AE Forum: Exclusionary Projects and Anthropological Analysis—
  Provocation—between Anti-Semitism and Islamophobia: Some Thoughts on the
  New Europe. American Ethnologist 32(4):499–508.
Butler, Judith
  1997 Excitable Speech: A Politics of the Performative. London: Routledge.
Çaha, Ömer
  2005 The Ideological Transformation of the Public Sphere: The Case of Turkey.
  Alternatives: Turkish Journal of International Relations 4(1–2):1–30.
Calhoun, Craig
  1998 Actually Existing Cosmopolitanism. In Cosmopolitics: Thinking and Feeling
  Beyond the Nation. P. Cheah and B. Robbins, eds. Pp.1–19. Minneapolis: University
  of Minnesota Press.
———.2002 Imagining Solidarity: Cosmopolitanism, Constitutional Patriotism, and
  the Public Sphere. Public Culture 14(1):147–171.
Carucci, Laurence
  1984 Significance of Change or Change of Significance: A Consideration of
  Marshallese Personal Names. Ethnology 23(2):143–155.
Charny, Israel, ed.
  1984 Toward the Understanding and Prevention of Genocide. London: Westview
  Press.
Chao, Emily
  1999 The Maoist Shaman and the Madman: Ritual Bricolage, Failed Ritual, and
  Failed Ritual Theory. Cultural Anthropology 14(4):505–534.
Cheah, P., B. Robbins, and Social Text Collective
  1998 Cosmopolitics: Thinking and Feeling beyond the Nation. Minneapolis:
  University of Minnesota Press.
Çınar, Alev
  2005 Modernity, Islam, and Secularism in Turkey: Bodies, Places, and Time.
  Minneapolis: University of Minnesota Press.
Çınar, Alev, and Thomas Bender
  2007 Urban Imaginaries: Locating the Modern City. Minneapolis: University of
  Minnesota Press.
Clifford, James
  1994 Diasporas. Cultural Anthropology 9(3):302–338.
Cohen, Julia
  2008 Fashioning Imperial Citizens: Sephardi Jews and the Ottoman State, 1856–
  1912. Ph.D. dissertation, Stanford University.

Cohen, Mark
1994 Jews under Crescent and Cross. Princeton, N.J.: Princeton University Press.
Comaroff, Jean, and John Comaroff
2001 Naturing the Nation: Aliens, Apocalypse and the Postcolonial State. Journal of Southern African Studies 27(3):627–651.
Cooper, Samuel
1999 Names as Cultural Documents. In These Are the Names: Studies in Jewish Onomastics, vol. 2. Aaron Demsky, Joseph Tabory Raif, and Edwin Lawson, eds. Pp. 13–22. Ramat Gan: Bar-Ilan University Press.
Davidson, Deanna
2007 East Spaces in West Times: Deictic Reference and Political Self-Positioning in a Post-Socialist East German Chronotope. Language and Communication 27(3):212–226.
Dayal, Samir
1996 Diaspora and Double Consciousness. Journal of the Midwest Modern Language Association 29:46–62.
Delaney, Carol Lowery
1991 The Seed and the Soil: Gender and Cosmology in Turkish Village Society. Berkeley: University of California Press.
———.1995 Father State, Motherland, and the Birth of Modern Turkey. In Naturalizing Power: Essays in Feminist Cultural Analysis. S. J. Yanagisako and C. L. Delaney, eds. Pp. 177–200. New York: Routledge.
———.1998 Abraham on Trial: The Social Legacy of Biblical Myth. Princeton, N.J.: Princeton University Press.
Derrida, Jacques
1997 Politics of Friendship. London, New York: Verso.
de Saussure, Ferdinand
1986[1913] Course in General Linguistics. Charles Bally and Albert Sechehaye, eds. Roy Harris, trans. Peru, Ill.: Open Court Publishing Company.
Deshen, Shlomo A., and Walter P. Zenner
1996 Jews among Muslims: Communities in the Precolonial Middle East. New York: New York University Press.
Devellioğlu, Ferit
1999 Osmanlıca-Türkçe Ansiklopedik Lugat [Ottoman-Turkish Encyclopedic Glossaries]. Ankara: Aydın Kitabevi.
Dorn, Paméla J.
1991 Change and Ideology: The Ethnomusicology of Turkish Jewry. Ph.D. dissertation, Indiana University.
Douglas, Mary
1966 Purity and Danger: An Analysis of the Concepts of Pollution and Taboo. London: Routledge.
Du Bois, W. E. B.
2008[1903] The Souls of Black Folk. Rockville, Md.: Arc Manor.
Durak, Attila
2007 Ebru: Reflections of Cultural Diversity in Turkey. Istanbul: Metis.
Eco, Umberto
1984 Semiotics and the Philosophy of Language. Bloomington: Indiana University Press.

———.1992 Interpretation and Overinterpretation. Cambridge: Cambridge University Press.

Eisen, Arnold
2000 Rethinking Modern Judaism. Chicago: University of Chicago Press.

Eissenstat, Howard
2003 History and Historiography: Politics and Memory in the Turkish Republic. Contemporary European History 12(1):93–105.
———. 2005 Metaphors of Race and Discourse of Nation. *In* Race and Nation: Ethnic Systems in the Modern World. Paul R. Spickard, ed. Pp. 239–256. London: Routledge.

Elazar, Daniel, and H. Friedenreich, B. Hazzan, and A. Liberles, eds.
1984 The Balkan Jewish Communities: Yugoslavia, Bulgaria, Greece and Turkey. Lanham, Md.: University Press of America.

Elazar, Daniel Judah, and Morton Weinfeld
2000 Still Moving: Recent Jewish Migration in Comparative Perspective. New Brunswick, N.J.: Transaction Publishers.

El-Or, Tamar
2004 Tickets to the Opera: A Negotiation of Western Knowledge—Beyond Resistance or Reproduction. Anthropology & Education Quarterly 35(2):189–211.

Encyclopedia Judaica
1972 Cecil Roth, ed. New York: Macmillan.

Fabian, Johannes, and Matti Bunzl
2002 Time and the Other: How Anthropology Makes Its Object. New York: Columbia University Press.

Falzon, Mark-Anthony
2004 Cosmopolitan Connections: The Sindhi Diaspora, 1860–2000. Leiden and Boston: Brill.

Farhi, Moris
2005 Young Turk. New York: Arcade Publishing.

Favret-Saada, Jeanne
1980 Deadly Words: Witchcraft in the Bocage. Cambridge: Cambridge University Press.

Feldman, Jackie
2002 Marking the Boundaries of the Enclave: Defining the Israeli Collective through the Poland "Experience." Israel Studies 7(2):84–114.

Ferguson, James
1992 The Country and the City on the Copperbelt. Cultural Anthropology 7(1): 80–92.

Fernandez, James W., and Mary Taylor Huber
2001 Irony in Action: Anthropology, Practice, and the Moral Imagination. Chicago: University of Chicago Press.

Fish, Stanley
1980 Is There a Text in this Class? The Authority of Interpretive Communities. Cambridge, Mass.: Harvard University Press.

Fishman, Joshua
1988 Language and Ethnicity in Minority Sociolinguistic Perspective. Philadelphia: Multilingual Matters.

Fleminger, Madelon
    2003 Istanbul: The Jewish Municipality in the Turkish Million-Metropolis.
    Jüdische Allgemeine.
Foucault, Michel
    1972 Archaeology of Knowledge. New York: Pantheon.
Gable, Eric
    2006 The Funeral and Modernity in Manjaco. Cultural Anthropology 21(3):385–415.
Gal, Susan
    2002 A Semiotics of the Public/Private Distinction. Differences: A Journal of
    Feminist Cultural Studies 13(1):77–95.
Gal, Susan, and Judith Irvine
    1995 The Boundaries of Languages and Disciplines. Social Research 62(4):967–1001.
Geertz, Clifford
    1973 The Interpretation of Cultures. New York: Basic Books.
Gerber, Jane S.
    1992 The Jews of Spain: A History of the Sephardic Experience. New York: Free Press.
Gerber, Jane S., and International Center for University Teaching of Jewish Civilization
    1995 Sephardic Studies in the University. Madison, N.J.: Fairleigh Dickinson
    University Press; London; Cranbury, N.J.: Associated University Presses.
Gluck, Carol, and Anna L. Tsing, eds.
    2009 Words in Motion: Toward a Global Lexicon. Durham, N.C.: Duke University
    Press.
Goffman, Erving
    1959 The Presentation of Self in Everyday Life. Garden City, N.Y.: Doubleday.
    ———.1981 Forms of Talk. Philadelphia: University of Pennsylvania Press.
Goldberg, Harvey, ed.
    1996 Sephardi and Middle Eastern Jewries: History and Culture in the Modern
    Era. Bloomington: Indiana University Press.
    ———.1997 Names in Their Social Contexts: An Anthropological Perspective. In
    These Are the Names: Studies in Jewish Onomastics, vol. 1. Aaron Demsky, Y. A.
    Raif, Joseph Tabory, and Edwin D. Lawson, eds. Pp. 53–64. Ramat Gan: Bar-Ilan
    University Press.
Goldberg, Harvey, and Chen Bram
    2007 Sephardic/Mizrahi/Arab-Jews: Reflections on Critical Sociology and
    the Study of Middle Eastern Jewries within the Context of Israeli Society. In
    Sephardic Jewry and Mizrahi Jews. Peter Y. Medding, ed. Pp. 227–256. Studies in
    Contemporary Jewry, 22. Oxford: Oxford University Press.
Greenhouse, Carol, and K. Roshanak, eds.
    1998 Democracy and Ethnography: Constructing Identities. In Multicultural
    Liberal States. Pp. 1–24. Albany: State University of New York Press.
Gruber, Ruth
    2002 Virtually Jewish: Reinventing Jewish Culture in Europe. Berkeley: University
    of California Press.
    ———.2009 Beyond Virtually Jewish: New Authenticities and Real Imaginary Spaces
    in Europe. Jewish Quarterly Review 99(4):487–504.
Güleryüz, Naim
    1992 The History of the Turkish Jews. 2nd edition. Istanbul: self-published.

Gültekin, Ayşe Orhun, ed.
    2009 Istanbul 2010 European Capital of Culture Program.
Gumpert, Matthew
    2007 "Everyway That I Can": Auto-Orientalism in Eurovision 2003. *In* A Song for
    Europe: Popular Music and Politics in the Eurovision Song Contest. Ivan Raykoff
    and Robert Dean Tobin, eds. Pp. 147–157. Burlington, Vt: Ashgate.
Gupta, Akhil, and James Ferguson
    1997 Culture, Power, Place: Explorations in Critical Anthropology. Durham, N.C.:
    Duke University Press.
Gutmann, Matthew C.
    2002 The Romance of Democracy: Compliant Defiance in Contemporary Mexico.
    Berkeley: University of California Press.
Gürsel, Zeynep Devrim, dir.
    2009 Coffee Futures. 22 min. Documentary Educational Resources. Watertown,
    Mass.
Habermas, Jürgen
    1989[1962] The Structural Transformation of the Public Sphere. T. Burger and F.
    Lawrence, trans. Cambridge, Mass: MIT Press.
———. 1997 Kant's Idea of Perpetual Peace, with the Benefit of Two Hundred Years'
    Hindsight. *In* Perpetual Peace: Essays on Kant's Cosmopolitan Ideal. James Bohman
    and Matthias Lutz-Bachmann, eds. Pp. 113–153. Cambridge, Mass.: MIT Press.
Habib, Jasmin
    2004 Israel, Diaspora, and the Routes of National Belonging. Toronto: University
    of Toronto Press.
Hall, Stuart
    1980 Encoding/Decoding. *In* Culture, Media, Language: Working Papers in
    Cultural Studies. Stuart Hall et al. eds. Pp. 128–138. London, Hutchinson.
Hanks, William F.
    1986 Authenticity and Ambivalence in the Text: A Colonial Maya Case. American
    Ethnologist 13:721–744.
Haraway, Donna Jeanne
    1988 Situated Knowledges: The Science Question in Feminism as a Site of Discourse
    on the Privilege of Partial Perspective. Feminist Studies 14(3): 575–599.
Harris, Tracy
    1982 Reasons for the Decline of Judeo-Spanish. International Journal of the
    Sociology of Language 37:71–97.
———. 1994 Death of a Language: The History of Judeo-Spanish. Newark, N.J.:
    University of Delaware Press.
Hart, Kimberly
    1999 Images and Aftermaths: The Use and Contextualization of Atatürk Imagery
    in Political Debates in Turkey. PoLAR: Political and Legal Anthropology Review
    22(1):66–84.
———. 2009 The Orthodoxization of Ritual Practice in Western Anatolia. American
    Ethnologist 36(4):735–749.
Harvey, David
    2000 Cosmopolitanism and the Banality of Geographical Evils. Public Culture
    12(2):529–564.

Haskell, Guy H.
   1994 From Sofia to Jaffa: The Jews of Bulgaria and Israel. Detroit: Wayne State University Press.
Hayırlı, Dilek
   2004 Sefarad Grubundan Athena'Ya Taşlama [Sefarad Group Hints at Critique of Athena]. Zaman. http://www.zaman.com.tr/haber.do;jsessionid=0DCFB9CBC23 95A50A6C6448EFBCB0DA0?haberno=14653, accessed August 16, 2010.
Hazar, Nedim, dir.
   2004 Yakın Ada Uzak Ada Burgazada [Nearby Yet Far Away—the Isle of Burgaz]. 60 min. Troya Medya. Turkey.
Heilman, Samuel C., and Steven Martin Cohen
   1989 Cosmopolitans and Parochials: Modern Orthodox Jews in America. Chicago: University of Chicago Press.
Henkel, Heiko
   2007 The Location of Islam: Inhabiting Istanbul in a Muslim Way. American Ethnologist 34(1):57–70.
Heper, Metin
   1992 Strong State as a Problem for the Consolidation of Democracy: Germany and Turkey Compared. Comparative Political Studies 25:169–194.
Herzfeld, Michael
   1982 When Exceptions Define the Rules: Greek Baptismal Names and the Negotiation of Identity. Journal of Anthropological Research 38(3):288–302.
   ———.1987 Anthropology through the Looking-Glas: Critical Ethnography in the Margins of Europe. Cambridge: Cambridge University Press.
   ———. 1997 Cultural Intimacy: Social Poetics in the Nation-State. New York: Routledge.
   ———.2002 The Social Life of Reality: A Review Article. Comparative Studies in Society and History 44(1):186–195.
Herzog, Hanna
   1987 Contest of Symbols: The Sociology of Election Campaigns through Israeli Ephemera. Cambridge, Mass.: Harvard University Press.
Hill, Jane
   1998 Language, Race, and White Public Space. American Anthropologist 100(3): 680–689.
   ———.2000 "Read My Article": Ideological Complexity and the Overdetermination of Promising in American Presidential Politics. In Regimes of Language: Ideologies, Politics, and Identities. P. Kroskrity, ed. Pp. 259–292. Santa Fe: School of American Research Press.
Hodder, Ian
   1982 Symbols in Action: Ethnoarchaeological Studies of Material Culture. Cambridge: Cambridge University Press.
Houston, Christopher
   2001 Islam, Kurds and the Turkish Nation State. Oxford: Berg.
İçduygu, Ahmet, and B. Ali Soner
   2006 Turkish Minority Rights Regime: Between Difference and Equality. Middle Eastern Studies 42(3):447–468.

Ignatowski, Clare
    2004 Multipartyism and Nostalgia for a Unified Past: Discourses of Democracy
    in a Dance Association in Cameroon. Cultural Anthropology 19(2):276–298.
İnalcık, Halil
    2002 Foundations of Ottoman-Jewish Cooperation. *In* Jews, Turks, Ottomans: A
    Shared History, Fifteenth through the Twentieth Century. Avigdor Levy, ed. Pp.
    3–14. Syracuse, N.Y.: Syracuse University Press.
Inoue, Miyako
    2004a Introduction: Temporality and Historicity in and through Linguistic
    Ideology. Journal of Linguistic Anthropology 14(1):1–5.
————. 2004b What Does Language Remember? Indexical Inversion and the
    Naturalized History of Japanese Women. Journal of Linguistic Anthropology
    14(1):39–56.
Irvine, Judith T.
    2004 Say When: Temporalities in Language Ideology. Journal of Linguistic
    Anthropology 14(1):99–109.
Kaganoff, Benzion
    1977 A Dictionary of Jewish Names and Their History. New York: Schocken.
Kahn, Joel
    2003 Anthropology as Cosmopolitan Practice? Anthropological Theory 3(4):403–415.
Kamhi, Jak
    2007 Letter to Abraham Foxman, Anti-Defamation League. Istanbul, August 22.
Kamhi, Jak V., and Harry Ojalvo
    1997 500. Yıl Vakfı Sergisi [Exhibit of the Quincentennial Foundation]. Istanbul:
    The Quincentennial Foundation.
Kandiyoti, Deniz
    2002 Introduction: Reading the Fragments. *In* Fragments of Culture: The Every-
    day of Modern Turkey, Deniz Kandiyoti and Ayşe Saktanber, eds. Pp. 1–24. New
    Brunswick, N.J.: Rutgers University Press.
Kaplan, Sam
    2003 Nuriye's Dilemma: Turkish Lessons of Democracy and the Gendered State.
    American Ethnologist 30(3):401–417.
Karimova, Nigar, and Edward Deverell
    2001 Minorities in Turkey. Occasional Papers 19:1–24.
Karmi, Ilan
    1996 The Jewish Community of Istanbul in the Nineteenth Century: Social, Legal
    and Administrative Transformations. Istanbul: Isis Press.
Kasaba, Reşat.
    1997 Kemalist Certainties and Modern Ambiguities. *In* Rethinking Modernity
    and National Identity in Turkey. Sibel Bozdoğan and Reşat Kasaba, eds. Pp. 15–36.
    Seattle: University of Washington Press.
Kastoryano, Riva
    1992 From Millet to Community: The Jews of Istanbul. *In* Ottoman and Turkish
    Jewry: Community and Leadership. Aron Rodrigue, ed. Pp. 253–277. Bloomington:
    Indiana University Press.
Kasuto, Yasmin
    2003 Arap dünyasında demokrasi arayışı [Searching for Democracy in the Arab
    World]. Şalom, January 8:8.

Katriel, Tamar
1986 Talking Straight: Dugri Speech in Israeli Sabra Culture. Cambridge and New York: Cambridge University Press.

Keane, Webb
2003a Second Language, National Language, Modern Language, and Post-Colonial Voice: On Indonesian. *In* Translating Cultures: Perspectives on Translation and Anthropology. P. G. Rubel and A. Rosman, eds. Pp. 153–175. Oxford: Berg Publishers.

———. 2003b Semiotics and the Social Analysis of Material Things. Language and Communication 23(3–4):409–425.

Kertzer, David
1988 Ritual, Politics, and Power. New Haven, Conn.: Yale University Press.

Keyder, Çağlar
1997 Whither the Project of Modernity? Turkey in the 1990s. *In* Rethinking Modernity and National Identity in Turkey. Sibel Bozdoğan, ed. Pp. 37–51. Seattle: University of Washington Press.

Kirshenblatt-Gimblett, Barbara
1998 Destination Culture: Tourism, Museums, and Heritage. Berkeley: University of California Press.

Komins, Benton J.
2002 Cosmopolitanism Depopulated: The Cultures of Integration, Concealment, and Evacuation in Istanbul. Comparative Literature Studies 39:360–385.

Kripke, Paul
1981[1972] Naming and Necessity. Malden, Mass.: Blackwell.

Kugelmass, Jack, ed.
1988 Between Two Worlds: Ethnographic Essays on American Jewry. New York: Cornell University Press.

Kugelmass, Jack, and Annamaria Orla-Bukowska
1998 "If You Build It They Will Come": Recreating an Historic Jewish District in Post-Communist Kraków. City and Society 10(1):315–353.

Kunt, Metin
1982 Transformation of *Zimmi* to *Askeri*. *In* Christians and Jews in the Ottoman Empire: The Functioning of a Plural Society. Benjamin Braude and Bernard Lewis, eds. Pp. 55–68. Teaneck, N.J.: Holmes and Meier Publishers.

Kuper, Adam
1999 Culture: The Anthropologists' Account. Cambridge, Mass.: Harvard University Press.

Kymlicka, Will
1995 Multicultural Citizenship. Oxford: Oxford University Press.

Lakoff, Andrew
2008 The Generic Biothreat, or, How We Became Unprepared. Cultural Anthropology 23(3): 399–428.

Landau, Jacob
1993 Jews, Arabs, Turks. Jerusalem: Magnes Press.

Lavie, Smadar
1993 The One Who Writes Us: Political Allegory and the Experience of Occupation among the Mzeina Bedouin. *In* Creativity/Anthropology. Smadar Lavie, Kirin Narayan and Renato Rosaldo, eds. Pp. 153–183. Ithaca, N.Y.: Cornell University Press.

Lazaroff, Tovah, and Yaakov Katz
  2003 Turkish Terrorists Send Jews Vicious Shabbat Greeting. Jerusalem Post, November 20:2.
Lederman, Rena
  2006 AE Forum: IRBs, Bureaucratic Regulation, and Academic Freedom—Provocation—Introduction: Anxious Borders between Work and Life in a Time of Bureaucratic Ethics Regulation. American Ethnologist 33(4):477–491.
Lehmann, Matthias
  2005 Ladino Rabbinic Literature and Ottoman Sephardic Culture. Bloomington: Indiana University Press.
Lempert, Michael, and Sabina Perrino
  2007 Entextualization and the Ends of Temporality. Language and Communication 27(3):205–211.
Lévi-Strauss, Claude
  1963 Structural Anthropology. New York: Basic Books.
———.1966 The Savage Mind. Chicago: University of Chicago Press.
Levy, André
  1997 Controlling Space, Essentializing Identities: Jews in Contemporary Casablanca. City and Society 9(1):175–199.
———.1999 Playing for Control of Distance: Card Games between Jews and Muslims on a Casablancan Beach. American Ethnologist 26(3):632–653.
Levy, André, and Alex Weingrod, eds.
  2005 Homelands and Diasporas: Holy Lands and Other Places. Stanford, Calif.: Stanford University Press.
Levy, Avigdor
  1992 The Sephardim in the Ottoman Empire. Princeton, N.J.: Darwin Press.
———.1994 The Jews of the Ottoman Empire. Princeton, N.J. and Washington, D.C.: Darwin Press; Institute of Turkish Studies.
———. 2002 Jews, Turks, Ottomans: A Shared History, Fifteenth through the Twentieth Century. Syracuse, N.Y.: Syracuse University Press.
Lewis, Bernard
  1953 The Impact of the French Revolution on Turkey: Some Notes on the Transmission of Ideas. Paris: Librairie de Méridiens.
———.1984 The Jews of Islam. Princeton, N.J.: Princeton University Press.
———. 2001 The Emergence of Modern Turkey. 3rd edition. New York: Oxford University Press.
Lewis, Geoffrey
  1999 The Turkish Language Reform: A Catastrophic Success. Oxford and New York: Oxford University Press.
Liss, Sara
  2004 The Jews of Istanbul. http://www.zeek.net/feature_0401.shtml, accessed March 21, 2011.
Loewenthal, Robyn
  1996 Censorship and Judeo-Spanish Popular Literature in Studies on Turkish-Jewish History. In Studies on Turkish-Jewish history: Political and Social Relations, Literature and Linguistics: The Quincentennial Papers. David Altabé, Erhan Atay, and Israel Katz, eds. Pp. 181–191. Brooklyn, N.Y.: Sefer-Hermon Press.

Losche, Diane
  2001 What Makes the Anthropologist Laugh? The Abelam, Irony, and Me. *In* Irony in Action: Anthropology, Practice, and the Moral Imagination. James W. Fernandez and Mary Taylor Huber, eds. Pp. 103–117. Chicago: University of Chicago Press.
Luhrmann, Tanya
  1989 The Magic of Secrecy. Ethos 17(2):131–165.
Mahmood, Saba
  2005 Politics of Piety: The Islamic Revival and the Feminist Subject. Princeton, N.J.: Princeton University Press.
Mallet, Laurent-Olivier
  2008 La Turquie, les Turcs et les Juifs: Histoire, Représentations, Discours et Strategies. Istanbul: Isis Press.
Mandel, Irvin
  2004 Mozotros Ailesi [Our Family], vol. 4. Istanbul: Gözlem Gazetecilik.
Mandel, Jonah
  2010 Turkey Boosts Security for Jews. Jerusalem Post, March 6. http://www.jpost .com/JewishWorld/JewishNews/Article.aspx?id=177341, accessed June 18, 2010.
Mandel, Maud
  2003 In the Aftermath of Genocide: Armenians and Jews in Twentieth Century France. Durham, N.C.: Duke University Press.
Mandel, Ruth Ellen
  2008 Cosmopolitan Anxieties: Turkish Challenges to Citizenship and Belonging in Germany. Durham, N.C.: Duke University Press.
Marcus, George E.
  1999 Paranoia within Reason: A Casebook on Conspiracy as Explanation. Chicago: University of Chicago Press.
McLeod, J. R.
  1999 The Sociodrama of Presidential Politics: Rhetoric, Ritual, and Power in the Era of Teledemocracy. American Anthropologist 101(2):359–373.
Mills, Amy
  2006 Boundaries of the Nation in the Space of the Urban: Landscape and Social Memory in Istanbul. Cultural Geographies 13(3):367–394.
  ———.2007 Gender and Mahalle (Neighborhood) Space in Istanbul. Gender, Place and Culture 14(3):335–354.
  ———.2008 The Place of Locality for Identity in the Nation: Minority Narratives in Cosmopolitan Istanbul. International Journal of Middle East Studies 40:383–401.
  ———.2010 Streets of Memory: Landscape, Tolerance, and National Identity in Istanbul. Athens, Ga.: University of Georgia Press.
Molinas, Ivo
  2002 Demokrasi sınavına çıkıyoruz! Şalom, October 2:3.
Moore, Sally Falk, and Barbara G. Myerhoff
  1977 Secular Ritual. Assen: Van Gorcum.
Navaro-Yashin, Yael
  2002 Faces of the State: Secularism and Public Life in Turkey. Princeton, N.J.: Princeton University Press.

Neyzi, Leyla
    2002 Remembering to Forget: Sabbateanism, National Identity, and Subjectivity in Turkey. Comparative Studies in Society and History 44(1):137–158.
    ———. 2005 Strong as Steel, Fragile as a Rose: A Turkish Jewish Witness to the Twentieth Century. Jewish Social Studies 12(1):167–189.
Oğuzlu, Tarık
    2010 The Changing Dynamics of Turkey–Israel Relations: A Structural Realist Account. Mediterranean Politics 15(2):273–288.
Ong, Aihwa
    1999 Flexible Citizenship: The Cultural Logics of Transnationality. Durham, N.C.: Duke University Press.
Örs, İlay
    2002 Coffeehouses, Cosmopolitanism, and Pluralizing Modernities in Istanbul. Journal of Mediterranean Studies 12(1):119–146.
    ———. 2006 Beyond the Greek and Turkish Dichotomy: The Rum Polites of Istanbul and Athens. South European Society & Politics 11(1):79–94.
Ossman, Susan
    2006 Suburban Battles and Dystopian Cosmopolitanisms. Anthropology News 77(1):5.
Ovadya, Silvio
    2002 Yeni hahambaşı nasıl seçilecek? [How Will the Next Chief Rabbi Be Elected?] Şalom, August 14:7.
Öztürkmen, Arzu
    2001 Politics of National Dance in Turkey: A Historical Reappraisal. Yearbook for Traditional Music 33:39–143.
Özyürek, Esra
    2004 Miniaturizing Atatürk: Privatization of State Imagery and Ideology in Turkey. American Ethnologist 31(3):374–391.
    ———. 2006 Nostalgia for the Modern: State Secularism and Everyday Politics in Turkey. Durham, N.C.: Duke University Press.
    ———. 2007 The Politics of Public Memory in Turkey. Syracuse, N.Y.: Syracuse University Press.
Paley, Julia
    2001 Marketing Democracy: Power and Social Movements in Post-Dictatorship Chile. Berkeley: University of California Press.
    ———. 2002 Toward an Anthropology of Democracy. Annual Review of Anthropology 31:469–496.
Pamuk, Orhan
    2005 Istanbul: Memories and the City. Maureen Freely, trans. 1st American ed. New York: Alfred A. Knopf.
Parmentier, Richard J.
    1987 The Sacred Remains: Myth, History, and Polity in Belau. Chicago: University of Chicago Press.
    ———. 2007 It's About Time: On the Semiotics of Temporality. Language & Communication 27(3):272–277.
Partridge, Damani
    2008 We Were Dancing in the Club, Not on the Berlin Wall: Black Bodies, Street

Bureaucrats, and Exclusionary Incorporation into the New Europe. Cultural Anthropology 23(4):660–687.

Peck, Jeffrey M.
2006 Being Jewish in the New Germany. New Brunswick, N.J.: Rutgers University Press.

Peirce, Charles Sanders
1931–1958 Collected Writings, 8 vols. Charles Hartshorne, Paul Weiss, and Arthur W. Burks, eds. Cambridge, Mass.: Harvard University Press.

Penslar, Derek
2000 Introduction: The Press and the Jewish Public Sphere. Jewish History 14 (1):3.

Phelan, Peggy, and Jill Lane, eds.
1988 The Ends of Performance. New York: NYU Press.

Phillips, Anne
1994 Dealing with Difference: A Politics of Ideas or a Politics of Presence? Constellations 1(1):74–91.
———.2007 Multiculturalism without Culture. Princeton, N.J.: Princeton University Press.

Pigg, Stacy Leigh
1996 The Credible and the Credulous: The Question of "Villagers' Beliefs" in Nepal. Cultural Anthropology 11(2):160–201.

Pinto, Baruh
1997 What's behind a Name? Istanbul: Gözlem.
———.2004 The Sephardic Onomasticon. Istanbul: Gözlem.

Pollock, Sheldon, Homi K.Bhabha, Carol A. Breckenridge, and Dipesh Chakrabarty
2002 Cosmopolitanisms. In Cosmopolitanism. Carol A. Breckenridge, Sheldon Pollock, Homi k. Bhabha, and Dipesh Chakrabarty, eds. Pp. 1–14. Durham, N.C.: Duke University Press.

Potuoğlu-Cook, Öykü
2006 Beyond the Glitter: Belly Dance and Neoliberal Gentrification in Istanbul. Cultural Anthropology: Journal of the Society for Cultural Anthropology 21(4):633–660.

Pratt, Mary Louise
2004 Security. In Shock and Awe: War on Words. Bregje van Eekelen, Jennifer Gonzalez, Bettina Stotzer, and Anna Tsinz, eds. Pp. 140–141. Berkeley, Calif.: North Atlantic Books.

Rabinow, Paul, and George Marcus, with James Faubion and Tobias Rees
2008 Designs for an Anthropology of the Contemporary. Durham, N.C.: Duke University Press.

Rapport, Nigel
1997 Transcendent Individual: Towards a Literary and Liberal Anthropology. London and New York: Routledge.

Rapport, Nigel, and Ronald Stade
2007 A Cosmopolitan Turn—or Return? Social Anthropology 15(2):223–235.

Rasmussen, Susan
1993 Joking in Researcher-Resident Dialogue: The Ethnography of Hierarchy among the Tuareg. Anthropological Quarterly 66(4):211–210.

Reisman, Arnold
  2006 Turkey's Modernization: Refugees from Nazism and Atatürk's Vision. Washington, D.C.: New Academia Publishers.
Richardson, Tanya
  2008 Kaleidoscopic Odessa: History and Place in Contemporary Ukraine. Toronto: University of Toronto Press.
Rodrigue, Aron
  1990 French Jews, Turkish Jews: The Alliance Israélite Universelle and the Politics of Jewish Schooling in Turkey, 1860–1925. Bloomington: Indiana University Press.
  ———, ed. 1992 Ottoman and Turkish Jewry: Community and Leadership. Bloomington: Indiana University Press.
  ———.1993 Images of Sephardi and Eastern Jewries in Transition: The Teachers of the Alliance Israélite Universelle, 1860–1939. Seattle: University of Washington Press.
  ———. 2005 Sephardim and the Holocaust. Washington, D.C.: United States Holocaust Memorial Museum, Center for Advanced Holocaust Studies.
Rodrigue, Aron, and Nancy Reynolds
  1995 Difference and Tolerance in the Ottoman Empire. Stanford Humanities Review 5(1):80–90.
Rosaldo, Renato
  1989 Culture and Truth: The Remaking of Social Analysis. Boston: Beacon Press.
  ———.1994 Cultural Citizenship and Educational Democracy. Cultural Anthropology 9(3):402–411.
Roskies, David G.
  1999 The Jewish Search for a Usable Past. Bloomington: Indiana University Press.
Rozen, Minna
  1996 Yeme Ha-Sahar: Perakim be-Toldot Ha-Yehudim Ba-Imperyah Ha-'Otomanit. Tel-Aviv: ha-Katedrah le-heker Yahadut Saloniki ve-Yavan: ha-Makhon le-heker ha-tefutsot, Universitat Tel-Aviv.
  ———.2002 A History of the Jewish Community in Istanbul: The Formative Years, 1453–1566. Leiden and Boston: Brill.
Rumford, Chris
  2003 Resisting Globalization? Turkey-EU Relations and Human and Political Rights in the Context of Cosmopolitan Democratization. International Sociology 18(2):379–394.
Rymes, Betsy
  1999 Names. Journal of Linguistic Anthropology 9(1–2):163–166.
Salzmann, Laurence, and Ayşe Gürsan-Salzmann
  2010 Travels in Search of Turkey's Jews. Istanbul: Libra Yayınevi.
Sandalcı, Defne
  2003 On Anti-Semitic Attacks. Turkish Daily News, November 18. http://www.hurriyetdailynews.com/h.php?news=reflections-after-a-horrifying-event-2003-11-18, accessed March 3, 2011.
Şaul, Mahir
  1983 The Mother Tongue of the Polyglot: Cosmopolitism [sic] and Nationalism among the Sepharadim of Istanbul. Anthropological Linguistics 25(3):326–358.
Schaffer, Frederic
  1997 Political Concepts and the Study of Democracy: The Case of Demokaraasi in Senegal. PoLAR: Political and Legal Anthropology Review 20(1):40–49.

Schechner, Richard
  1985 Between Theater and Anthropology. Philadelphia: University of Pennsylvania
  Press.
Scheper-Hughes, Nancy
  1995 The Primacy of the Ethical: Propositions for a Militant Anthropology.
  Current Anthropology 36(3):409–440.
Schild, Robert
  1998 Burgazadası: Bir Canlı Etnografik Müze. Istanbul Dergisi 26.
  ———.2004 Adalar'da "Cok kültürlülük" Var mı? August 15. http://www.radikal.com
  .tr/ek_haber.php?ek=r2&haberno=3777.
Schleifer, Yigal
  2003 Turkish Jews Dig Out after Bombs. Jewish Journal, November 20. http://www
  .jewishjournal.com/israel/article/turkish_jews_dig_out_after_bombs_20031121/,
  accessed March 3, 2011.
  ———.2004 Et Tu, Turkey? Jerusalem Report, November 15:25.
Schmelz, U. O., Paul Glikson, S. J. Gould, Universitah ha-'Ivrit bi-Yerushalayim.
  Makhon le-Yahadut zemanenu, and Institute of Jewish Affairs
  1983 Studies in Jewish Demography Survey for 1972–1980. New York: Published
  for the Institute of Contemporary Jewry, the Hebrew University, Jerusalem, and
  the Institute of Jewish Affairs, London, by Ktav Pub. House.
Schmitter, Phillipe, and Terry Lynn Karl
  1991 What Democracy Is . . . and Is Not. Journal of Democracy 2(3):75–88.
Scott, James C.
  1990 Domination and the Arts of Resistance: Hidden Transcripts. New Haven,
  Conn.: Yale University Press.
Scott, James C., John Tehranian, and Jeremy Mathias
  2002 The Production of Legal Identities Proper to States: The Case of the Permanent
  Family Surname. Comparative Studies in Society and History 44(1):4–44.
Scott, Joan Wallach
  2007 The Politics of the Veil. Princeton, N.J.: Princeton University Press.
Secor, Anna
  2004 "There Is an Istanbul That Belongs to Me": Citizenship, Space, and Identity
  in the City. Annals of the Association of American Geographers 94(2):352–
  368.
Seni, Nora
  1994 The Camondos and Their Imprint on 19th-Century Istanbul. International
  Journal of Middle East Studies 26:663–675.
Shaw, Stanford
  1991 Jews of the Ottoman Empire and the Turkish Republic. New York: New York
  University Press.
Sheffer, Gabriel
  1994 Ethno-National Diasporas and Security. Survival 36(1):60–79.
Shokeid, Moshe
  1988 Children of Circumstances: Israeli Emigrants in New York. Ithaca, N.Y.:
  Cornell University Press.
Shryock, Andrew, ed.
  2004 Off Stage/On Display: Intimacy and Ethnography in the Age of Public
  Culture. Stanford, Calif.: Stanford University Press.

Silverstein, Brian
2008 Disciplines of Presence in Modern Turkey: Discourse, Companionship, and the Mass Mediation of Islamic Practice. Cultural Anthropology 23(1):118–153.
Silverstein, Paul, and Ussama Makdisi
2006 Introduction. *In* Memory and Violence in the Middle East and North Africa. Ussama Makdisi and Paul Silverstein, eds. Pp. 1–26. Bloomington: Indiana University Press.
Simmel, Georg
1950 The Sociology of Georg Simmel. Glencoe, Ill.: Free Press.
Singer, Milton
1980 Signs of the Self: An Exploration in Semiotic Anthropology. American Anthropologist 82(3):485–507.
Soysal, Levent
2001 Diversity of Experience, Experience of Diversity: Turkish Migrant Youth Culture in Berlin. Cultural Dynamics 13(1):5–28.
Soysal, Yasemin N., T. Bertilotti, and S. Mannitz
2005 Projections of Identity in French and German History and Civics Textbooks. *In* The Nation, Europe, and the World: Textbooks and Curricula in Transition. Hanna Schissler and Yasemin N. Soysal, eds. Pp. 13–34. New York: Berghahn Books.
Spolsky, Bernard
2004 Language Policy. New York: Cambridge University Press.
Stade, Ronald
2007 Cosmos and Polis, Past and Present. Theory, Culture & Society 24(7/8): 283–285.
Stadler, Nurit, Eyal Ben-Ari, and E. Mesterman
2005 Terror, Aid and Organization: The Haredi Disaster Victim Identification Teams (ZAKA) in Israel. Anthropological Quarterly 78(3):619–652.
Steedly, Mary Margaret
1996 The Importance of Proper Names: Language and "National" Identity in Colonial Karoland. American Ethnologist 23(3):447–475.
Stein, Sarah A.
2003 Making Jews Modern: Yiddish and Ladino Press in the Russian and Ottoman Empires. Bloomington: Indiana University Press.
———.2006 Asymmetric Fates: Secular Yiddish and Ladino Culture in Comparison. Jewish Quarterly Review 96(4):498–509.
Stillman, Norman A.
1995 Sephardi Religious Responses to Modernity. Luxembourg: Harwood Academic Publishers.
Stillman, Yedida K., and George. K. Zucker
1993 New Horizons in Sephardic Studies. Albany: State University of New York Press.
Stoler, Ann L.
2002 Colonial Archives and the Arts of Governance. Archival Science 2(1):87–109.
———.2008 Along the Archival Grain: Epistemic Anxieties and Colonial Common Sense. Princeton, N.J.: Princeton University Press.
Stratton, Jon
2000 Coming out Jewish: Constructing Ambivalent Identities. London: Routledge.

Sutherland, Anne
1994 Gypsy Identity, Names and Social Security Numbers. PoLAR: Political and Legal Anthropology Review 17(2):75–84.

Sutton, David
1997 Local Names, Foreign Claims: Family Inheritance and National Heritage on a Greek Island. American Ethnologist 24(2):415–437.

Tanabe, Akio
2007 Toward Vernacular Democracy: Moral Society and Post-Colonial Transformation in Rural Orissa, India. American Ethnologist 34(3):558–574.

Taussig, Michael
1999 Defacement: Public Secrecy and the Labor of the Negative. Stanford, Calif.: Stanford University Press.

Teibel, Amy
2009 Jews in Muslim Lands Anxious over Gaza War. Boston Globe, February 16. http://www.boston.com/news/world/middleeast/articles/2009/02/16/jews_in_muslim_lands_anxious_over_gaza_war, accessed March 21, 2011.

Todorova, Maria Nikolaeva
1997 Imagining the Balkans. New York: Oxford University Press.

Toktaş, Şule
2006a The Conduct of Citizenship in the Case of Turkey's Jewish Minority. Comparative Studies of South Asia, Africa and the Middle East 26(1):121–133.

———.2006b Perceptions of Anti-Semitism among Turkish Jews. Turkish Studies 7(2):203–223.

———.2006c Turkey's Jews and Their Immigration to Israel. Middle Eastern Studies 42(3):505–519.

———.2007 Citizenship and Migration from Turkey to Israel: A Comparative Study on Turkish Jews in Israel. East European Quarterly 41(2):117–148.

Tsing, Anna L.
1993 In the Realm of the Diamond Queen: Marginality in an Out-of-the-Way Place. Princeton, N.J.: Princeton University Press.

———. 2005 Friction: An Ethnography of Global Connection. Princeton, N.J.: Princeton University Press.

———.2009 Adat/Indigenous: Indigeneity in Motion. In Words in Motion: Toward a Global Lexicon. Carol Gluck and Anna L. Tsing, eds. Pp. 40–67. Durham, N.C.: Duke University Press.

Türeli, İpek
2010 Ara Güler's Photography of "Old Istanbul" and Cosmopolitan Nostalgia. History of Photography 34(3):300–313.

Turkish Daily News
2002 Can a Song Divide or Unite a Country? September 4. http://www.hurriyet dailynews.com/h.php?news=can-a-song-divide-or-unite-a-country-2002-09-04, accessed March 3, 2011.

Türköz, Meltem
2007 Surname Narratives and the State-Society Boundary: Memories of Turkey's Family Name Law of 1934. Middle Eastern Studies 43(6):893–908.

Turner, Victor
1974 Dramas, Fields and Metaphors: Symbolic Action in Human Society. Ithaca, N.Y.: Cornell University Press.

Tuval, Shaul
    2004 ha-Kehilah ha-Yehudit be-Istanbul, 1948–1992 [The Jewish Community in
    Istanbul 1948–1992]. Jerusalem: World Zionist Organization.
Valins, Oliver
    2003 Stubborn Identities and the Construction of Socio-Spatial Boundaries: Ultra-
    Orthodox Jews Living in Contemporary Britain. Transactions (Institute of British
    Geographers) 28:158–175.
Varol, Marie-Christine
    1989 Balat, faubourg juif d'Istanbul. Istanbul: Isis Press.
vom Bruck, Gabriele, and Bodenhorn Barbara, eds.
    2006 An Anthropology of Names and Naming. Cambridge: Cambridge University
    Press.
Walzer, Michael
    1997 On Toleration. New Haven, Conn.: Yale University Press.
Wardle, Huon
    2000 An Ethnography of Cosmopolitanism in Kingston, Jamaica. Lewiston, N.Y.:
    E. Mellen Press.
Weiker, Walter F.
    1988 The Unseen Israelis: The Jews from Turkey in Israel. Lanham, Md.: University
    Press of America; Jerusalem: Jerusalem Center for Public Affairs/Center for Jewish
    Community Studies.
    ———.1992 Ottomans, Turks and the Jewish Polity: A History of the Jews of Turkey.
    Lanham, Md.: University Press of America.
Weiss, Adina
    1975 The Jewish Community of Turkey. Jerusalem: Center For Jewish Community
    Studies.
Werbner, Pnina
    2005 The Place Which Is Diaspora: Citizenship, Religion and Gender in the
    Making of Chaordic Transnationalism. Journal of Ethnic and Migration Studies
    28(1):119–133.
    ———. 2006 Understanding Vernacular Cosmopolitanism. Anthropology News
    47(5):7–11.
    ———, ed.2008 Anthropology and the New Cosmopolitanism: Rooted, Feminist and
    Vernacular Perspectives. ASA Monograph, 45. Oxford: Berg Publishers.
White, Hayden
    1982 The Politics of Historical Interpretation: Discipline and De-Sublimation.
    Critical Inquiry 9(1):113–137.
White, Jenny B.
    2002 Islamist Mobilization in Turkey: A Study in Vernacular Politics. Seattle:
    University of Washington Press.
Whorf, Benjamin
    1956 Language, Thought, and Reality. Cambridge, Mass.: MIT Press.
Williams, Raymond
    1980 Marxism and Literature. London: Oxford University Press.
Wortham, Stanton E. F.
    2005 Socialization beyond the Speech Event. Journal of Linguistic Anthropology
    15(1):95–112.

Yardımcı, Sibel
  2007 Festivalising Difference: Privatisation of Culture and Symbolic Exclusion in Istanbul. EUI Working Papers, Mediterranean Programme Series.
Young, Iris Marion
  1989 Polity and Group Difference: A Critique of the Ideal of Universal Citizenship. Ethics 99(2):250–274.

INDEX

Page numbers in italics represent illustrations.

Labor Disorders in Neoliberal Italy: Mobbing, Well-being, and the Workplace
Noelle J. Molé

Inside Tolerance: Jewish Life in Turkey in the 21st Century
Marcy Brink-Danan

Hypersexuality and Headscarves: Race, Sex, and Citizenship in the New Germany
Damani J. Partridge

Secularism Soviet Style: Teaching Atheism and Religion in a Volga Republic
Sonja Luehrmann

Political Crime and the Memory of Loss
John Borneman

Marcy Brink-Danan is Dorot Assistant Professor of Judaic Studies and Assistant Professor of Anthropology at Brown University.

Printed and bound by CPI Group (UK) Ltd, Croydon, CR0 4YY

13/04/2025

14656547-0003